Be Seeing You

Hubert O'Hearn

ISBN: 1530975476
ISBN-13: 978-1530975471

Four Freedom Publishing 2016
Ireland – Canada – United States of America

First Edition

DEDICATION

Even with all the advantages of retrospect, and a lot of witnesses
dead and gone, you can't make your life look as if you intended it
or you were consistent. All you can show is how you dealt with
various hands.

- Christopher Hitchens

CONTENTS

ACKNOWLEDGMENTS

Most of the pieces in this book have appeared in other publications over the years in slightly different form. Where necessary I have edited or updated the content. I wish to acknowledge and offer my thanks for the support of the following (in no particular order): The Thunder Bay Chronicle-Journal (esp. editors Claire Stirling Young and Ian Pattison), The Herald de Paris et Cie, American Blues Scene Magazine, Winnipeg Review, San Diego Book Review, San Francisco Book Review, Tulsa Book Review, Shelf Unbound, Hispanic News Online.

Also to a very few special people who helped create the stories behind these stories, in no particular order: Lawrence Siddall, Connie Christianson, Marnie Roberts, Miranda Huckle, Bradley Gibson, Audrey Petticrew, Amanda Held, Kimberly Mc Innis, Audrey Petticrew.

Introduction

Perhaps my favourite quote of all time is something Elia Kazan
said upon the debut of the repertory ensemble which he helmed at
Lincoln Center in New York in the early nineteen sixties.
Referring to directing, Kazan noted that if prior to the start of any
production any director was forced to take the time to write down
the thousands of decisions that would have to be made by him
over the coming weeks no one would ever again direct a play.
However wrong the old boy was in testifying before HUAC
during the communist witch hunt, he was correct in that
observation about life.

Kazan's comment kept returning to my mind as I selected the
materials presented here in **Be Seeing You**. If I had looked with
perfect foresight forward from any notable passage marker in my
early life – let's say on my high school or university graduation
day – and made a similar list, well honestly I think I would have
gone into the nearest study, locked the door behind me and
removed a vintage pistol from its case before doing what defeated
generals and insane poets have done for ages. Life really is like a
blind man groping his way up a steep, shale-ridden mountain
until he reaches the summit where the nearer sun opens his eyes
at last in sight. He turns around, looks down at the cliffs, crags
and shifting pebbles falling to the valley below and then lifts his
face to God and screams, 'You had me do *what!?!?*' That all said
and without either further ado or *a Dieu*, Welcome to my world!

This collection is actually the result of several people asking me to
write a memoir. Objectively I can see their point. After all, I have
done a fair bit of living including before, between and after having
clinically died twice. That by the way is a play whose third act is

bound to be a stinker. Speaking of plays, I've also founded a successful theatre, written six hit shows and acted in God only knows how many more as I stopped counting after I got past fifty opening nights. Then there were the years I spent working in politics; a dozen more covering music, golf and television for the newspapers; and then founding my own publishing company.Oh and let's see, there was the tragedy of watching my fiancée drop of a brain aneurysm right in front of me and then when we were separated because it was determined against my wishes that I could not cope with her on-going therapy, I moved to Ireland then to England then to Northern Ireland and finally (I hope) back to Ireland. I have been comfortably wealthy and desperately impoverished.

And yet, when it comes to a formal memoir to tell you the truth I just find my life much too boring to ever want to spend months and months writing about it. I know how all the stories end so there's no adventure in it, only work and who in heck needs more of *that*?

Instead, what I've found is that over the course of many years I actually have recorded my life for your dining and dancing pleasure. There are the reviews, the newspaper columns, poems and plays and a whole lot of what-nots. You see, I always write personally, even when reviewing a book. Granted, for that reason the number of publications accepting of my work becomes limited yet I find it honest to dot the pages with the word I. Everything one writes is in one way or another an opinion and all opinions are subjective, so why pretend towards objectivity when such a thing does not exist? I want the readers to have a sense of who is lecturing them. If my persona seems to be that of someone you find agreeable, then read on. If you think I'm an ass, well who am I to prove you wrong?

It has been quite a process sorting through all the material as it is amazing how many vivid memories one can have that still may be forgotten. In selecting the material, I have put the memoir idea on a shelf in a rear storeroom; it's there yet largely to be forgotten. If I started to arrange these pieces to follow the path of my life in linear fashion, you would have an awful mish-mash of a review followed by a poem followed by a television column, followed by two more reviews, a play, a column – well I think you see my point.

What I have chosen are selections that I believe accomplish two things: One, they are examples of the best writing I have done (with one caveat that I'll get to); and two, they cover all my major interests save for golf.

In my heart of hearts I have always been a sportswriter. Sorry if that disappoints. For a brief time I was a golf columnist, with that period ending when the snow came along and buried the courses in my hometown of Thunder Bay, Ontario. I no longer have the computer on which I wrote those columns and many, many more pieces between 1996-2010. To be brutally frank, there is no damn way I am going to pay to access the on-line archive of newspapers for which I wrote. Besides, one should always leave room for a volume two.

There are of course quite literally hundreds of people and publications that deserve a note of gratitude. We are all sculpted by the hands which touch the clay of our lives. Those who touch with harm make us wise; those who touch with love make us even wiser. I am taking the risk of naming a few names in this book's dedication even while knowing a month from now I will be racked with guilt for missing someone so obvious. Also, I certainly cannot name past lovers for those who took my place in warm and pleasant beds may have uncomfortable questions to ask of gentle women who deserve only peace after the turbulence of our times. So here in this Introduction I am only going to thank the two professionals I trusted to look over this manuscript and told me what to keep, what to lose and what was typo. Thank you

Hubert O'Hearn

to Christie Parry and Patricia Gregory.

What's that? You want to know the meaning of the title? **Be Seeing You** is derived from the farewell used by Patrick McGoohan's Number Six in the greatest television series ever made, The Prisoner. After all, we're all just living in The Village and trying to discover who put us here and why. As such, for the past twenty years my sign-off on the vast majority of things I have written has been ...

Be seeing you.

April 8, 2016

Kilkelly, Ireland

Friends

(For the past six years, the brilliant comedy actor and writer Lydia Cornell has been my best friend, confidante and personal philosopher. She is the kind of woman who will take a phone call at 4AM and stay on the line for three hours if she thinks a friend needs help. She is first in this collection not because she is famous, but because she is kindness personified. Oh, and she makes me laugh too. That is damn important in life. The following is the first time I ever wrote about Lydia, back in the spring of 2011 for the Thunder Bay Chronicle-Journal.)

Lydia Cornell: Angel

Inside Television #555
Publication Date: 5-27-11

About My Friend, Lydia Cornell

In thinking about this column, I started leafing through my internal photo album. I basically only have an internal one - I've never been all that big on taking pictures. Somehow having admissible evidence right at your fingertips of who was and wasn't where you should have been tends to block that pleasant coat of strawberry icing that the imaginative memory uses to coat the past. Things are always so much sweeter in retrospect. One never remembers pain nor pleasure quite as accurately as the feeling at the time.

But thinking back has its advantages too, provided that the meditative mood is infrequent, special and pleasant. Nostalgia therefore is best eaten like raw oysters; infrequently and with vodka close by. And yes, that imaginative memory supplies the sweet sauce mixed with dashings of horseradish and lemon.

In doing this *nostalgie des temps perdu* today, I realized that although I have had many unusual friends, I haven't actually had many unusual friendships. As to the first - well, when you spend the better part of your adult life in the company of theatrical and other arts folk, the crowd tends to be livelier than most of the usual, nine-to-five professions. In my case, the following types people have been considered in that haloed circle of one's true friends; there are or have been (no I'm not ranking) magicians, puppeteers, writers good and writers not so good, the occasional politician who should have been an actor, and a lawyer-activist who was an actor and may well be again. Then there are the musicians and technicians certainly; journalists, actors male and female, and a small group of improvisers who were my favourite gang of gangs. You get some lively evenings this way.

Yet, by and large, the friendships themselves weren't or aren't unusual. You meet, find a common interest in that you've both at least heard of Frank Lloyd Wright, Stan Musial or the contribution of Zeppo Marx to the greater good of the whole. And so, you hit it off. Then comes laugh laugh laugh, argument, settle, laugh, what did you mean by that, laugh laugh, do some really stupid thing together, laugh uproariously, someone moves someone gets married, dear god he's an idiot, why hang around with him, hot sex episode hot sex episode, guilt, normal, not quite, someone dies, you him or the person who was the sun that held the planets that held the moons dies. You drift.

Same as you. (Just to clarify, I have not had hot sex episodes with all my friends. They have however had hot sex at some point with someone, as have I and at some discussion or another the topic has come up. Just to clarify.) All that said, a my friendships have been the usual sort in that one and the other work or recreate together, meet at one another's homes or common bars and at the very least actually know one another.

One of the very best friends I have ever had I've never met, not live and in person. Yet she is one of the kindest yet courageous, talented yet giving people I have ever known. Her name is Lydia Cornell. I hope you'll enjoy our story.

Did her name ring a bell, pluck a string, sound a tinkling note? If you're say thirty-five or over, there's a good chance that your thoughts formed a phrase starting, *Wasn't she the one who* - The answer is, yes she is.

There was a series on ABC in the early 80s called **Too Close for Comfort**. It starred Ted Knight, who had been a white hot property after his run as one of the ultimate second bananas in history from his role as incompetent news anchor Ted Baxter on **The Mary Tyler Moore Show**. He lost a lot of that heat after the six-episode disaster of **The Ted Knight Show** zeppelined into the ground. (Ted, playing Roger Dennis, ran an escort service in New York. Yes exactly. In 2011 you might have a runaway hit; in 1978 on American broadcast television, not bloody likely.) So after he had a couple of relaxing therapy experiences as a guest on **The Love Boat**, ABC thought there was still money in Ted Knight's name. Arne Sultan was hired as the showrunner to get Ted Knight's new comedy series on the air in the fall of 1980. Sultan, by the way, had been a major writer on **Gilligan's Island, Get Smart,** and **Barney Miller** so he knew how to do funny.

The set-up of **Too Close for Comfort**, for those who might need further reminding, is that Ted played Henry Rush, a cartoonist whose creation was Cosmic Cow. Henry had two young adult daughters with his wife Muriel. The two daughters lived together in separate quarters in the same house below their parents. This makes Daddy nervous, as the daughters are quite attractive. Fitting the conventions of the day, the daughters were loving and compatible opposites. There was the lovely and smart brunette Jackie (played by Deborah Van Valkenburgh) and the eye-poppingly lovely not-so-smart blonde Sara played by, you guessed it, Lydia Cornell.

A broadcasting or media student could turn out a reasonably passable paper in the comparisons between **Too Close for Comfort** and its slowly expiring ABC colleague sitcom **Three's Company**. A quick Cliff's Notes version:

Three's Company: Two gorgeous roommates, smart brunette and slightly thick blonde
Too Close for Comfort: Sisters. Otherwise, check.

Three's Company: Annoying landlord always spying to make sure no wild sexual shenanigans were going on.
Too Close for Comfort: Landlord is also Dad.

Three's Company: The late John Ritter played Jack Tripper the male comedy lead, who the landlord thinks is gay.
Too Close for Comfort: Jim J. Bullock plays Monroe Fiscus, who is an unattached and well-groomed single male in San Francisco who never makes a pass at the Rush sisters. Exactly.

That said, formulas in television exist for a reason. Audiences like them. One can work ones's way through the intricate family relationships of a Eugene O'Neill play to relax the mind – good luck with that – or one can watch the old guy get out-smarted and exasperated by the gay guy. If the writing is good and the characters likable, the show will succeed. Television is as simple as checkers to understand for rules, yet as difficult to win as a checkers tournament.

Too Close for Comfort had a very nice run of it. 129 episodes in all, with the first three seasons running on ABC and the final three in syndication - this in an age where syndicated scripted series were still very much a rarity.

I remember the show well. Very much a comedy for a family audience, my Mom always hoped that Ted Knight would wear a sweatshirt from her alma mater, the University of Wisconsin. A smart running gimmick was that Knight would wear a different college or university sweatshirt every week, with this becoming a badge, or at least an iron-on, of honour for the selected. My granddad would laugh his head off at Munro. As for me, I was 21 at the time, so as for my interests... Exactly.

There were a couple of things I could never figure out about the show. Even at age 21 I could see Cosmic Cow as a great marketing angle, so I never understood why we so rarely saw the hand puppet Henry Rush used to talk to while drawing his panels. The other puzzle was why the parts of the daughters kept being cut back. As an audience, we never really got to see Jackie and Sara realize their characters' lives, which I still think was a wasted opportunity. When the show died along with Ted Knight in real-life in 1986, there was hopeful talk of a spin-off featuring the two sisters and Munro, but Ted Knight's estate which owned the rights puzzlingly did not want to pursue a cash cow after Cosmic Cow so that was the end of that.

As to Lydia herself, she has a really unique place in the history of television. I mentioned that she was (I'll get to the 'is' in a few paragraphs) eye-poppingly beautiful, but that requires further description. Her eyes were turquoise dreams of dreams of soft warm seas, the hair so gold that one felt that gold must have a perfume, and of course the figure that launched a thousand posters. She was the last of the 'innocent sex symbols'. My most-admired novelist from England, Martin Amis, wrote in last year's **The Pregnant Widow** a character named Scheherazade; an impossibly beautiful and voluptuous young blonde woman who was unaware of her own power. **The Pregnant Widow** was set in 1970 mostly, at the first full dawn of the sexual revolution where a beautiful woman could be still be beautiful and unaware of her beauty. Sara Rush was of that line, but by 1986, no one would ever believe it again. Madonna had warmed up her lungs and Kelly Bundy was about to stride onto the set of **Married...with Children**. Sexy could no longer be played innocently.

So time passes, as it tends to do unless everything churches and physicists have told us is all an inside joke. Lydia never yet re-achieved the white hot fame of being Number Two in poster sales to Farrah Fawcett. By the by, I never had one. I tended more towards the singers in my youth - Linda Ronstadt and Stevie Nicks guarded my bedroom like defending Valkyrie while I slept.

Still, Lydia kept working and continues to do so. She refined her comedic skills and developed as a writer. I invite the reader to do a search on YouTube for 'Lydia Cornell True Love' to see a very good selection from her one-woman show. She does not have the brassiness of the standard stand-up comic. Her voice is burnished copper and copper is a much mellower metal than brass.

Surely by now the reader is wondering, why am I telling you about all this? Is this just (...checking word count) going to be 2500 words or so of Where are They Now? Well yes; well no. Because here's the thing about Lydia: nothing - absolutely nothing I have told you about her looks and career have anything to do with what is important about her as a person. Her career just granted her the opportunity to do all the important things in her life. Fame, you see, is a renewable passport to performing good works.

And this is what drew me to her in the first place. As anyone who has ever read much of my work over the years knows, I have grown frustrated and tired over the obsession with Bad Celebrity.

The slogan for TV used to be borrowed from Dr. Timothy Leary: Turn on, Tune In, Tune Out. Now it's more like: Be bad, Be worse, Be famous. Charlie Sheen has as much place in an article about Lydia Cornell as Donald Trump at an ashram, but for the life of me I truly fail to understand why anyone would pay money to go to a Charlie Sheen 'concert thingie' when they know the show is so bad people walk out on it by the hundreds? The only defence is that this is what the audience is trained to think: celebrities are like Japanese Emperors or Vatican Popes - they are incapable of error, even when wrong, and must be adored.

So my quest in that part of my writing practice that is Inside Television is to try and bring out stories of Good Celebrity. Because the public eventually turns, you know. I suspect that part of the reason why the ratings of reality TV are rising against scripted series is that scandals make celebrities look like a clan of mud pigs that one no longer wants clopping their muddy trotters across the carpeting.

I like to write about happy things. Nothing pleases me more in writing than the fact that a story I did about Alyssa Milano working to bring clean water wells to Africa is still the most-read story I've ever done.

So what is so great about Lydia Cornell? It reminds me of a story the great Charles Grodin told on his CNBC talk show about Marlo Thomas. Marlo, who played maybe the first independent woman on a comedy sitcom - **That Girl!** - has been a well-known supporter of liberal causes for decades. Marlo talked Grodin into show-doctoring a play that was about an important issue or some such, because, as Grodin said straight-faced into the camera: "When Marlo gets involved with something and asks you to get involved, you have to say yes. You have to get involved because when Marlo gets involved (slightest pause, stares at camera) she's involved." Lydia Cornell also gets involved.

It would have been on Twitter that I first ran across her, 25 years nearly since **Too Close for Comfort** closed down for good. And for the life of me, I can't even remember now what the cause was she was promoting. There are so many: Autism, Brain Injuries, Young Women in Crisis, Disabled Veterans, Substance Abuse and others. Lydia had her run with booze - it was the 80s, everyone not only had a run with something, usually it was a race against mortality. Lydia is one of the strong ones. She has not had a drink in 15 years and is the picture of perfect health. More on that too.

Anyway, I was looking for celebrities with interesting stories to tell in these columns. So I did a Google search and found out some fascinating things about the woman who would become my dear friend. She had become quite political, or at least openly political - co-hosting a radio show in Las Vegas, and through it and her Politically Hot blog Lydia had engaged in a glorious pissing match with Ann Coulter. For those who might not recognize the latter name, if Dick Cheney had transsexual fantasies (and one truly hopes he does; it would explain so much) he would imagine himself as Ann Coulter.

Now call me shallow, but when I find intelligent, bold and charitable people at the car wash, let alone the entertainment industry, I want to get to know them. So I contacted Miss Cornell and asked if she would care to grant an interview to me about her career from **Too Close to Comfort** to her present-day success. The response I received was both personal and kind. We would do the interview when there was time, which was fine by me.

I also then joined Lydia's Facebook page. If there was going to be time to get to know the interview subject better, then I should spend the time doing so. And without a whisper of exaggeration, Lydia's wall is my favourite page on the Internet - well there is also the football page at guardian.co.uk, but a man must have his idle pleasures.

Lydia has a great friends' list. as they aren't public personages per se I think it would be wrong to single out names, but although all sides of an issue are represented, there is usually a tone of respect between disagreeing parties. If that respect is lost through crude or callous remark, the offender is promptly smacked across the lips with -

Love? Yes, love. No one talks about love, peace and letting go of anger more than Lydia. Life has not been all mandolins and rainbows for Lydia. Her beloved younger brother Paul died a tragic death from a drug overdose. Lydia found the body. Two divorces, being a single Mom, trying to be taken seriously as a bombshell with a brain - any or all of these things could build a bullet casing around the heart, but not with her. She actually practices what is preached.

I know that Lydia has a great book in her. *(2016 update – darn right she does and I've read its first draft)* Its theme will be a celebrity and how that can be both a cancer yet also a vehicle for good works. There has not been a weekend or scarcely a week when this wonderful person has not been attending a charity event, or counseling young women, or just being like Roy Scheider in All That Jazz while looking in the mirror and saying 'It's showtime folks!' before dressing herself in the showbiz regalia and making an appearance in support of a friend. Lydia is a proud mother, a staunch and faithful friend, and claims to have the ability to speak Klingon. When we eventually do have our interview, I intend to put this to the test. *(It actually took us close to three years before we had a real, formal interview. That was after maybe two hundred hours of Skype calls.)*

Lydia also has a regular chat show on Ustream. That show too is a joy, running on Wednesday evenings from 9:30-11:30 eastern time. The show, Lydia Live is in the process of a set and presentation upgrade from just Lydia along with a webcam, her iPhone, and a desk lamp for lighting; but I hope it doesn't lose the charm the present show has. Interesting people talking about interesting things in interesting ways don't necessarily have to be famous. As I say, good writing and likable characters make for successful television. And for my money, Lydia is actually much more beautiful now than in her sitcom heyday. The eyes now are not directed to hide their intelligence and she exudes the much-envied look that comes from healthy living. If you watch the show you will see how her inner peace absolutely glows. This is not just the verdict of a friend talking about a friend; Lydia Cornell is more beautiful than ever, physically and intellectually.

I absolutely love this woman, no more so than when our email relationship had got to the point where she asked about Kimberly - my fiancee who was struck by a brain aneurysm a year ago February. Kimberly lost her short term memory and is still funny and loving and beautiful and the subject of all my dreams and wishes, but will never again be who she was. So I told Lydia about the Love of My Life and the words of prayer that came back were genuine and beautiful. You want to know evidence of when someone cares? When they pray for you. From that moment on she became one of the few who form the eccentric circle I love to call my best friends. She has calmed my rage, raised my hopes and made me laugh. My prayer is that everyone who reads this can say now or someday, 'She sounds just like my friend.' God bless Lydia Cornell. God blesses us for knowing her. God will bless us for being like her.

Be seeing you.

(As you'll see later, the brilliant Irish singer-songwriter Ciara Donnelly has become my musical collaborator on various stage plays we have co-authored. This is how we met.)

Ciara Donnelly: Ireland's Next Music Star

For: American Blues Scene, April 2014

-

(A significant part of the joy in moving to a new country is discovering the gems of its culture, those acts and personalities that have not made an impact on North America ... yet. This is the story of a singer/songwriter of incredible intelligence and talent who I first noticed by watching, of all things, a televised singing competition. Onwards!)

The whole question of the worth of televised singing competitions as an identifier of real talent is one that can be debated forever without hope of a final resolution. The first opinion, the highly negative one, squints hard at the various Idol, Voice and X Factor shows as manufacturing pseudo-stars the same way as a fast food chain manufactures cheeseburgers – emphasis on the cheese. On the other hand, there is for instance Beth Hart who won the first edition of Star Search and she is has developed into a role model for independent female artists worldwide. Ultimately, TV singing contests are a tool to get visibility and in that way they are as viable as singing on the sidewalk outside a record label's home office, or desperately shoving a homemade CD into a limousine's window just before the tinted closing glass crushes the aspiring musician's fingers.

For Ciara Donnelly, age 25 from Waterford, Ireland the Voice of Ireland was one step towards separating herself from the legions of Irish singer-songwriters who wish to emerge from the clouds and crowds and into the sunshine of success. Ciara considers herself an 'underground musician' and as such in the ballpark of Voice coach Niall Breslin, aka Bressie. As Ciara said, 'If you're going to put yourself being judged by the whole nation, with the whole stream of social media that can give you abuse or give you Craic, the obviously you're trying to to get something out if it. You're not doing it for the fun.'

Ciara was chosen as a late walk-on by a panel of four DJ's from 2FM, Ireland's top-rated radio station. That however was a simple recognition for the hard work Ciara had applied to her talent. As she said when asked why an independent artist would enter a manufactured TV singing competition, 'If I didn't need it I wouldn't be here.'

Beyond the Voice of Ireland though, which leave us face it is a show which only Irish readers recognize and few have seen worldwide, Ciara is representative of an artistic dedication that stares in the face of the sexist prejudices of the music industry and in staring it down says, 'Why not me?' Pubs and clubs in Ireland pay a meagre living and as her Voice of Ireland coach, the gifted producer and musician Niall Breslin said to her, 'I'm dedicated to breaking talent out of our small country.'

Breslin, known as Bressie, continues to support Ciara's talent beyond the scope of the television show, marking her as the breakout star she has become. 'Bressie calls me his little Dusty Springfield. And he was really funny about it when we were talking about it last week when we were between rehearsals and stuff. Which is a great compliment. I really love Dusty Springfield. She was so original. Actually, her family are from Tralee in Ireland and some of her ashes were scattered over the burn in Tralee, when she died. So I come out with all of this stuff and he goes, "How do you know all this stuff, you freak?"'

Ciara formally studied language and its nuances in her college education in Theatre at both the Universities of Cork as well as Dublin. 'A lot of my songs are metaphorical, which comes from my interest in literature. I don't think you should ever be so direct with a song, because you're giving it to other people. So it should never be all about you.' It is both the intonation as well as the richness of words that informs Ciara Donnelly's ethic. Her favourite Shakespearean play being The Tempest, and favourite poem T.S. Eliot's The Love Song of J. Alfred Prufrock one can see and hear the influence of her studies in such vivid verses as the following from her whimsical, allegorical song Circus:

You will never find her in the desert barren land
Or find peace in the arms of someone else's hands
But traveling man you are something
And the lions cry and cry for what's gone and what's to begin
And Nelly sings her songs and lullabies
Of circus games and how elephants die

She has continued in acting with an appearance in a soon to be released independent film, as well as making a day-to-day living as a fashion journalist. Film though, in her words is 'too clinical. Hold on, we're going to do this another fifty times. That's not acting.' It lacks the organic, live nature of theatre or a live musical performance. In addition, this woman of many talents is also schooled in ballet to an expert level. Yet if she had to sacrifice the others for one, that which remains would be music. As she said, 'I think just mentally, having withstood the struggle of the last couple of years must mean that I really care about music.'

Caring requires an attitude of perfectionism, as that is a necessity in this often cruel business of music. There is no accommodation for weakness or sentiment, not for the true artist. Ciara made clear that for her back-up band she has no patience for the lazy, the by-the-numbers player, or for those who sadly succumb to stage-fright. Having gambled her youth and her career on music, there is no place for either the casual or the complacent. Is that perhaps too strong? Some might think so. Yet we accept such an attitude from men as strength, so why should we not accept it from women as determination?

With Ciara Donnelly, it all begins with the voice; not the Voice of Ireland, rather her true voice. It slithers around and embraces lyrics like an embracing, friendly serpent. It rasps, it calls, it sounds a horn calling attention to all within its range. At the same time, her left hand signs an interpretive cobra's dance, supplying a visual commentary on her lyrics' aural meaning. And when her brilliant blue-green eyes open and stare, an audience is drawn into her songs' truth and live the life of a song with her. With regards to the care of her vocal instrument, she said, 'We came off a nationwide tour last year and the boys had been drinking all night and smoking this and that, and I got home and said, "I cannot speak!" It was really tough, so I definitely started warming up a lot. Any vocalist will tell you, we hate to warm up. It's so boring. I mean the guitarist doesn't have to warm up. It isn't fair! But I do warm up the voice. It takes me a good forty-five minutes to really be singing properly, constantly. Probably because of the huskiness of my voice as well; to get a cleanness from it and ensure that it will last, definitely I have to do a lot of warm-ups.'

It is not an easy life, being a musician in a small nation such as Ireland. Gigs in small pubs and clubs are a satisfying classroom for learning one's craft, yet not a breakthrough in themself. However, Ciara has emerged. Nominated twice for Best Songwriter awards as well as the Emerging Artist category at England's world-famous Glastonbury Festival, she is now well on her way. She longs to expand beyond her beloved country's borders and make her impact on the American music market. 'People are always saying music is dead. Music is not dead! Go and see a show. Don't just go to a cinema and pay all that money. Go and see something that's real. Maybe the labels are dead. (laughs) And also I want people to start respecting the musician. Even songwriters. People go into a bar and they're not listening. It's definitely an abuse of the music industry. That's really hard to see, and music is not dead but music will die if musicians get disheartened. I haven't got disheartened yet, I'm still hangin' on! But people say, you know, "Why do you go on The Voice? Why are you messin' up, or messin up the scene?" But you know, those are the people that aren't going out and seeing shows. They aren't feeding the music scene, they're just sitting around at home on Twitter and giving out on everything.'

With regards to expanding her market, specifically into the US, Ciara says, 'I want to make that jump across the pond more than you know!' Plans are already in the works for her to headline an Irish Invasion Concert in New York City in the near future, by which time Ciara's second album will have been released to her devoted and growing fan base. Ciara Donnelly: the successor to the late Rory Gallagher, Bono and Dolores O'Riordan as Ireland's next great gift to the world of passionate music.

Ciara Donnelly's EP can be heard and downloaded at:
http://yellowbridge.bandcamp.com/album/yellowbridge-ep

(Over the past four years I have said countless times that I will

know that I've finally made it as a writer when I have an invitation to read at the greatest book salon in the world. That salon is held at Vicki Abelson's home in Los Angeles. This is the story behind that salon and the remarkable woman who hosts it.)

photo ©carlosalejandro

Vicki Abelson Wants to Save Your Mind! Yes!

Herald de Paris, November 3, 2012

THUNDER BAY (Herald de Paris) — The origin of this story is slightly complicated while the rest of it is pretty straightforward, so let's get the slalom course out of the way first in this combined Alpine event.

In this internet world it's a constant wonder how many people we know that we don't actually 'know', you know? As life has happened to turn out, my dearest friend in the world is the wonderfully talented actress and equally talented writer Lydia Cornell. Among Lydia's Facebook friends is one Vicki Abelson, who I assume has her settings set so that her status updates can be seen by friends of friends. (By the way, is just me, or doesn't all this friends and friends of friends business make you feel that we're all a bunch of Quakers? Pass the oat bowl!) So I'm sat back on the couch late one night last week and enjoying the evening's fourth martini – ha ha! I kid! It was the fifth – when I see an update from Vicki thanking everyone who had come out to her latest meeting of Vicki Abelson's Women Who Write Literary Salon. 'Vicki Abelson's Women Who Write?', I said, 'What's that?' And, after I quieted the dog from barking, because Daddy is talking to The Invisible People again, I started Googling.

Eventually I found some YouTube clips of Vicki's past Women Who Write events and I was equally engaged, intrigued and delighted.While it is demonstrably true that there has never been an entertainment or media industry more adaptable to challenges than book publishing – it has after all thrived in the face of theatre, vaudeville, daily newspapers, magazines, movies, radio, television and now the Internet – it is always a business under challenge and seeking an audience for its product. Once one actually starts reading for pleasure, of course one is hooked; but that is a hard hook to bait after the joy of words has been drummed out of the soul by undertaker-like school teachers who rip the living breath out of Keats, Dickens and Fitzgerald in the quest for test-able questions. Ugh. Read? I'd rather you tear my lips off.So Vicki's series of authors invited into her home and speaking to an audience of 50 or 60 women (It's a very nice house and I am indeed sucking up for an invite) struck me as an excellent way of getting writers over with the public. A little food, a little chat, a little music, a lot of words, and these 60 women are going to tell at least 10 friends each about the wonderful time they had with say Fred Willard reading from his screenplay and that in turn creates a buzz. Well, so would wine, but there is none at Vicki's events. The intoxication is cerebral, not physical.

What? Oh you noticed that Fred Willard isn't a woman? Well aren't we the observant one! We'll get back to that, trust. Now stop interrupting, I'm on a roll here.

I messaged Vicki and said, 'You know you're doing an incredible service to publishing and authors? Having people into your home to personally interact with writers is worth a thousand Barnes and Noble book signings, and as a professional book reviewer, thank you for continuing my employment.'

Anyway, she was flattered and touched and I was flattered and touched that she was flattered and touched, so after we had each confirmed all this flattery and touching, I decided that Women Who Write deserved a column. Which you are reading. In case you hadn't noticed. Hi there!

I asked Vicki ten questions, as transcribed below:

1) When did Women Who Write get started?

Tuesday September 23, 2008.

2) Why did you start it?

I had just started the second draft of my first novel, Don't Jump. I wanted to hear it, to read it aloud, and workshop it into a play. I was fairly new in LA and had no idea how to get stage time to do so. At 413 pages, doing a few random minutes here and there would have taken decades. My wise editor, David Tabatsky, suggested I find a restaurant with a private room, invite other writers and local mommies, eat lunch and read.

3) Why did you decide to hold it in your home?

At first I sought a venue. It was problematic for a number of reasons. Noise and distractions for one. Or is that two? Plus, I was going to have to guarantee approx 25 women who would pay $25 for lunch each month. That felt like an awful lot of pressure. I was in a book club that met at a friend's home periodically… she had a comfortable living room with lots of seating. I asked if she'd be willing to host my mid-day soirees. She generously agreed. I'm not sure I ever would've gotten started otherwise. I had a big empty living room that sat 4. Almost all of our furniture is still in New York. The first three salons were held at her home. The last of three was almost cancelled the night before the event, when our hostess wasn't sure she'd be home. I considered bagging the whole thing after that. Asking someone to be available for my thing every month was too much to ask, and having to depend upon someone else's schedule was too much stress for me. I asked a local church if I could borrow some chairs and moved it to my house in January of 2009. That's when the magic started.

4) Who was the first writer to appear? How'd that go?

Erika Schickel and Kathleen Wilhoite were scheduled. I found out the day before the salon that Kathleen was on hold for an acting gig. I'd been planning it for a couple of months and was kind of panicked, but it was great. We had a potluck brunch — food is a major element to Women Who Write. Breaking bread, breaks barriers. Ericka read from her You're Not The Boss of Me, and I read the prologue and first chapter of Don't Jump. Twenty-five women attended (ironically). We had a fantastic, provocative discussion following the readings. And, that became a mainstay — topics borne from the art shared, unplanned "coincidences." On a whim, I wrote a recap that evening and sent it off to those that attended and those who couldn't make it. They also became a mainstay.

5) It's Women Who Write, but it's not just women. When did you decide to let the boys play too and why?

Soon after moving it to my house, Facebook friend, Tom Bergeron, announced his upcoming book, I'm Hosting as Fast as I Can!: Zen and the Art of Staying Sane in Hollywood. I sent him a note lamenting how I wished he could read for us. He said he'd wear a dress. On the spot I decided that since I'd made the rules, I could break them. Tom was willing, there was no way I wasn't going to seize that opportunity. Since we were having a man, I decided why not two, or three? I reached out to Evan Handler, red hot with Sex and The City and Californication and his memoir, It's Only Temporary: The Good News and the Bad News of Being Alive. He agreed. And then TV writer and comedian, Ron Zimmerman reached out to me. Tom read his book for the first time to us, the day it dropped. And we got the "R" rated version. It was a brilliant day. I thought at the time that I'd have men once or twice a year. Little did I know that incredible male authors and performers would avail themselves to us often and in abundance. The audience however, has remained women only, until this past August, when we ventured north to The Henry Miller Memorial Library in Big Sur, at the invitation of Michael Nesmith. At his urging to take some risks and grow the thing, we did it in the expansive great outdoors, with boys in attendance, and it felt still, remarkably like home.

6) You've also had 'non-traditional' writers like songwriters and screenwriters appear – what was your thinking behind expanding the tent as it were?

Just shy of two years in, Lori Lieberman wrote to inquire if I'd consider her reading her poetry or song lyrics. When I realized that she'd penned Killing Me Softly. I asked her to sing it and another song of her choice. She did — in New York in July 2009. (For the first three years I held the salon twice a year in Manhattan.) It was thrilling. Opening with music set a new tone. When I returned to LA in the fall, Lori came to the salon to be a woman amongst the women. I wanted the LA women to experience her. With her permission, I asked a neighbor if we could borrow a guitar. Lori opened and killed again. We haven't had a Women Who Write without opening with music, since. Angelica Page Torn was the first to read from a screenplay of a film that she'd written and starred in which was about to premiere. Academy Award Nominee, Michael O"Keefe, another Facebook friend, had a book of poetry about to drop, when he agreed to read. Women Who Write is not just great writing, it's also great performances, and that factors greatly into who I book. Personality is also essential. Following the musical performance and readings we have discussion, on topics that are borne from the art. It's provocative, profound and transformative for the audience and, the writers.

7) I doubt if you're making a nickel off this. Why do you keep doing it?

It cost me money for the first three years. And, I gave out swag every month, courtesy of WWW guardian angel, Rick Smolke, of Quick Impressions in Chicago. Out of necessity, in the last few months, I started to presell tickets. I'd much rather have the money come from sponsors.

8) I'll never ask you who was the 'best' guest because you won't answer that, nor should you. That demeans everyone else. But who surprised you? Who made you think, 'Holy sh!t, I knew you were good, but I didn't know you were THAT good.'

My mind's been blown more times than I can say. Across the board, the talent has been stunning. Every month we say this was the best, and every month we mean it. There's always an element of magic. I think the women bring out the best in everyone. Carl Reiner did over two hours for us and said it was one of the greatest shows of his career. It was an absolute love fest. Harry Hamlin was a huge surprise. He is the sexiest man alive. Breathtaking. He was such a good sport, a brilliant, forward-thinking activist. Steven Weber was amongst our most gifted readers. His piece on his date with Ann Coulter was a finely crafted tour de force not soon to be forgotten. MacKenzie Phillips had the room in empathetic tears. She was vulnerable and generous with her heart. We had so much fun with Robert Morse, one of the sweetest men, ever. Not to mention, one of the most talented. Phil Rosenthal killed us. Hysterical! Taylor Negron was a revelation... I had no idea the depth of his talent as a writer and a performer. Michael Nesmith, performing for the first time in a long time, previewed his then upcoming UK solo tour for us, with his band in full production, and treated us to spoken word intros for each song, written specifically for the occasion. It was a completely unexpected, mind-blowing treat. Now I want to go through the list and tell you what was special and wonderful about every one of our readers. Because they all were. Every single one of them. Except for... never mind. KIDDING!

9) Who would you love to get for Women Who Write that you haven't got so far?

Anne Lamott is a dream. Traveling Mercies is one of my favorite books. Steven Stephen King. His On Writing is my bible. I just connected with Da Chen. I'm thrilled that he's agreed to read. Tina Fey. I'm reading Bossypants now, laughing out loud at every other line. I've been working on Micky Dolenz for two years to sing and read. Janis Ian. Marianne Williamson. Dr. Drew. Keith Richards, what a book! What a life. I lean to those who tell a personal story. Gifted writing is a thrill to read, but not necessarily to have read. I seek those who reveal themselves and who know how to do so effectively. Women Who Write is a grand entertainment and sharing of deep truths. The grand trilogy of dreams: Garry Shandling, Albert Brooks and Steve Martin. I shan't rest until I get them to my living room. And then there's Larry David. Sigh.

10) Last – and I want to get YOU over too, kid – tell me about your writing, what you've done, what you're working on. Don't get modest on me!

I started out as an actress, segued to comedian, and then became a rock promoter and publicist. I left the business to have children. While pregnant I started writing for me. A screenplay, first. Buried in a drawer somewhere. Post 911, in the midst of personal trauma, I began writing Don't Jump. I call it a novel, it's more a fictionalized memoir. I swear to some of it. It was never my intention to take anyone down. I had a journey I was burning to document. A women's quest to find her place and purpose amidst sex, drugs, rock n' roll and celebrity. An inside look from an outsider. No one will know where I took liberties. I intend that as a protection for all my characters. I took no such liberties with Andi's internal journey. Every thought, every feeling is genuine. My greatest hope is that reader fills their toolbox as Andi does. And, laughs a bit along the way.

I had a publishing contract with a very small publisher that came and went twice from neglect. I was lent a hand by one of the most successful writers in the world, but to date it hasn't translated to a deal as yet. She encouraged me to self-publish, as she is now doing with her back catalogue. Another small publisher is reading Don't Jump now. We'll see where that leads. I've been sitting on a completed manuscript for too long, It's time, no matter what I have to do. I can't move on to the next book until I have this one on its way.

I write for Huffington Post, although, I've yet to submit the last piece I had approved ages ago. It's hard for me to justify writing without financial compensation, but, the benefits for me of having my pieces as the lead stories in their sections, making the Huff Po front page each time, and being featured on the Yahoo home page, opened the door for me to a new audience.I optioned a music reality show to Telepictures a few years ago, and have an advocate who perhaps will help it find new life. I shot a pilot pitch for a half hour comedy, Hey Vicki. It's my take on Curb, meets Larry Sanders, meets Lucy, meets Vicki, in as much as Women Who Write is the show within the show. It's my ongoing quest to get guests, and how I constantly embarrass myself personally and professionally. That sounds really arrogant, I should only be so lucky to ever be uttered in the same breath as those shows. The commonality, I hope, will be truth, no matter how unattractive. I co-wrote a dramedy, long before Weeds, about pot addiction and the road to recovery, which I still have believe in. And then, of course, there's Vicki Abelson's Women Who Write. Shortlisted for Oprah's OWN, I'm still not sure why we're not on there. Maybe, because we need an uncensored venue. HBO, SHOWTIME? I have interest from an internet channel, and, an agent about to pitch it— wide. It's been my dream to go live to a global audience who could participate — live— in the discussion.

As whack as it sounds, I do much of my daily writing on The Facebook. I found my voice there, and continue to cultivate it on a daily basis. Almost all of the readers who have graced my living room, I approached on FB. It's a powerful networking vehicle, as well as an extraordinary connector of humanity. I've made innumerable friendships that have come off the wall and enrich my life, daily. I documented and was comforted through the passing of my father, share the exploits of my amazing kids, promote my work and that of those I admire and respect, give voice to just about every thought and feeling I have, and, through daily practice, have learned to say it my way. I'm an acquired taste, not for everyone. I'm uncensored and snarky. I love The Facebook. I love LA. I'm as shallow as a puddle.

photo ©carlosalejandro

*(Update: Vicki's book **Don't Jump** was released in 2015 and it is a wonderful read in the tradition of Carrie Fisher's **Postcards From the Edge**. Buy a copy. Aloha!)*

(For a brief yet enjoyable time, I was a wrestling correspondent for PWTorch.com, one of the leading internet information sources, or dirt sheets as they are called in the trade. As a wrestling fan since childhood it has been my pleasure to have met and interviewed many of these great actor-athletes. One became a dear friend – April Hunter.)

(Over 18) Official site: AprilHunter.com
Wrestling/Pinup Downloads: AprilHunterPPV.com

April Hunter: A Body of Work

Herald de Paris, January 17, 2012

In a very real, visceral way it pains me to do this, however I know I need to make the case for this woman's profession before profiling the woman herself. Why? Because I know from personal experience that if the title of this article read as it properly should, April Hunter: Wrestler, it's highly likely you would have not read it. You have a clear conception that professional wrestling is low-rent, uncultured entertainment suitable only for trailer park boys and girls who serve in diners; the people for whom The Education

System Has Failed. To which I reply, bollocks.

Like a newly-appointed diplomat in a Henry James novel, please allow me to present my credentials. In my past live theatre career I have had precisely 108 Opening Nights as an actor, Director, Writer and/or Producer. I have trained who knows how many dozen actors, some of whom have gone on to juicy and profitable careers. I have studied Stanislavsky and Sandy Meisner, directed works by Anton Chekhov and Noel Coward, and yes indeed I played Hamlet. And played him damn well. I know of what I speak. Here is my bottom line: Professional wrestlers are the greatest actors of them all. It's not even close.

I well recall my first year acting class at Queen's University in Kingston, Ontario. We were all sat cross-legged on the grey all-weather carpeting in the studio and the professor, Bud Burkom, asked everyone what role they would most like to play and what actor's career they would most like to emulate. The women had a variety of parts, although their ideal actress became a recurring musical theme. Katharine Hepburn. Katharine Hepburn. Katharine Hepburn. Finally Bud said, in delicately, 'If anyone else mentions that broad's name I'm gonna scream!'

I can't remember a professional wrestler ever referring to a woman as a 'broad'. (Lauren Bacall did, but she of course was not a professional wrestler.) All bracketed humour points aside, here are the points of evidence:

> - Katharine Hepburn never had to perform in high school gyms or Legion halls
> - Katharine Hepburn never had to take a chair shot
> - Katharine Hepburn never had to perform with a broken nose
> - Katharine Hepburn never had to tell an entire story with no scripted words, just her body to work with to convey meaning

Katharine Hepburn never had bones broken by a fellow actor,

never had to take painkillers, and had a union to protect her.

Take the worst case scenario of any or all of the above, and April Hunter has been there, done that, and she's coming back for more Brother. She is Katharine Hepburn with muscles.

I watched a series of April's matches on YouTube in preparation for this profile; not watching them as a mark (the wrestling term for a hardcore fan who pretends to be an insider to this carnival-borne world), but as a theatre director. What is the message? What is the technique? How successful is the execution?

April Hunter approaches the ring in a calm, confident, sexual swagger. Hers is an energy of supreme confidence, yet not isolated but rather self-contained. She makes eye contact, she acknowledges fan support, she high-fives, hand slaps, hugs, points and smiles. She is on the side of those in the audience who are on her side. With the slow roll of her toned torso she lets the room in on her secret, speaking wordlessly with looks and movement, 'Oh, I'm gorgeous. You know it. I like that you know it. But you can't have it. Unless I say you can have it.' Nobody's fool. Nobody's tool.

I can't say as I have lost friends over my fascination with professional wrestling; I do however know that I've lost admirers. What is perhaps my most treasured email was sent by a former student who became a friend. It began, 'I've lost all respect for you' and carried on from there. I loved its honesty. You can't teach understanding until someone admits that he doesn't understand.

Besides, Ernest Hemingway and Norman Mailer both loved bullfighting. You tell me how the public, ritual slaughter of cattle is a higher calling than the enjoyment of wrestling and I'm willing to listen. You won't win the argument; I am simply willing to listen to it.

Back to April. I watch as she calls out, in what is called an 'in-ring promo' a rather skinny, frightfully bleached young woman named Talia Madison. Talia would later achieve fame as Velvet Sky in the TNA Impact promotion, known for wriggling her ass over the middle rope of the three-rope ring while the camera zooms in for a shot of tight-covered pudenda.

Why has there never been a band called Tight Covered Pudenda? Lost opportunity.

Thankfully, that was only a brief digression. Coming back to the ring, set in what looks like a high school gymn-atorium with a whiter audience than a Tea Party rally, April continues her promo. I am impressed.

Here's the Dirty Truth about acting. I'm not the first to have noticed this. Michael Shurtleff in the best single volume on acting I've ever read (Audition) devotes a chapter to it; and every casting director knows it, although few are loathe to comment as it is nearly impossible to define the abstract. The Dirty Truth is that some have it, and It can be refined; others don't. We're talking about charisma.

Charisma is the Great Unteachable. Speaking for myself as an acting coach, I can teach timing, energy, listening, stage movement, even how to read a script for nuance and meaning … I can't teach charisma. In all of the arts, that may be the one skill that one is either born with (and enjoys); or isn't born with (which isn't to say you can't have a nice career anyway).

Leave us face it - there are people on stage or on screen that you enjoy watching more than others. That little innocuous 'more' speaks shelves of volumes. Shurtleff talks about it in his book: there are people that the eye naturally tracks; you want to know what this person is going to do next.

I continue watching April's matches on YouTube. The more I watch, the more I realize that she has the quality of charisma. In some forty years of an on-and-off relationship between me and wrestling, I have never seen a better female wrestler.

Now, why I was catching up on these old matches - done for the most part for regional promotions that pop up, have a run of two or three years then morph into something else - is that she has never worked for Vince McMahon's WWE. No Monday Night Raw, no Smackdown, no national exposure since she broke into the business with WCW during its death throes in 2000. These aspects of her career would be major topics when I interviewed April.

So the question must be in your mind: If I hadn't actually seen April Hunter work, why was I profiling her? Why not Trish Stratus, likely the best-known woman wrestler in the world who is now a successful TV presenter on a variety on non-wrestling shows? Why not Sunny, or Sable, or George Clooney's squeeze du jour Stacy Keibler?

The answer is that journalism operates a lot like horse race betting: you go with hot tips. I knew that I wanted to profile a wrestler as part of this Women of the Year series. If part of my purpose is to learn how women are striving and thriving in what still is, in James Brown's words, A Man's Man's Man's World, there aren't many more male-dominated professions than the wrestling world. I asked three people whose opinions I trust; a wrestling manager, a writer, and a friend who is a devoted fan: Who would you like to see me interview? They all said April Hunter because she has a story to tell and she deserves the push. Good enough for me.

I do want to comment further on April's in-ring work. The good part about the smaller promotions as compared to WWE is that the former actually let the women wrestle for a time longer than a beer commercial. That has been a long-standing gripe of mine and I used to write about it when I wtote a weekly column for a major wrestling website (pwtorch.com). My theory on management in general is to hire the best people you can, then get out of the way and let them do their jobs. In WWE (and to a slightly lesser extent in its chirpy, smaller competitor TNA Impact) women's matches have an average length from bell to bell of about a minute. Strange. We'll come back to that.

Anyway, April is a masterful worker. She goes from move to move with tremendous pace, uses her strength - she is built like an Olympic pentathlete - and remembers to sell for her opponent. (You likely have no idea what that means. Selling means that when your opponent hits you, remember to show that it hurts. If your opponent has mashed your leg in a chair early in the match, don't be skipping along like nothing happened two minutes later. You would be amazed at how many professionals forget about this one. Hulk Hogan for one has made a career out of it.)

Work rate is hugely important, yet it isn't everything. It is that charismatic quality that separates April Hunter from the pack. She communicates her story with imagination and the full shelf of the emotional toolbox. When working as a heel (villain) she mocks her opponent with humorous disdain. When working as a babyface (hero), especially when wrestling men, she creates a pastel of fear, pain and determination while never ever wandering off into the cartoon-land of pulling faces and swooning like Sarah Bernhardt.

To be completely honest with you, if I was still in the theatre business I'd cast her in a heartbeat. Given three weeks' rehearsal she'd be phenomenal as Nora in Ibsen's A Doll's House.

Beyond wrestling, there were two other aspects of April's career I needed to catch up on before our conversation. One is her work as a Fitness model and a titleholder in professional Form and Fitness competitions. To say the minimum, at five foot nine in height with long red hair framing brilliant hazel eyes and a strong yet supple figure that would make a valkyrie weep in envy, she has the necessary equipment. She has won the Ms. Fitness Philadelphia competition and medaled at the NPC Junior Nationals. An international spokesperson for various nutritional supplements, she has also featured regularly in fitness and bodybuilding magazines. In other words, the girl's ripped.

The final part of April Hunter's career and the one that I suspect will generate the most hits for the on-line version of this profile, is that she is also a nude model, with her own website www.aprilhunter.com . Yes, if you would like to see what this astoundingly beautiful woman, who appears a good ten years younger than her actual thirty-seven years, looks like without her clothes on, you can do that for a small membership fee. And because you're going to ask anyway I'll tell you yes, of course I looked. I am utterly devoted to my fiancee, who sadly is disabled with a loss of short-term memory (that may come in handy here), however research is my life.

We must digress for a paragraph or three. I would ask April about the nude modeling in our interview; it is after all a substantial contributor to her income and she was in Playboy before she was in WCW. Nudity actually led to wrestling; a combination of which I'm quite sure D. H. Lawrence would have approved. If you don't get the reference, do look up Sons and Lovers. It's very good.

It would be disingenuous of me to ignore the nudity issue. You and I have known each other for at least five or ten minutes now, so we've established an honest relationship. (Well actually, you know a lot more about me while I know not a thing about you; but why let accuracy stand in our way?) The nude modeling was the one thing about April's career that made me hesitate in choosing her for this profile. What would the neighbours think? (The house next door is currently vacant. Next.) What would the prospective in-laws think? (A larger issue, hopefully ignorable. Next.) What would my editor think?

Yes, that was the potential sticking point. While I'd been given the luxurious go-ahead to write about whatever I wanted it might not be the prudent move to test the rippability of the envelope quite so soon. Here we are though, some two thousand words in and I'm not turning back now.

If journalism is about anything it needs to be about asking questions that others might not ask. For all the sniggering about the internet being a money machine built on porn, who ever asks the models in a serious way how they feel about being part of that industry? Additionally, in watching April Hunter's video updates I had also discovered that she knows a wealth of information about health, fitness and lifestyle issues that would inform this paper's readers and improve their lives. It would be the height of hypocrisy and shabby ethics to ignore all that just because April gets her kit off for the cameras.

As the brilliant French General Ferdinand Foch said in the midst of World War One's Battle of the Marne, 'Hard pressed on my right; center is yielding; impossible to maneuver. Situation excellent, I shall attack!' I was ready for the interview.

The Interview

I began our Skype interview by asking April how her Mom was doing. April had actually retired from wrestling after 2007, then returned to it in 2009 after her Mom was diagnosed with Stage Four lung cancer. That sadly reminded me of Christopher Hitchens' laconic statement when he was diagnosed with Stage Four esophegeal cancer, 'The bad part is that there is no Stage Five.'

April, who lives now in Clearwater Florida with her husband, the wrestler known as J. D. Maverick, travels regularly back to Pennsylvania where her mother is receiving treatment in a hospice. She said, 'That's why I came back to wrestling. I needed the money to help her out and to be able to get back as often as possible, at least once a month.' *(Update: Erna Kyle passed away in 2014.)*

Related to that, I'd noticed some comments April had made about the Japanese health cares system in relation to the American. As a Canadian I was curious as to the Japanese variant to the single-payer system. 'Well, just one comparison, an MRI in Japan costs

$160. Here in the US it's over $1500. They have a combination of public and private health care that I like. You do pay something, like $25 for an exam, which I think is good because that stops people from just coming in for nothing and filling up the system.'

With that as an ice-breaker - I wanted her to know that this wasn't just another wrestling interview - I of course then asked the standard question of all wrestling interviews. how did she get into the business? She had been in Playboy before WCW, so how did that transition work?

'It was really easy. They came to me. People had said to me before that I should go into wrestling, because I'm five nine and I'm athletic. Plus I was getting old for modeling at that time.' (*Interruption - she was 26. If 26 is old then I am an Egyptian Pharaoh.*) 'WCW approached me after the Playboy shoot and asked me to join so I did.'

April studied wrestling with a true legend, Wladek 'Killer' Kowalski. If you think that wrestling is all make-believe and no one ever gets hurt, I invite you to Google 'Kowalski + Yukon Eric + ear'. If you don't want to Google that, I think you can fill in the blanks yourself. So how did April come to learn wrestling with the trainer of Triple H and Chyna (Joanie Laurer)? He did not take on many students.

'I'd been in WCW for nine months and I actually left WCW when they said they didn't really know what was going on for us girls and then had the interview with WWE and their writers...which is how I was referred into Killer Kowalski's school. Kowalski was really hard to track down, so WWE tracked him down for me. He was in Boston so I packed up and moved to Boston the first week of September, just when all the students were arriving. It was crazy. Let me tell you,don't move to any university town during that time!!'

It surprised me more than slightly that April had been with a major wrestling company (at its peak, WCW's Monday Nitro drew ratings in the 6.0-7.0 category which if replicated would put it in the Top Ten in 2012) for nine months when on her own volition she decided to learn how to actually wrestle. You'd like to think that would be a prerequisite if only for safety's sake. Did anyone mentor her in WCW, say, 'Hey kid let me help you with this'?

'No, not really. Not at all actually. The girls really don't help one another. They're all just concerned about themselves.' And yes, I found that to be sad.

So why had she never been signed by WWE? I think I've made it clear in this article that April Hunter is the best female wrestler I have ever seen. My only speculation was that Vince McMahon seems to sign women who do *not* look like athletes (q.v. Kelly Kelly, Maryse, Maria Kanelis, it's a long and dubious list). Was that it?

'No one's ever really told me, but what I've heard is that because I'm tall they didn't want me standing next to some of the male wrestlers because I'd make them look short.'

What about TNA Impact? April has done a couple of appearances for them and the rumour is that they offered, and she turned down, a contract offer. Is that true?

'Yeah, it is. Here's why I turned it down. One, they only offered $300 a show -'

Wait. What!?! A lousy three hundred bucks? Was that the same for TV tapings?

'That was for TV. But what really stopped me was there was no health care coverage. In order to hire me, I had to sign a waiver that would not have them responsible for any injury I might get on the job. AND the pay was lousy, with no healthcare or benefits. So even though lots of people, friends even said, "Hey are you *sure*?", there was just no way.'

Now that was really appalling to me, particularly as TNA is that rarest of wrestling promotions, one owned by a woman - Dixie Carter of Panda Oil. No, not Dixie Carter of Designing Women. Three hundred dollars is a lousy reward for the risk wrestlers take every time they enter the ring, where quite literally their health and life is in the hands of their competitor.

Speaking of which, there was an experience I was curious about. Wrestlers do *not* have long life spans. WWE needs to rush people into its Hall of Fame before they are age 60, because not too many wrestlers live to see 60. As Bret Hart said in his brilliant autobiography Hitman (one of the 10 best autobiographies I have ever read by anyone in any profession), 'Is wrestling real? The outcome is pre-determined but the pain is real.' So how is it being married to a wrestler and watching J. D. in the ring, knowing all the things that can go horribly wrong?

'You watch it differently. You're watching it for their forearms, are they right? You know the spots so you're watching for that. Like, "Hey the manager's supposed to be there! Why's he late?" Then at home we're always checking our forms and criticizing one another. "What's this look like?" "No that's wrong." It gets pretty interesting. (*laughs*)'

My other point of curiosity related to the death of WCW. I have read many, many accounts of how that company fell apart - 1996, top of the ratings; 2001, dead. I have never read a woman's perspective on the implosion. So how much of a mess was it?

'We used to use a phrase in the industry. It was indie-rrific. Honestly, you'd arrive at one o'clock for a TV show, to get into your gear and make-up and you'd sit around and at six o'clock there still wouldn't be a match order taped to the wall. The show would be on at eight o'clock and stuff would still be being torn off the wall and changed. You never knew what you were doing.

'Then there was the travel. You'd get this FedEx envelope and it would tell you to get to the airport to go to wherever and you'd go. Then there would be no ticket there, but eventually there would be a ticket for like eleven hundred dollars, in coach, which was a lot of money in 2000, while for another fifty bucks you could have traveled first class. Then you'd get in after midnight and have to drive another 2-3 hours to get to the hotel near the venue...because WCW didn't play many big cities. We did outer areas. ' Clearly, a smooth-running operation.

On to the 'nudity issue'. Feminists would undoubtedly decry April for objectifying women, so how does she react?

'I don't hurt others with what I do, and it allows me freedom with my time. These things matter to me. Sure I end up working all day and night half the time and hurting MYSELF, since people can't tell the difference between being a centerfold and being a porn star, but hey...I don't apologize to anyone for doing what I have to do to take care of my Mom, put a roof over my head and food on the table. I don't care. I'm doing what I need to do. My Mom never cared about the nude modeling. She can't watch me wrestle though. I had to wrestle a lot of men in my career and my Mom came to one show where I was in a battle royal with a bunch of men and one of them was giving me chops in the corner and she just couldn't watch.'

What about fitness? April Hunter's career and income depends on keeping herself in fine tune. What are her tips for others?

'OK, the first one is a no brainer: Avoid soda. Duh. There's zero nutritional value in it and nothing but harmful chemicals to be gained.
2. Get more sleep. You probably need it.
3. Use smaller plates and eat less. As we get older, we need less food.
4. At restaurants, take home 40%.
5. What you eat matters far more than going to a gym. Diet is 80% of what you look like. Eat clean 6 days a week, then have a nice cheat meal.

6. If you're over 30, cut back/cut out your starchy carbs. You probably don't need them & they cause excess weight gain.
7. If you're drinking, stick to vodkas and wine.
8. Realize that on some days you just can't do it all. That you need time for yourself...and don't feel guilty about it. You need to recharge yourself to be at your best for those around you. "Should the airplane cabin pressure drop, put your own mask on first, before helping those around you." '

Last but in no way least to me, give my 'regular' career as a book reviewer, I knew that wrestlers are massive readers. They are constantly en route here and there and crossword puzzles get boring. So what books would April recommend to readers?

' I read so much and love so many books. OK, I've found a few to be really helpful:
1. *The Art of Non Conformity* by Chris Guillebeau. If you've ever been told to "Get a real job!", you may want to read this book.
2. *Bonjour, Happiness!* by Jamie Cat Callan. How to age gracefully and the tips and tricks that French women do to achieve this, compared to American women who tend to just give up and fall apart.
3. *Eat Right 4 Your Blood Type* by Dr Peter D'Adamo. Most of us are eating wrong for our types, which is part of the reason there's so much chronic disease. For example, type A's are very evolved and cant handle meat. They tend to have softer teeth (more dental problems) and don't produce enough stomach acid to break down meat. They are meant to be vegetarians. If you're type A and don't know this, you may be inadvertently causing yourself stomach issues. Type O's are hunter/gatherers. They do well with protein, fats and produce. They are not meant to eat starchy carbs or dairy, both cause weight gain and they're predisposed to diabetes. It sounds a little insane, but after seeing my family battle so many chronic illnesses, I gave it a shot and found that I dropped weight without trying and had more energy.'

In summary? I can't think of an interview subject I've enjoyed more.

(Since this interview, April has gone on to develop her skills as a writer. Without question, she is perhaps both the bravest and the most purley talented newcomer I have ever come across. She writes with a searing intensity and language so vivid it bursts like fireworks. Look for her work, coming soon.)

Books

(I became a book reviewer somewhat by accident. In late 2009 a friend asked me if I could possibly write a newspaper review of her daughter's book. Even though I already had my television column and had been covering all manner of arts subjects for several years, I had never reviewed a book. The editor was fine with it, so why not? The Chapters Books outlet in Thunder Bay sold out all its copies within a week after my review ran on the Sunday. Huh, imagine that? That started what is in many ways the best part of my career. I can read whomever and whatever I want, and learn about anything. In many ways reviewing has been a bonus – and free! - university degree. Below are some of my favourites from the past seven years.)

The Waterproof Bible

Andrew Kaufman (Random House Canada, 2010)

I believe it was at the point where the green-skinned gill breathing Aquatic humanoid was carjacking the white Hondo Civic sedan from a Halifax parkade in order to drive herself to Manitoba to save her mother from the fate of being an air breathing hotel proprietress that I realized things were getting a little weird in the story. This required a certain shifting of my critical perspectives shall we say. Andrew Kaufman's new novel *The Waterproof Bible* is, the more I think of it, a subversive little book with a message far beyond its plot. In his writing a book that would seduce people into reading about Aquatics in stolen cars who otherwise never would, I have to congratulate the author. I do love a good subversive.

The subversion comes in the story's set-up. I am about to describe to you the part that Jennifer Aniston should absolutely play if she has even the slightest interest in being a real actress, either that or just hire Sandra Bullock again. Kaufman has a background in film by the way. As that art compels its practioners to think cinematically all day every day, I'd bet my bottom dollar that he was definitely setting up a sweet romantic comedy.

Rebecca Reynolds has an interesting capability. Whatever emotions she is feeling - anger, satisfaction, fear, and so on - everyone around here also feels. This being the case since birth, everyone in her life knows about it, so it's treated as a ho hum fact of life by people around her. Secret identities have been done to death anyway. Rebecca also has learned to control this, by taking tchotchkes from awful moments in her life (e.g. the hospital bracelet when her mother was sick), putting them in shoe boxes and they in turn would block her specific feelings about those moments from returning and so being transmitted ever again. Well there's *one* way to control your emotions. If it worked for all of us, cold storage lockers would propagate like field mice.

Nonetheless, that is a perfectly charming device. Throw in the separated husband who still loves Rebecca, off building them a sailboat in the middle of the Manitoba prairies and we have a plot that could be filmed tomorrow.

But that plot sucks you in to the Aquatic science fiction religion debate. Not that there is anything wrong withe the sci-fi plot, but I stuck with it to find out what would happen with Rebecca. The story never really properly gets back to her - she virtually vanishes for a hundred pages or so - but the ride is fascinating enough. Oddly enough, the literal ride of the narrative includes rest stops in Pass Lake and Upsala that I have sparked in myself. That was a pleasant surprise.

There was one brilliant thought in an interesting and occasionally quite funny book. "(T)he only difference between a happy ending and a sad ending is where you decide the story ends." What a refreshing way of handling life and summarizing one's feelings about death and the hereafter. A formula for coping, by the book.

(I have what I call my Wall of Fame hanging in my sitting room. It is a series of framed autographs with any two word phrase chosen by my favourite writers. Martin Amis started it all when he sent me a wonderful 'Piss Off' that hung on the inside of my front door; thus it was the last thing guests saw before leaving. Victoria Coren is a member of my Wall of Fame, based upon our exchange after the following review was published.)

For Richer for Poorer

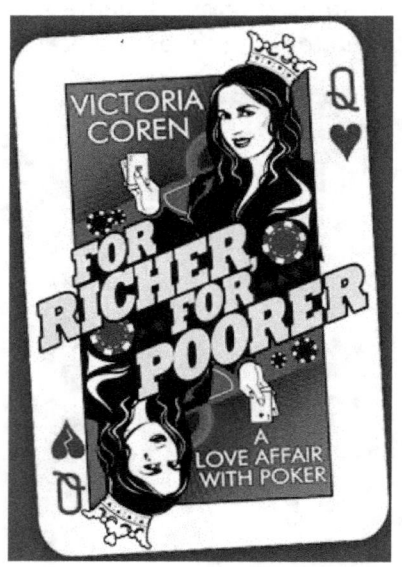

Victoria Coren (McClelland and Stewart, 2010)

I like to think of myself as a pretty fair game player. I won the Queen's University backgammon tournament a couple of decades ago, have fine card sense in euchre and can hold my own in other rummy or trump games. And yes, I play poker on-line (never, ever for money as I achieved that self-awareness when I'd regularly get fleeced in the high school cafeteria playing classic five card draw) winning about one out of five sit-n-go tournaments I enter. But I would never, ever play at the same table as Victoria Coren for I know that the evening would end in defeat and my being destitute - if not of money, at least of spirit.

Coren has written a funny, thorough and emotionally bare biography of her career as a poker player. What makes For Richer for Poorer stand out amidst the annual shoveling out of sports and game biographies is that Coren is a professional in the arts of observation and writing. Still only 37 she could just as easily have written a biography of her 'other' career, that of a columnist for The Guardian in London as well as its weekly off-shoot The Observer.

I've been a fan of Coren's since well before reading this book, so I admit to a pre-disposition for enjoyment of this work. Then again, what's the point of picking up a book if you don't think you're going to enjoy it? They are rather more expensive than a small bag of a new flavour of potato chips that one might or might not like.

What I've enjoyed about Coren over the years is the glorious invention she has brought to her work. Here is a short anecdote quoted from wikipedia:

n December 2008, Coren revealed that she had instigated a hoax in order to trap a group who turned up to memorial services for people they had actually never met. She created the fictitious and recently deceased Sir William Ormerod, and placed an advertisement in the main British newspapers for his memorial service "followed by a drinks reception". Coren reported that the group duly applied for tickets claiming to have known the late Sir William.

Now you have to agree that has more journalistic imagination than anything you've likely read in your local Canadian daily in the last five years. But Britain, for all that Fleet Street is damned actually has a competitive and profitable newspaper industry and either because of that or as its reason British newspapers demand writers who are brave, sharp, opinionated and blisteringly sharp of wit. If Oscar Wilde was re-born he'd be writing the society page. And for my money The Guardian is the best paper of any and Victoria Coren is an excellent first exhibit.

But back to the cards. Coren is still the only woman to have won a Euporean Poker Tour event, winning 500,000 pounds at the London tournament in 2006. She is also a frequent on-air analyst and interviewer on the various poker shows which proliferate television in the UK, much as they do in North America. The luck that supports her skill is that she straddles two poker eras - the traditional card room and the modern internet.

Like me, Victoria Coren was regularly fleeced in her teens. Unlike me, she responded to the challenge and kept going. She eventually found her home base at a Tuesday night game at the Victoria Casino - the Vic. This game was populated by the sort of characters as vividly described by Coren in For Richer for Poorer as Damon Runyon would have, had he been British and they been fictional. And amidst all these Guys was the one Doll: Victoria Coren.

She became a very good player and as a successful journalist was able to afford to keep on playing and learning. British journalism also pays better than North American. That also helps the industry in general if you want to attract quality away from the magazine and internet competition. More to the point, Coren became good enough to become a tournament player, of both the celebrity and hard-boiled pro variety.

The characters absolutely bubble off the page. There sits the great Phil Hellmuth, the biggest winner in the history of the Las Vegas based World Series of poker, babbling like an idiot about a music album he wants to put out featuring rejected cuts by famous artists. Would he have written any of the songs? No. Why would people buy it? Because he, Phill Hellmuth would have endorsed it.

There is also a wonderful conversation with the ever-brilliant novelist (and poker player) Martin Amis:

Before his heat I asked Amis why he likes poker. I have asked a lot of people this question over the years and the answer is usually 'Oh, you know, the thrill, the money.' Amis replied: 'People often compare politics to chess, but it's closer to poker because egos are involved. On a chessboard, the properties and powers of a bishop are permanently fixed. In poker, it's all wobbled through the prism of personality.'

But For Richer for Poorer is not all big names and glitzy casinos. There is the emotional displacement she feels when she realizes that she has substituted cards for relationships and children. *(Update: Since this review was written Victoria married the English actor and wit David Mitchell, They had their first child, a daughter, in 2015.)* When she does fall in love - with a decidedly uncommitted fellow player against all her better instincts - she is destroyed emotionally. Strangely, and yes understandably, it is only the serious illness of her father that makes her re-enter life with fresh enthusiasm.

This is truly an excellent book for anyone with even the mildest interest in poker or the human psychology of game players. And do look at Victoria Coren's other work at www.guardian.co.uk. And that's the final word.

(I rarely write a negative review as my opinion is, Why waste a reader's time reading about a lousy book? However, sometimes a publication asks me to review a specific book and then I am morally compelled to write honestly. The following is an example of what I'm like when I don't like something. Take cover.)

Tell-All

Chuck Palahniuk (Doubleday Canada 2010)

It couldn't have taken much more than two hours to read Chuck Palahniuk's new novel, 'Tell-All.' It is a slight book at 179 pages, but then again so was The Great Gatsby. To draw a parallel with a quiet different recreational activity, size doesn't matter; it's what you do with it that counts. I'm seriously considering suing. In that two hours I could have held my wife's hand, played baseball with our border collie, or cleaned the basement. Instead I spent that two hours at first intrigued but then rapidly and overwhelmingly annoyed.

So annoyed, in fact that I'm breaking a personal rule. I write these reviews for three reasons: money, free books, and I want to encourage people to read and expose their souls to the work of some absolutely brilliant people who write about worlds that are both familiar and strange in their blossoming of the human condition.

Equally however - and this will be a rarity, I promise - it is valuable to intermittently look at what is a complete sham foisted off on the public as something cool in its cutting edge fantasy. A book like Tell-All gives cutting edge fantasy a bad name. The literary descendants and admirers of Kurt Vonnegut should be gathering pitchforks as I write. And it's not like Palahniuk is a lousy writer either. He has nine other novels published, with the best known being Fight Club (yeah, the Brad Pitt and Edward Norton movie). Tell-All just feels infernally lazy.

Let me present some evidence. Here is a typical paragraph from Tell-All. The bold-faced words and names are as they appear in the book. The "Lilly" referred to is the late author Lillian Hellman, who appears as a recurring character. I'll get to explaining that. Read on:

'On page one of the screenplay, **Robert Oppenheimer** puzzles over the best method for accelerating particle diffusion until Lillian stubs out a **Lucky Strike** cigarette, tosses back a shot of **Dewar's whiskey**, and elbows Oppenheimer away from the rambling equation chalked the length of a vast blackboard. Using spit and her **Max Factor** eyebrow pencil, Lilly alters the speed of enriched uranium fission while **Albert Einstein** looks on. Slapping himself on the forehead with the palm of one hand, Einstein says, "Lilly meine liebchen, du bist eine genious!"'

Now I'll be the first to say that there is something brilliant in that. But that's it. It's Bret Easton Ellis minus that annoying plot thingie. Well that's not entirely fair. There is a plot to Tell-All. Sort of.

The story is narrated by Hazie Coogan, the major domo of Miss Kathie Kenton, an aging actress who has bought herself youth at the hands and on the table of plastic surgeons. She takes on a lover, Westward Calton Westward III. Hazie and Miss Kathie discover that Westward plans on putting out a tell-all biography of Kenton whose last chapter is her death. Which as various attempts at her life are derailed because Hazie and Kathie have read the book, he has to write different last chapters, whose plots are derailed etc. Thus cleaned up, the story will make a fine movie. And maybe that's the point of this review. When it comes out; see the movie, burn the book.

You see, the writing really shouldn't get in the way of the story. I have a deep suspicion that Tell-All is intended as a parody of a Dominick Dunne book: lots and lots of very famous smart set people doing horrible things to one another. I rather hope not. Given that the flowers on Dunne's grave have not even had time to wither after his passing, it would be the literary equivalent of stabbing someone in his back and a dead back at that.

But if not aimed directly at Dunne, Tell-All certainly takes aim at his imitators - everyone from the aforementioned Ellis to Gore Vidal to Jackie Collins. And endless name-dropping is certainly a feature of that whole genre of books. The reason for the boldfacing in Tell-All is to absolutely shriek each instance of name or name brand droppings. Droppings is indeed the word for it. But even in the 'real' tell-alls, the Dominick Dunne books, the name-dropping gets tedious: all the shops where every table setting was bought, those lists of who was sat at the surrounding tables in the Copacabana while Sinatra sang on stage.

To work, parody needs to be a condensation of the unusual or grating elements of the subject being parodied. Parodies are damnably hard to sustain over length, which is why there are few parody movies that can really stay funny from start to finish as Airplane! did a long time ago. The genre is best made for sketch comedy. Once one starts to do a full-length parody, those grating elements become even more grating because now they're being shouted at rude length.

Worse yet, the fatal flaw of Tell-All is that there is no counter to the grating noise of all the names. And they literally become noise as Pahlaniuk frequently writes little triptych sentences like, *Snarl, bark, screech* (italics as in the book). A countering influence, say one prominent voice in the book that doesn't get bold-faced brand names all littered about, is vital to parody. You need a babyface to expose the heels. That is the point of parody, otherwise it is just bleating mockery. The Pythons knew it, which is why there were all those Majors barking out that all this needs to stop, it's too silly. That's a parody: point out something's characteristics in a humorous fashion then have someone say that the subject is horrible and should be shunned. There.

Finally, the whole business of Lillian Hellman popping up and being a bold-faced lying fantasist is, well, troubling. Granted there was the infamous feud and lawsuit withy Mary McCarthy but ... it is both obscure, pointless and mean. And that's the final word.

The Balfour Declaration: The Origins of the Arab-Israeli Conflict

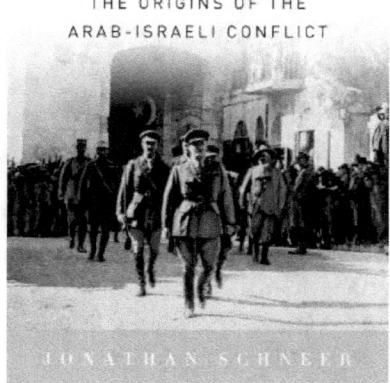

by Jonathan Schneer (Bond Street Books, 2010)

It was a fairly simple statement.

"His Majesty's government view with favour the establishment in Palestine of a national home for the Jewish people, and will use their best endeavours to facilitate the achievement of this object, it being clearly understood that nothing shall be done which may prejudice the civil and religious rights of existing non-Jewish communities in Palestine, or the rights and political status enjoyed by Jews in any other country."

A mere sixty-eight words issued as a letter from British Foreign Secretary Arthur Balfour to the Baron Walter Rothschild in November 1917; yet as Jonathan Schneer states clearly in the sub-head to this excellent political history, the origins of the mistrust between and among the Muslim world, the West and Israel all can be seen to begin here.

This is history at its most gripping - the history of the diplomacy, secrecy, risk and battle that led to the declaration by the predominant Western Power that Zionism would find a protected home in Palestine. I would argue that *The Balfour Declaration* deserves a place next to *The Seven Pillars of Wisdom* by T.E. Lawrence (as in "of Arabia") as an essential book for understanding what went on in the Middle East during World War One and how it went on.

There is such a narrow canyon between the cliffs of academic history and popular history. To traverse it successfully, the writer must supply all the first-hand evidence and document sifting that academia requires, while giving the non-term paper writing casual reader a crisp narrative with memorable characters. The late Barbara Tuchman was a master of this territory. Schneer is not the literary stylist Tuchman was - his prose is solid and thoughtful, on the level of the well-written editorials of a major serious newspaper. But good enough I say. He may not move you to tears with his poetry, but he won;t move you to tears from boredom either.

Schneer knows how to tell an incredibly complex story of opposing goals and personalities and make it comprehensible. His art, and his book's blessing, is that he excels at making the people involved tangible for the reader. His research has led him to pull the precise episodes and quotes that make, dare I say it, history come alive. An example, from page 234:

If the principals were satisfied, however, some of the lesser figures were not. They shared neither Hussein's faith in Sykes nor Sykes's faith in Sykes. Colonel Cyril Wilson, for one, felt deep unease. When the king read the statement, "it struck me as possible that the sharif [Hussein], one of the most courteous of men, absolutely loyal to us and with complete faith in Great Britain, was verbally agreeing to a thing which he never would agree to if he knew what our interpretation of what the IRAQ situation is to be." He took Sykes aside: "Does the Sharif [Hussein] know what the situation at Baghdad really is?"

For this was the third point of the triangle. Emir Hussein had chosen to place his trust in Britain and defy the *jihad* against the Entente powers pronounced by the Constantinople-based caliph, the supposed leader of they Muslim peoples. Hussein and his sons organized and led the famed Arab Revolt, tying down and disrupting the Ottoman armies in a return for the promise (Hussein thought) of an Arab Kingdom stretching from present-day Saudi Arabia through Syria, Lebanon and - oh dear - Israel.

Had that promise been made or had it not? The evidence Schneer presents suggests that the boundaries were intentionally fudged by Sir Henry McMahon in a series of secret correspondences with sharif Hussein. At worst, and as alluded to in the excerpt above, Hussein thought part of his envisioned kingdom might be under a British protectorate for a time, during which Britain would pay the kingdom a recompense. This is what he thought Britain's plan was for Mesopotamia, which we know as Iraq. It wasn't.

Meanwhile back in London, under the charismatic leadership of Chaim Weizmann, Zionism managed to work its way into favour with the Foreign Office, the War Cabinet and Prime Ministers Asquith and Lloyd George. Add into the mix characters such as Lawrence of Arabia (Schneer shrewdly reminds the reader of scenes from David Lean's movie), the aforementioned Sykes - rather the Henry Kissinger 'leave it all up to me' diplomat of his day - and settings that sprawl across Europe, the Middle East and a guest appearance by the occasional American and you have a tale that is as suspenseful as a James Bond story.

There is much, much more here than can ever be covered in one review. And although Schneer clearly believes that Hussein and the Arabs were the wronged party, the Zionists themselves are not placed in blame when Hussein gets a much shrunken version of his kingdom in return for two years of battle. The Zionists never knew of the promises made to Hussein, just as Hussein never knew of the promises made to the Zionists.

An exceptional study of a critical time. Recommended to anyone who has, or wished to have, an opinion about the Middle East today. And that's the final word.

Interview with Jonathan Schneer (The Balfour Declaration)

Date: September 16, 2010

San Francisco Book Review

I don't believe in coaxing or coercing an interview subject into discussing matters that they would rather not, thank you very much. If there's not enough interesting topics remaining to talk about, then why on earth would I want to interview them or for you to read about them? We all have things or even opinions that we don't necessarily choose to wave about like a knight's pennant. the exception of course is politics and politicians for whom there is no closed season.

Still, I was initially surprised when Dr. Johnathan Schneer, graduate of Columbia University and specialist in modern English history seemed reluctant to discuss Middle East Relations, given that his excellent new book The Balfour Declaration is about the origins of the now century old political conflict between Arabs and Jews. Was the delivery of the document stating that His Majesty's Government was supportive of the idea of a formal Zionist presence in Palestine, later becoming Israel, a good thing or not?

I'd say it's rather hard to sit on the fence on that one.

Still, I chose not to press the issue, after trying the roleplaying exercise of asking if he were a member of David Lloyd George's

War Cabinet, how might he have voted? Schneer laughed heartily. I guess no one had tried to ask it that way before.

He said, "I'm trying very hard to get to the bottom of what happened. the historian's job is not to take sides." That I suppose is why Political Studies programs exist - political scientists are historians who take sides.

I had another suspicion that I didn't raise. There is an insane hatred running rampant in the world. To come down firmly on a lightning rod such as the rationale for Israel's existence is to impale one's self on that lightning rod. And to be frank, I'm not so sure I'd state my own opinions on so volatile an issue to a journalist I hadn't met and whose work I might not know; given that a misquote or an exaggeration by an eager writer could lead to God only knows what consequences.

But anyone whose working title for his rich and compelling narrative was Dragon's Teeth (Schneer's son told him it sounded like a kung fu book) has got some thoughts on the subject. Perhaps another time.

As to what we did discuss, there was much of interest there. I asked who his intended audience was, the academic world or a more general audience, and The Balfour Delcaration is indeed a general interest work. There has been academic interest of course. Scheer said, "Some academics have reviewed it in non-scholarly settings. The response has been very positive. As always, they can find something to criticize. One criticism is that I didn't spend time on the Christian Zionist movement."

The what?

He continued, "There are (Biblical) historians who have said that the Jews should gather in Palestine before the Second Coming." As both the British Prime Minster Lloyd George and the Foreign Secretary Arthur Balfour were members of churches which shared that belief, the line of reasoning goes that this was a motivation for the eventual note endorsing Jewish Zionism. Schneer feels that although Lloyd George and Balfour "were probably pleased" this would have been more of a happy coincidence than a compelling argument forcing their geo-political decisions.

It is a fascinating story, with shifting alliances between Britain and Zionism, Britain and the Arabs, Britain and France. There were what I referred to as diplomatic James Bonds conducting secret negotiations and Lawrence of Arabia sweeping across the desert with the Arab revolt against the Ottoman Empire.

What is the lesson of the book and the times for the modern reader? Schneer has two lessons. One, that the British duplicitous behaviour left the atmosphere in Palestine filled with suspicion and hatred.

As to the second, "The second one has become more clear me over time was that the same way the people of Great Britain or the Ottoman Empire could not keep track of what their rulers were thking, nor did the rulers know what each other were thinking. Does Barack Obama tell Hilary Clinton everything he's thinking? ... People like us today should never take what leaders say for granted. I don't believe politicians have changed."

I thanked him for his great contribution to the understanding of the times - he was particularly pleased to have given the Turkish or Ottoman aspect its proper showcase. The conversation was as enjoyable as the reading of The Balfour Declaration. And that's the final word.

The Paris Wife

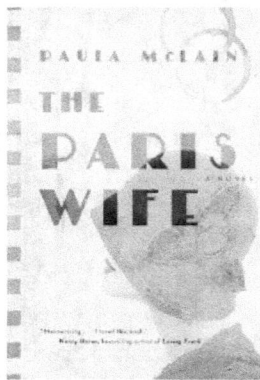

Paula McLain (Bond Street Books, 2011)

Gather round ladies and you shall hear why never to hold the heart of writers dear. That is the great *caveat* at the heart of Paula McLain's highly-anticipated novelization of the life and marriage of Ernest Hemingway and Hadley. That is the way it was. Ernest Hemingway and Hadley; not Ernest and Hadley Hemingway. Ernest Hemingway rather insisted on supporting acts rather than equal billing. That seems to have been a problem.

When I said highly-anticipated in the paragraph above, I very much included myself among the high. *The Paris Wife* was not just the scratch that satisfied the itch; it was the scratch accompanied by a finely poured martini and a loving coo in the ear.

I mark out for the Jazz Age and the authors who toasted it. Granted I more worship at the Altar of Fitzgerald than sing to the Organ of Hemingway, but I do have an intuition that Hemingway is being dismissed as a caricature and that is a travesty of literary justice.

There was an incredible irony behind my reading of *The Paris Wife* and it would be dishonest as a reviewer to not mention it. I know I do not have a fifth of the talent of Hemingway - this despite many fifths consumed in the hopes of finding it. Our similarities as writers extend to the comparison that we have both began sentences with the word 'The'.

However, I have slept in the old boy's bed.

It was exactly one year ago from this writing that I was staying in the Ernest Hemingway Suite at the Clarion Hotel on Sherbourne Street in Toronto. It is so named because the Hemingways lived there for a time in 1923 when Hadley was giving birth to their son Jack aka Bumby and Ernest was being badly mistreated as a regular free-lance contributor to the Toronto *Star*.

Having come this far, I now have to complete the story. Oddly, it will explain an important point about *The Paris Wife*. So bear with me, damn it. I had come to stay at the Clarion because my bride-to-be was undergoing emergency brain surgery, I had arrived with her on an air ambulance with the clothes on my back and the sole advantage that I did some work for a hotel chain. Therefore I was able to book in at the Clarion at a rate you'll never believe exists.

What amuses me in retrospect, is that I had alerted the book publishers to my temporary change of address, so that the books I had listed for review would arrive at the correct destination. At the precise, exact, perfect musical comedy moment as I was mentioning to the Desk Clerk that I might be expecting a package or two, the courier from Random House arrived with a fat box 'for Mister O'Hearn' as the manager of the Clarion was stepping out from his office and he - phew - absorbing all this said, "Would you like the Ernest Hemingway Suite, sir? No extra charge?"

It was an easy decision.

So I know what he saw in the morning, in the little wedge of a study behind bay windows that stared down - straight down - the street that ironically houses the offices of the great Canadian publishing houses. As I suspect there were less thousand storey Delta Hotels in the 1920s than in 2010, Hemingway would have also have been able to see the Star building at 1 Yonge Street. I suspect the author glowered when he glanced.

At the time, I wondered why there was an Ernest Hemingway Suite *and* a Hadley Hemingway Suite. Having read *The Paris Wife*, now I know.

There is a danger in reviewing or even reading novels of historical fiction. Much like the enjoyment of professional wrestling, one can get lost in what is fiction and interpret it as reality. What one is reading in this novel is Paula McLain's version of events recorded by diaries, letters and the recorded observations of others in diaries and letters. This is the Danger Land for a writer.

If inventing conversation is an Art (and it is) then the danger is in the Art being caught in the crossfire between the mercenary 'Ain't Necessarily So' forces and the 'Don't Speak Ill of The Dead' Gestapo. In other words, one must read *The Paris Wife* not as absolute or perhaps even probable truth, but at the least as possible truth. And in other words again, Ernest Hemingway is presented as a character based on a character who created characters based on character. And so on.

So what then is one left with for absolute certainty in '**The Paris Wife**'? Well, at its most basic level you have an instructional warning against seeking comfort with *l'artiste* in a well-written story populated by famous, charismatic persons.

Paula McLain makes what is, I think, the shrewd choice of casting Hadley Hemingway (the great man's first wife) as the novel's narrative voice. As she is presented as non-vindictive - indeed a shy and if not simple then non-complex St. Louis girl - we tend to receive her take and description of events as Truth. Were the narrative personage to have been the Objective Anonymous , we would become bogged down with arguments of fact, whereas if the narrator had been Ernest Hemingway, we as readers would have been expecting a perfect (and impossible) simulation of the Hemingway style. Because Hadley is a largely unknown-beyond-her-name historical figure, then who better to describe the goings on? She is a Nick Carraway who gets to sleep with the author.

Even if one argues with the 'He said/She said' evidence and 'How insane was Ezra Pound' digressions, the nut of the story of *The Paris Wife* still bursts out of its shell. Artists are the Obsessed who can draw/write/design. Anything that gets in the way of the Obsession must be destroyed.

This doesn't lead to healthy personal relationships. Although there is no clear passage in Paula McLain's novel to illustrate this, one is left with the absolute feeling that Ernest fell for the simplicity of Hadley because she was a woman he could overwhelm in a way he never could his mother. Later, he leaves Hadley because (in the novel's world) he could actually hump and dominate a worthier opponent in Pauline, his second wife.

There is much good to be said about *The Paris Wife*. The writing is solid throughout and in particular Paula McClain does a fine, fine job in lightly describing what a usual Hell and occasional Heaven it was being a friend of a sodden, violently abusive F. Scott Fitzgerald's.

The lesson though- ah dear, the lesson though - is that no matter how much a writer loves you, you my dear are grist to his mill, possible solution to his problems, pinata to his fears. You're along until his next model of the Perfect Future thrusts its hips his way.

I loved it.

Be seeing you,

H

(This review was sheer indulgence for me as I have given away many copies of The Groucho Letters to my closest friends over the years. I bear tribute in the following.)

The Groucho Letters: Letters From and To Groucho Marx

(Simon and Schuster, 1967)

Yes, you read that right. *The Groucho Letters* was first published in 1967 and if the author is planning a book-signing tour any time soon it's going to rouse the interest of the Executors of his estate. But sometimes I think it is of equal value for a reviewer to draw your attention to the obscure or forgotten as well as to the hot and touted. Reviews don't always have to be about the Next Big Thing when there are Present Big Things or Past Big Things that have the same qualities of bigness and, er, thingness as the hot new arrival.

If I knew lots about websites and 'arranging things' I'd do a separate section for these called Blasts From the Past. But I don't know lots about websites so you'll have to hunt. I'll include that Blasts From the Past somewhere in the text of future reviews of this type so you can find them using the search engine elsewhere on this page. There, I've done my best.

So why *The Groucho Letters* for the first in this series? I first read it when I was about 16 years old. I'm on my third copy now, purchased from Alibris as I wanted it in hard cover so perhaps this one will last. It is still the funniest book I have ever read.

For years, literally, I would keep one of my earlier copies in the bathroom. No wonder the paperback bindings finally expired from bubble bath suffocation. But I could do with *The Groucho Letters* what serious-minded Protestants do with the Bible - open to a random page and find inspiration. Here, let's play together.

I randomly opened to page 223 and there was a letter from the late David Susskind. Susskind was a talk show host in the 1960s through the 1980s. Imagine a liberal melding of Charlie Rose and William F. Buckley and you'd have the picture about right. So from a letter to Groucho written March 26, 1964:

I miss John F. Kennedy, but have begun to reconcile to the homey-folksy ways of Lyndon Johnson. For a brief time it seemed as if literacy, intellect, sophistication and style were going to become respected aspects of American life, but I guess it was not to be. I find it more than passingly interesting that the first foreign dignitary received by President Johnson, President Segni of Italy, was entertained with an evening of hootenanny. Anyway, I am rambling like crazy and with no provocation whatsoever.

Perhaps uniquely among books of collected letters I have read (and they are great snoopy fun, now aren't they?), Groucho's correspondents were as sharp with the return volleys as was the master server of sarcasm. T.S. Eliot, who shared with Groucho loves of baseball and boxing - yes *that* T.S. Eliot - James Thurber and Garson Kanin were all men who knew the business end of a pen and how to wield it.

There too, Groucho's letters put to rest any speculation that his best stuff was done by writers. Without a smidgen of disrespect to S.J. Perelman, Leo McCarey or anyone else associated with the Marx Brothers, Groucho was a creation all right, but he was his own creation. He is just as sarcastic, just as witty, just as gifted with satire on the page as he was in the movies or 'You Bet Your Life.'

There had been previous evidence to that effect. On an appearance on 'What's My Line?' a panel show where the celebrities tried to guess the occupation of Mystery Guests, Groucho asked some plumpish male Tammany Hall fat cat, "Are you a crooked politician? ... Or is that redundant?" One would pay dearly to hear that one asked at a Leaders' Debate.

It would be wrong to leave you with my words when Groucho Marx's words are literally at hand. I again shall choose randomly ...

From a letter to Arthur Sheekman (comedy writer) sometime in the 1940s whilst on vacation in Maine:

In the evening we sit around a fireplace with nothing to drink (unless it's my house), very little to smoke (unless it's my house) and nothing to eat (unless I buy it), and discuss what's the matter with the theater. Is it dead? and where is the road gone to.

[A Guest] makes a three-hour speech against Equity, and then I defend it in a speech not lasting over five minutes. I would make a longer speech but I am two years behind in my dues and I can't seem to get my heart into it.

The Absolutist

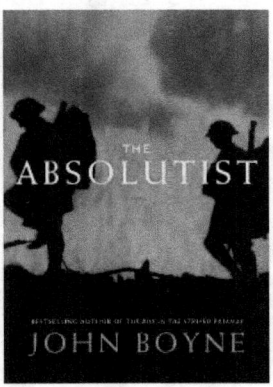

John Boyne (Doubleday Canada 2012, Hardcover)

For: Herald de Paris

There is a poem by Siegfried Sassoon written to his fellow 'war poet' Robert Graves called A Letter Home. Here is a section of it:

*You and I have walked together
In the starving winter weather.
We've been glad because we knew
Time's too short and friends are few.
We've been sad because we missed
One whose yellow head was kissed
By the gods, who thought about him
Till they couldn't do without him.*

When I read and reviewed Nicholas Murray's *The Red Sweet Wine of Youth*, which told the story of the generally all too brief lives of the World War One poets the question occurred to me as to why on Earth any homosexual man ever took up arms in that conflict. There is a larger issue of course - why does any man ever take up arms in any conflict, however let's leave that one aside. Consider:

when the war started in 1914 it had been less than 20 years since Oscar Wilde had been sentenced to Reading Gaol and it would be a half a century before the sodomy laws were amended. If a country rejects one's own interests and desires, how is that country worth killing for and dying for?

That issue is never directly addressed in *The Absolutist*, yet it looms over the plot like rain cloud over the trenches in France. This indeed is one of the strengths of John Boyne's novel and indicative of a noble trust Boyne has in his readers. He allows us the pleasure of discovery through contemplation. No irony is ever stated, merely alluded.

For instance, referring back to the earlier question, no one ever pretended that World War One was fought in the interests of freedom and democracy. Any misconception along that line that the modern reader may have has been imposed by later re-writers of history. Instead, as a doomed war objector named Wolf states,

Yes, there are issues at stake, political issues, territorial issues, over which this war is being fought, and there are legitimate grounds for complaint, I dare say, but there is also such a thing as diplomacy, there is such a thing as the concept of right-thinking men gathering around a table and sorting their problems out. And I don't believe those avenues have been exhausted yet.

Political issues and territorial issues. The war was fought over land and control of land. However, if the land was the metaphorical damsel in distress she completely rejects the knights coming to her rescue. The land literally eats the trench-bound armies who have scarred it with their eight-foot deep trenches. Lice and vermin chew the soldiers. The rain drowns them. The mud buries them. Their efforts are rejected.

Of course, God help anyone like Wolf who points out anything like that. One has two choices. Fight, and likely be killed; or object and either become a stretcher bearer whose life-span averages 10 minutes, or be reviled by those back home in England who have had their own sons and husbands killed. Not much of a choice now, is it?

This magnificent, emotionally-shattering novel has both the structure and dialogue of an outstanding theatre piece. I truly would much prefer to see an eventual adaptation than the inevitable movie. All those guns and sweeping camera shots will distract rather than enhance the interior life of Boyne's story.

The structure is a to and fro between 1919 and 1916. The novel's lead, Tristan Sadler, is a 21 year old returned veteran who has finally recovered from his emotional traumas sufficiently enough to seek out the sister of a fallen friend named Will Bancroft. Will had kept all the letters sent to him by his elder sister Marian and Tristan felt she should have them back. The 1916 scenes are Tristan's remembrances of the Aldershot training ground and eventual deployment to the front. Each time frame deserves commentary.

The scenes between Tristan and Marian contain some of the finest, emotionally real conversation I have read in years. This is not the false reality of Balzac or Updike wherein everything is stated precisely and nothing is misunderstood. Life's not like that. Instead, things are misunderstood - names are mispronounced, statements are misinterpreted, assumptions are wrong. If you follow the conventions of stale modern novels and guess where it all might lead, you will find that you are deliciously incorrect. Now, I do have to give Boyne one little slap on the wrist. Having a scene in a public house called Murderers given the central events of this novel is thicker than a forgotten pot of gravy left too long on the stove. Well, Boyne is Irish as am I so I understand. Sometimes we just can't resist a big winking joke.

As to the scenes of war - I have never read better. I only partially understood why my grandfather never told war stories; now I do. The dirt, the fear, the exhaustion, the cruelty, the madness, the slow countdown as a platoon of 20 at Aldershot dwindles to 12, to 11, to 10, to 9 …

Still, the soldiers seek identity and humanity even though to a random observer they are all the same. In a splendidly insane scene, the troops are visited by a General after capturing a few hundred yards of that scarred and muddy land. Their commander, a Sergeant Clayton makes sure that they are clean but not *too* clean for the inspection. There must be just the right amount of dirt on the face and uniform. All are the same, except of course all are unique. Tristan's claim to fame is that he is able to hold out his hands rock steady for up to eight minutes. By 1919 he suffers from a tremor in his right hand, specifically his right index finger - you know, the one you use to pull a trigger.

My task here is almost complete and I am feeling quite a sense of relief as I did not want to give away more of this plot than was necessary. Much like John Boyne, I want you to discover for yourself, rather than being led alone like a cart horse. That said, when a year or so has passed and The Absolutist has received its full glory, I want to write again about this novel and I relish conversations to be held with intelligent friends who have read this book. This wondrous, intelligent novel is the perfect marriage of art and entertainment. It will leave you both numb and sparkling with life. As near to a perfectly written a story as it gets.

Be seeing you.

(My politics are proudly left-wing. Reviewing had a lot to do with that, particularly after reading well-articulated books like the following and absorbing their authors' arguments.)

HOPELESS:
Barack Obama and the Politics of Illusion

Jeffrey St. Clair & Joshua Frank, editors (AK Press 2012, Trade Paperback)

For: The Herald de Paris

(Before beginning the writing of this review, I know that by the end it is one that will make no one happy almost, except the publisher and authors of this book. Republicans, Democrats, left, right and the mushy center may all feel rightfully offended. That of course is why Hopeless is vital reading and that is why I choose to write this review as viscerally as I know I will. Onwards. H.O.)

It was the late spring about to turn into the summer of 2008 the last time I was in London, that city so very mannerly in its ancient traditions where for a gala dinner one does not rent a tux for there it is hanging in the closet next to crisply-ironed french-cuffed shirts for which there are choices of cufflinks in a well-arranged bureau drawer beside folded, not rolled, calf length thin black socks. Thus properly attired, the attendees could now commence drinking and swearing in gentlemanly fashion.

The topic of the night among the guests who had come from across the UK, the Irish Republic, France, Germany and a good number of African nations was George W. Bush. The American President had arrived in town two days before to the delight of no one, particularly travelers for he had tied up all the airspace above London, obviously including Heathrow Airport, for hours so that he could make a grand helicopter descent to the grounds of Windsor Castle. Like the pussycat of the children's rhyme, he'd been to London to visit the Queen. It would have been a 15 minute limousine ride tying up only a few avoidable roads, but that wasn't quite grand enough for the Imperial Presidency.

Indeed, I learned that Bush had become a rather good punchline for any misfortune great or small. Among some minor accidents during the dinner portion of the night, a member of the wait staff neglected to bring a salad to a guest, a Cambridge-educated Englishman of Pakistani heritage who had the most marvelously florid purple spotted bow tie and matching cummerbund. 'Blame Bush,' he harrumphed to much toasting and guffaw. Later, the salt cellar ran out and in one voice, two men turned to one another and tweedle-dummed 'Blame Bush.' More toasting.

Before the toasting led to the usual sex jokes – as it happened to be an all-male table, that was an inevitability – as the token North American of the group I was urgently asked my opinion of the upcoming American Presidential election. John McCain had already clinched the Republican nomination over Mitt Romney (which guaranteed a prediction I also made that night that Romney would be the 2012 nominee), but Barack Obama had not

yet sealed victory over Hillary Clinton. In the interest of honest reviewing, by the way, I should tell you that I was cheering for Hillary from my observation post of Canada. *(Update: I've rather changed my mind on that one.)*
Anyway, I told the group, "Don't worry about a thing. Barack Obama will win the nomination, will trounce McCain in the general election and everything will be all right."

Well now. Romney in 2012; Obama to win in '08; and everything will be all right. I guess I'll have to go along with Meat Loaf that two out of three ain't bad. Things are not all right. Things are the antithesis of all right. And that is why Hopeless is a vital, necessary book to read.

Let us be clear about something. Although this collection of sharply written, devastating short essays – none longer than 16 pages and most only 4 – is about Barack Obama, *Hopeless* is not really 'about' Barack Obama any more than Beckett's Waiting for Godot is about Godot. Actually, now that I've written it, that parallel is even more telling than I first thought.

I believe it was the great former war correspondent of the New York Times, Chris Hedges who first coined the term Brand Obama. To summarize Hedges' thoughts, Obama is but the latest false saviour who presents himself as that which he has no intention of becoming; the elusive saviour/knight come to rescue the shining white city on the hill. The marketing and splendid rhetoric promises much, while the delivery is next to nothing. Godot never arrives to rescue the two sad clowns.

There are examples of this on very nearly every page of *Hopeless*. Riffing open the book at random, here is one from a February 2011 essay by economics professor Ismael Hossein-Zadeh, called Inside Obamanomics:

Prior to his recent u-turn on the regulation-deregulation issue, President Obama shared this near unanimous view of the destructive role if the excessive deregulation of the past several decades and, indeed, strongly supported the need to bolster regulation: "It's time to get serious about regulatory oversight," Mr. Obama argued as the Democratic nominee for President; and again, "...this crisis has reminded us that without a watchful eye, the market can spin out of control," as he stated in his inaugural speech.

Splendid stuff! Surely we could look forward to a freshened version of the Glass-Steagall Act which separated commercial and investment banking to be re-instated after being rather stupidly repealed during the Clinton Administration? The lessons of 1929 having been re-learnt in 2008's collapse, the solutions of 1933 would fast approach. Well, not quite. A few lines later, we read:

Accordingly (Obama) issued an executive order on 18 January 2011 that requires a comprehensive review of all existing government regulations. On the same day, the president wrote an op-ed piece for the Wall Street Journal *in which he argued that the executive order was necessary in order to "remove outdated regulations that stifle job creation and make our economy less competitive."*

Not quite the same exciting rhetoric, now is it? The effect, by the way, was that the Wall Street Journal reported two days later that the Labor Department dropped a proposal on noise in the workplace that would have forced manufacturers to install noise-reducing equipment and the Food and Drug Administration retreated from plans to tighten rules on medical-advice approvals. Well isn't that great?! Allow workers to go deaf then sell them faulty hearing aids. How ever will they be able to hear all those grand speeches?

There are hundreds of examples. The appointments of former Goldman-Sachs and Citibank executives to most senior positions should have been a clue that Obama, in economist Michael Hudson's words (Obama's Sellout on Taxes), "has only done what politicians do: He has delivered up his constituency to his campaign backers – the same Wall Street donors who back the Republicans. What's the point of having a constituency, after all, if you can't sell it?"

Oh there's more, there is more. Incidentally, while reading each essay I kept the mind-set of trying to find a rationale for a defence of the administration's actions. It didn't go well. What of the case of Omar Khadr, the fifteen year-old Canadian captured outside Kabul in 2002. Khadr's trial was the first under the Obama administration. Chase Madar, a New York lawyer, notes in Torturing the Rule of Law at Obama's Gitmo, that "no nation had tried a child soldier for war crimes since World War II." When Khadr threw his grenade, as he confessed, he tossed "the grenade from his hospital bed at Bagram prison while heavily sedated, his chest wounds barely closed."

So what happened with Khadr? Well, he and his lawyers – once he was finally able to retain counsel – plea-bargained a sentence of eight years not including time served. The military tribunal essentially said, to hell with plea bargains, you get forty years in solitary confinement. For a child. Who acted in a war. Who was re-defined as a 'belligerent' rather than a soldier.

What of Obama's successes? The pattern essentially follows his pattern on the environment, wherein (the source here is editor Jeffrey St. Clair's Obama and the Man in the Hat) while the Department of Agriculture filled with ex-industry lobbyists authorizes, "the most ghastly of clearcuts in the most ecologically sensitive sites, such as the Bitterroot Mountains in Montana to the fast-dwindling ponderosa pine forests of Oregon's Blue Mountains", the environmental movement largely stays quiet and acquiescent. Why?

The pattern of political conditioning has been honed to perfection. Every few weeks the Obama administration drops the Beltway Greens a few meaningless crumbs – such as the reinstitution of the Clinton Roadless Area rule – which they gobble up one after another until, like Hansel and Gretel with groupthink, they find themselves hopelessly lost in a vast maze of Obama-sanctioned clearcuts. After that, they won't even get a crumb.

That, by the way, is a fine example of the lacerating and well-chosen prose found throughout *Hopeless*. I'll admit to a general sadness I have felt for years that the voices of Real journalists, the ones who write with passion grounded in thorough research; I thought that the children of Lincoln Steffens had all died. No, there are dozens of them in these pages, writing about every important aspect of American life with damning perspective.

So you say, it's all aboard the Romney train, then is it? Oh don't be an ass. As Gore Vidal noted years ago, there is no Republican Party or Democratic Party, there is just the Banks' Party. Or as Chris Hedges answered when I asked him recently if it made the slightest difference whether Obama or Romney won the next election, "No. Not at all." Both serve the same corporate interests; both have the same campaign contributors. It was recently noted that the U.S. ranks 138th worldwide in voter participation. The only surprising piece of information in that statistic is that I didn't know there were 138 democracies in the world (according to Wikipedia, there are actually 167).

Hang in there America. And fight back. Be seeing you.

Leonardo and The Last Supper

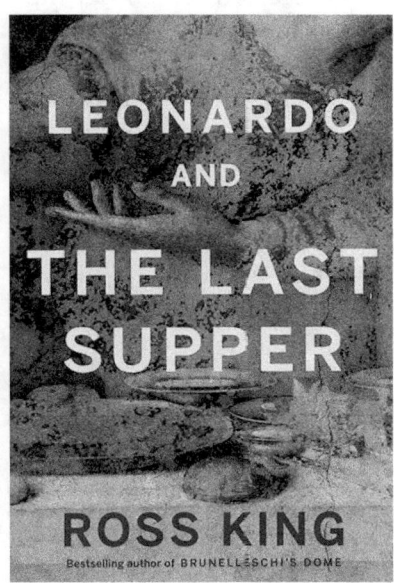

Ross King (Bond Street Books 2012, Hardcover)

For: San Francisco Book Review

I rarely write a review after speaking with the author. It seems like cheating somehow and of course the craft of book reviewing, wherein one is paid to receive free first editions and so improve one's home decor and intellect, is one beyond any hint of influence or corruption. Ahem.

In any event, I did speak to Ross King for an Audible Authors podcast in the time between finishing reading his book and writing this review. What I said to him, I say to you. What fascinates about this discussion of the creation of The Last Supper is that Leonardo Da Vinci's famous painting is *so* famous that one really does not see it for what it was; an astonishing new reality of form and content.

That is the value of *Leonardo and The Last Supper* – we are given the opportunity to see something familiar for the first time. That is not just a sly paradoxical phrase. It is much like famous geographical or architectural landmarks. You 'know' what the Grand Canyon, Niagara Falls, the White House or Eiffel Tower look like. I'm willing to wager that no one reading this piece can remember the first time they saw a print or televised image of any of them; yet I equally wager that no one reading this piece who eventually went to any of those places did not leave astonished at how there was so much more to it than was expected.

What is remarkable about the painting – we'll get to the painter in a paragraph or three – is that the disciples are not static, reflective, silent figures. There is tumult in the room at that moment when Christ announces that one of those present will betray him. Here is the perfect example of seeing the familiar for the first time. Tumult? Of course there would be tumult. If you were having dinner with your best friends and the host suddenly states that someone in the room was planning a murder, well I do think there might be a dropped salad fork or two. Wine might even be spritzed like a roomful of Jerry Lewis impersonators.

Yet, as Ross King points out, this is not how earlier versions of Last Supper images were presented. The disciples are seen as quite sedate, gazing out in reflection or even reading a book. No one contorts, writhes, leans in, has an expression of (in modern parlance) 'Say WHAT!?!'

So were those earlier imagists (there were both paintings and bas-relief friezes in existence) utterly ignorant? No. They were just obeying the terms of their contracts and probably equally a little overwhelmed by being tasked with depicting the holiest of holy figures. After all, Jesus had told the disciples that were blessed with the power to heal the sick, so seeing them as emotional and frenetic humans like the rest of us would seem debasing. Plus, these images were usually to be found in monasteries and convents, specifically their dining rooms or if you like, cafeterias. There were rather strict rules in those places, especially as King notes, in the Dominican monasteries. One did not talk, except for whomever read the prayers during the incredibly bland meal. Such ascetic environments should not be upset by turbulent, emotional images.

Harrumph, to hell with all that, Leonardo may well have said. Amongst his many other well-known talents, he may well have been the very first realist. Ross King speculates that Leonardo may well have been the world's first mountain climber (although I suspect that a farmer with a lost goat may have beaten him to it) as he did not want to drawn imaginary pastoral landscapes instead of the real thing. Leonardo was as obsessed with re-creating truth in his art as Ernest Hemingway would be in his writing nearly half a millennium later.

Therefore, when he was awarded the commission by the unofficial Duke of Milan (the discussion of Renaissance era politics in Italy alone makes this book worth purchase) to decorate a wall in a convent cafeteria, Leonardo set about making that depiction as real and as truthful as possible. In the 6000 pages of Leonardo's notes which have survived to our time – Hold! Let's think about that for a second.

6000 pages of notes? It is suggested by King that there used to be 20,000. If you added up and printed out absolutely every memo, email or Facebook status update you've ever written, would that even get close to 6000 pages? No, I didn't think so and no, me neither. What one person – you or me – might describe as obsession, a true creative artist such as Lenoardo would describe as profession.

Obsession is perhaps the key to what separates the great from the merely good. When awarded the contract to paint The Last Supper – and painting was very much a moonlight job for Leonardo, who saw his calling as engineering or weapons design – he goes out into the piazzas of Milan to sketch what groups of crowded men look like when they argue and discuss. Similarly, he purchases his first Bible to get the take on the event from the witnesses Matthew, Luke and John (Mark had either abandoned the cause or was caught in traffic – regardless, although he wrote about it, he was not present at the occasion). And from that he paints what is likely a true depiction of the emotion of the moment. Such is genius at work – seeing that which is 'known' as something new and then creating from that vision.

I'll admit that when Leonardo and *The Last Supper* first arrived in my mailbox, I thought that there was not anything new, beyond the trivial, between its covers. Oh brother was I wrong. I suspect Ross King's book will be appearing on College reading lists for decades to come although it is not – emphasis on the not – a dull, academic treatise. This is lively, intelligent history and will be nestled on my bookshelf of Best Histories forever.

Be seeing you.

Women's Bodies as Battlefield:

Christian Theology and the Global War on Women's Bodies

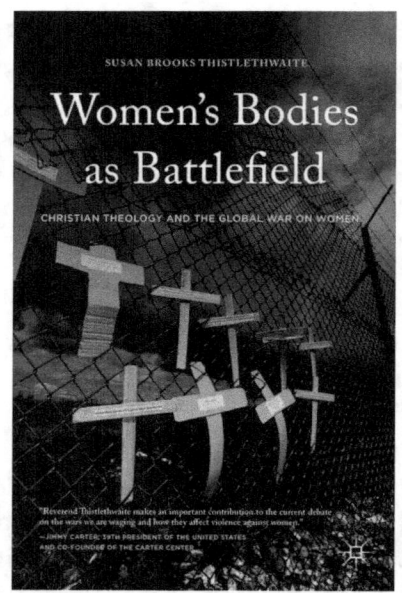

Susan Brooks Thistlethwaite (Palgrave Macmillan 2015, Hardcover)

For: San Diego Book Review

I place before you a series of propositions. If a third of the houses in your neighborhood were regularly burnt by arson, would you demand greater police and fire protection? I think you would. If a third of the children were struck down by communicable disease, year-in year-out, would you not take a deep interest into the cause of that illness and insist on more and better health care? Of course you would. Both the arsons and the pandemic would be widely reported, taken personally and force a re-assessment of public safety. I don't think anyone can really argue against my hypotheses.

However, 35% of all women worldwide are subjected to physical abuse at some point in their lives, often repeatedly and at the extreme of brutality. That is 35% regardless of nation, race or cultural origin. And yet we do not see these attacks on a third of humanity as a crime wave or an epidemic. The rape, beating or murder of women is seen as an exception, an outlier, perpetrated by random sick individuals. If the attacks occur during a declared state of war, then they are lumped together and seen as regrettable yet sadly predictable collateral damage. Heads shake mournfully, but then of course comes a response somewhere along the lines of, 'That is why the war must continue. So we can protect women's rights.' Ah.

As a matter of fact – and I do mean fact – women must not take the fight into their own hands. Did you know that according to a study released by The Michigan Women's Justice and Clemency Project, 'The average prison sentence for men who kill their intimate partners is 2 to 6 years. Women who kill their partners are sentenced, on average, to 15 years.'? It should be a topic rich in public discussion as to why this obvious imbalance of justice exists.

By and large though, that discussion does not happen which is the value of *Women's Bodies as Battlefield*. What Reverend Susan Thistlethwaite, a Professor of Theology at the Chicago Theological Seminary does is lay out in fine and painful detail precisely how it is that women are seen as beings are that are dangerous and justifiable spoils of power struggles.

What is stunning is how many of the deep thinkers throughout history, philosophers and artists alike, have taken the abuse of women as not only inevitable but also justifiable. A sampling:

Aristotle: *Females are weaker and colder in nature, and it is necessary to regard the female status as a deformity, though a natural one.*

St Augustine: 'He concludes that the act of rape brings shame to the one raped *"lest that act which could not be suffered without some sensual pleasure, should be believed to have been committed also with some ascent of the will."'*

Joseph Campbell: On the artistic depiction of rapes, '(R)apes over and over, *"simply dramatize the will of consciousness, portrayed with male power, imposed upon natural frailty."'*

You know, don't take it personally, it's just human nature. Shrug.

Where Thistlethwaite's book really soars and becomes indispensable is within her argument completely taking apart any theological justification for war. As the title of *Women's Bodies as Battlefield* implies, she equates abuse to war. However Thistlewaite also attacks the very concept of war itself and particularly how its consequences – the sight of ruined and dismembered bodies are kept away from our eyes lest we lose our taste for that mythical ruse of the 'Just War.'

I could go on and would most happily, however I would then be delivering to you a precis rather than a review of *Women's Bodies as Battlefield*. It is a deeply, deeply disturbing book as it literally questions the foundations of what we loosely term civilization. Yet, in order to not just observe a rape, a murder, an atrocity that flashes across the news as an isolated exception to common behavior – to instead witness that event as evidence of a larger crime, one has to be aware of the crime itself. Susan Thistlethwaite prosecutes her case with bravery, with calm passion and with eloquence. And if this sounds like a book you really don't want to read, because who wants to read such nasty things ... well that's just the point, now isn't it? Be seeing you.

(One of the great joys of moving to Ireland was discovering dozens and dozens of wonderful writers whose work has not yet been discovered in North America. I consider it part of my duty and loyalty to the nation that adopted me to rectify that situation. Rob Doyle is one of the best of the new Irish writers.)

This is the Ritual

Rob Doyle (Bloomsbury 2016, Hardcover and Trade Paperback editions)

For: San Diego Book Review, Writing.ie

When you strip away all the gloss and glitter, the high-wire plotting with acrobat characters, after the trumpets of hype are laid to rest in their velvet-lined cases what remains at the nut of a writer's art is reporting. See something that is worth knowing and convince a reader of that worth. Tell the truth and make it vivid. All the rest of it is marketing.

There are two generalized means of approach to this. The writer can travel to places and experience things that are both literally and psychologically foreign to the average reader in his horsehair-stuffed chair, or her comfy bed with the pillows plumped just so. Or, there are the dramas in the study and the fire in the bedroom, those familiar objects that look very unfamiliar indeed when an a torchlight held by the writer's hand causes them to cast monster-shaped shadows on bungalow walls. Is the art here or is it there, and where is there if not indeed here?

That doesn't make it easy of course, although given that in 2015 over one million books were published in English alone there seem to be one hell of a lot of people who think that just because they can speak a language they can write in it; most can't, or at the very least not well. This makes it rather difficult for the few hundred who can truly re-create a world on a page to get noticed at all. The task is rather like two top football teams, say Barcelona and Bayern Munich, trying to play an artful match on a pitch where the spectators were allowed to wander around, occasionally taking a punt at the ball. Can't someone *please* blow a bloody whistle and call security?

Rob Doyle is one of the writers who deserves a place on the team and I am therefore delighted that his short story series *this is the ritual* is the first book I am reviewing in 2016. Doyle you see takes a perspective on his work that is equal parts wisdom and mischief. Given that you're the sort of person who reads literary book reviews, I am quite sure you know the tale of Plato's Cave, so there is no need to explain that one for the nine millionth time. However, while most writers (including many very good ones) will create stories about the deception of the shadows or the blindness of the cave dwellers, Doyle is interested in the anonymous person who keeps the flame burning behind the drama. That's the real interesting person in the room; the wizard in the Oz chamber, the author himself.

For this reason, *this is the ritual* is not a short story 'collection' in the traditional sense. No, these nineteen pieces are a series that interweave and comment on one another with the effect of a scientist looking into a microscope only to see on his slide a smaller version of himself looking up through a telescope.

Doyle lets us know what he's up to in the very first story, 'John-Paul Finnegan, Paltry Realist'. Finnegan and the narrator are traveling from Holyhead back to Ireland after many years away on a not-at-all-ironically-named ferry Ulysses. On deck and with spray slapping about, they talk about books they have read, experiences they have had, and what expectations readers demand. They are also more than a bit edgy about returning to Ireland. The story thus becomes as whimsically elegant an apologia as you'll ever run across. Here's what I've been up to and I hope you like what I've done with it.

Doyle's cast includes many a character who are like the prophets writing on the subway walls in Simon and Garfunkel's The Sounds of Silence. The words may be wise, but who pays attention to spray paint philosophy? For instance, there's the nameless roll-up smoker found alone on an empty Ballymount Estate in 'No Man's Land' who expounds on Nietzsche between slugs of Dutch Gold beer. He summarizes with an eloquent description of despair that later reduces the narrator to such a quivering mess he asks his mother if he can sleep on the floor beside her bed:

'There's no plan any more. This is unprecedented. There is no father. There is no appeal. And hell, hell assumes its true fuckin significance. We're already there. I saw all this so fuckin clearly, durin a mushroom trip out here, one of the first times I came to this place. The mushrooms are like a technology, they let ye see what's happened to the world. Death is in everything now. I sat there cryin and screamin for hours. The entire sky was crushin me, all of outer space was pressin down on me. I was buried and I've never come back. I'm still buried. There is no surface, nowhere to claw back to. You're buried too, and ye know it, I can see it in ye. There is no father. There is no therapy. Do ye know how that feels?'

Well yes actually we do ... not that we like to dwell on those moments. That though is the writer's job, the ritual itself, to cause us to feel that which we prefer to bury for truth should never be buried. Mind you, truth-tellers are often uncelebrated or come to grim ends. The dubious fortune of being 'taken seriously' often seems utterly random, a point Doyle makes with his deeply satirical, wonderfully wicked creation Killian Turner. Much like Kurt Vonnegut Jr's Kilgore Trout – and if those matching KT initials are a coincidence, I'm my Aunt Nancy's cat – Turner is either a genius disguised as a fraud or a fraud disguised as a genius. *(Update: I later interviewed Doyle and asked him about this. He had never heard of Kilgore Trout. Therefore, I am indeed my Aunt Nancy's Cat. Meow.)* Turner is introduced in the story 'Exiled in the Infinite – Killian Turner, Ireland's Vanished Literary Outlaw'. Turner, an Irish writer, is described by a minor academic thusly: 'In fact, his body of work, taken as a whole, might be seen as Turner's lifelong project of effacing all marks of nationhood from his authorial voice and literary being.' Much like James Joyce or Samuel Beckett, Turner becomes a celebrated Irish writer by getting the hell out of Dodge, or at least out of Dun Laoghaire. He becomes a linking device in *this is the ritual*, popping up unannounced in the later stories, again much like Kilgore Trout in Slaughterhouse-Five or Breakfast of Champions.

The themes and interplay, the point/counter-point of story elements continue to work until what is formed is akin to a watertight woven basket. Nietzsche arrives again as a subject for a writer who never gets around to writing much as he never feels his research his sufficient. Doyle himself appears in character form, which is a device I usually use to club writers with a spade, however given the shot/reverse shot nature of *this is the ritual*'s dialogue about observing and writing, this is one time where the author deserves to appear on stage.

Finally, *this is the ritual* reminds of a favourite lesser-known film, Joe Gould's Secret, directed by and starring the criminally underrated Stanley Tucci. Joe Gould was a real-life charlatan, a for want of a better term hobo who was taken in, virtually adopted by New York's cognoscenti as he claimed to have written a nearly completed, nine million word long 'Oral History'. The book was the sociological equivalent of a physicist's theory of everything, except the book never existed. Joseph Mitchell of The New Yorker was one of those taken in by Joe Gould, writing two Profile pieces on him, one in 1942 and the second admitting the fraud in 1964.

After that second piece, Mitchell continued to go to his office at The New Yorker every work day, Monday to Friday, for another twenty years. He never wrote another word. In *this is the ritual*, Rob Doyle writes the book Joe Mitchell should have written emerging from that experience.

Brilliant.

Be seeing you.

Dangerous Obsessions

Bob Van Laerhoven (Anaphora Literary Press 2015, hardcover)

For: San Diego Book Review

The effects of a sudden recognition jolt from sleep somewhere in the misty border lands between déjà vu and memory, a false security disrobed as fear. I first sensed it at quite a young age, the first time I ever went to London. Our house in Canada backed onto a one acre park planted thickly with trees that bordered along its narrow curving dirt paths forming glades and green hollows, with shadows cutting across the light. So there I was in Hyde Park, stood next to my mother and I looked up and saw, I thought, the park at home. That tree here and that tree there and those branches here and there looked exactly – exactly! - like one a corner of that park in Canada. In that moment of recognition there was such an incredible compression of comfort, transportation, wonder, knowledge, objective and subjective thoughts all tumbled together like laundry in a dryer; all so remarkable that the trees in Hyde Park remain my most vivid childhood memory.

Books do that to you too, you know. The effect is not quite as startling as seeing familiar places in *un*familiar places because for one thing we're older and smarter and for another, with books we're consciously looking for links to readings past. It's rather more akin to a date with a new and attractive woman when she stands a certain way or says a certain phrase and there you are – exactly! - in the same moment except it is in the past with a different beautiful woman.

Dangerous Obsessions by Bob Van Laerhoven had precisely that same delicious effect on me, echoing the music of sweet songs past. It is a thin book containing five short stories, just thin enough that I am willing to forgive its publisher for not numbering its pages and so making me count them up. The pages themselves may not be quite so forgiving as they know have damp wrinkles on their right upper corners where I flicked them with my licked index finger. Dear Publishers – Don't do that again.

Malcolm Lowry only produced one complete novel during his adulthood – terminal alcoholism makes a man dead before his deadlines – but it was one hell of a novel. *Under the Volcano* is such a remorseless portrait of doom one can feel the stench of sulphur rising off each page. The effect was akin to reading Graham Greene while on acid. That was something I never tried – reading Graham Greene on acid – but I and its many fans have been looking for something like *Under the Volcano* ever since. I began reading *Dangerous Obsessions*, I metaphorically turned around to look at Hyde Park and I thought I'd been there before.

Doom is the great serpent of Fate and rare is the writer who dares get close enough to it to count its scales or allow himself the knowledge of how it feels when the serpent Doom wraps around the throat. For that is how Doom operates; it kills by a slow crushing of the larynx until the battle to draw a breath seems not worth the struggle. Doom is way beyond Fear. Fear is easy – a shock, a bite, sudden and severe but even when Fear kills it is done in as little time as it takes to light a cigarette. Doom and Fear both can kill the body, but Doom first kills the mind.

The Doomed reach a point before dying where choices, the weighing of morality become meaningless. However, knowing that Doom has won and so life is ending ends with one last choice – does one strike one last blow at the serpent, or perhaps hope it notices a meatier body nearby?

Bob Van Laerhoven has survived life among the Doomed. He has covered wars and revolutions and knows how how humans behave when morality is as impossible and foreign as a parkland glade untouched within a battlefield. He writes of soldiers, thieves, and Holocaust victims; women willing to give their bodies to save their families, men willing to die to spite their killers. And he does all that in language so vivid that you will believe you have seen it all before.

Thirty bucks is one sweet hell of a price to pay for five short stories. On the other hand, I put it to you this way: What's the difference between that fine butcher's steak that makes you drool at the memory of its tender, full-fleshed taste and the regular grade hamburger you season and pound into patties before burying it under cheese, relish and a thick bready bun? They're both just cow meat aren't they? *Dangerous Obsessions* is reading for the reading *gourmand*. I've waited a goddam long time to run across a writer who can make me feel both eager and brave to turn each page and I've finally found one. I salute you Bob Van Laerhoven. Your work reminds me of a park I thought I saw.

Be seeing you.

The Testament of Mary

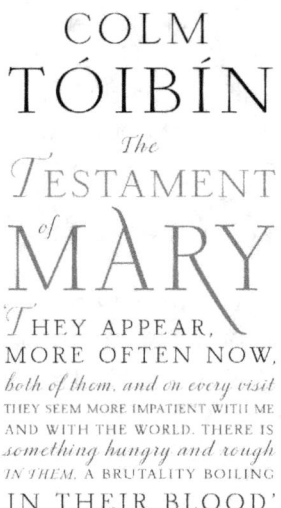

Colm Tóibín (Penguin Viking 2012, Hardcover)

I am certainly no one's idea of a religious scholar, however being raised a Roman Catholic and attending a Catholic elementary school, along with a few decades of reasonably regular attendance at Sunday Mass teaches a man a few things. Besides, the story of Jesus of Nazareth is pretty unavoidable in the Western world; we get long weekends to celebrate his birth (almost undoubtedly on the wrong day) and his death (occurring on a sliding date). His image and that of his mother Mary hang on the walls of many – likely most – homes in Ireland, the country I happily emigrated to a month ago. I see the little crosses hanging around the necks or off the ears of men and women alike. No matter how popular Charles Dickens is, I have never seen anyone wear a little guillotine around the neck to celebrate A Tale of Two Cities. So one develops a pretty good knowledge of Jesus and his family almost by osmosis, similar to the sun tanning the skin without one noticing until a watch and ring are taken off at night and there are pale bands on the hands where the rays could not penetrate.

I like this Mary, mother of Jesus as presented in Colm Tóibìn's novel. Well, *The Testament of Mary* is not really so much a novel as it is a dramatic monologue. Indeed a version of it was presented in Dublin in 2011 in a play called *Testament*. Twice short-listed for the Man Booker Prize (for *The Blackwater Lightship*, as well as *The Master*), Tóibìn is a brilliant master of the English language. This book begs to be read aloud and I suggest to you that auditioning actresses could do a lot worse than pulling passages out of The Testament of Mary and committing them to memory. For instance:

My son was already in custody, a real prisoner. He had allowed himself to be taken, and in this house during the hours that I spent with his followers they all seemed to feel that this was planned, part of a great deliverance that would take place in the world. I wanted to ask them if this deliverance would mean that he would not then be crucified, that he would be released, but they all, including Mary (her cousin), once she was in their company, spoke in a maze of riddles. No question asked, I knew, would elicit a straight answer. I was back in the world of fools, twitchers, malcontents, stammerers, all of them hysterical now and almost out of breath with excitement even before they spoke. And within this group of men I noticed that there was a set of hierarchies, men who spoke and were listened to, for example, or whose presence created silence, or who sat at the top of the table, or who felt free to ignore me and my companion and who demanded food from the other women who scampered in and out of the room like hunched and obedient animals.

'Fools, twitchers, malcontents and stammerers'; Well wouldn't you feel pretty much the same disgust and barely lidded hatred for a crowd of people bribed by your own Temple to cast a vote condemning your only child to death? No matter what centuries and centuries of religious iconographers may insist on – Mary as benign and loving figure gently loving the world – the real Mary was definitely mortal and mortal mothers tend to get a bit tetchy when their children are about to be crucified. Just by allowing Mary to step away from the halo so we readers can get a good look at her makes me want to stand up and applaud. Much like Philip Pullman's *The Good Man Jesus and The Scoundrel Christ*, what *The Testament of Mary* gives us is a plausible, excellently described alternate version of events.

Of course, what really makes me smile is that Tóibìn is more than just a little subversive within his text. Mary tells her tale (she does not go into the issue of the manner of Jesus' conception, in case you were wondering) from her own personal Elba, somewhere across a sea where she is spirited by nameless guardians or apostles after her son's execution. She is constantly pumped for information by her guardians/captors so they can continue refining what presumably are the Gospels. Interestingly, she never drops the names of Matthew, Mark, Luke or John; neither does she ever state the name of any of the other Apostles. They were just her son's 'followers', a rather noisy rabble that he used to bring home to preach and argue with. Again, her feelings are much like those of a modern mother who brings home his lager lout mates for pizza and Nintendo. Her memory is affected by her emotions. As she freely admits to one of the guardians, 'I told him before he departed that all my life when I have seen more than two men together I have seen foolishness and I have seen cruelty, but it is foolishness that I have noticed first.' Well I certainly have no argument with that judgment; how about you?

So in a similar yet opposite manner to how he treats Mary, Tóibìn demystifies the apostles by making them, for all intent, anonymous. They hide. A lot. And they alter Jesus' story. A lot. A dream that Mary and her cousin Mary have simultaneously – that of going to a well and finding that Jesus has been revived and has left his grave – becomes fact. After all, he had come to visit the hiding apostles and stuck around for three days before heading back to his real father, God. There were no other witnesses.

Therefore you must be wondering and perhaps assuming that Jesus was a magic act at best, with all his feats and miracles made up by earnest, pious scribblers. Not quite. The raising of Lazarus is described in exquisite, gripping detail:

Slowly the figure dirtied with clay and covered in graveclothes wound around him began with great uncertainty to move in the place they had made for him. It was as though the earth beneath him was pushing him and then letting him be still in his great forgetfulness and nudging him again like some strange new creature jerking and wriggling towards life.

The whole story of The Testament of Mary turns on this incident; and yes it does feel churlish to describe the raising of the dead as a mere incident. Yet, that is the way it would have been reported back to the Roman and Jewish authorities by the spies and stranglers watching Jesus and it sets to play the events leading up to the execution of Jesus. Mary alludes to rumblings of discontent amongst the Jews in Palestine against both the colonial power and its taxation, as well as their own compliant rabbinate. Now with Jesus able to raise the dead, my my! '

Some people say that the Romans wish to overthrow the teachers, and others that the teachers are behind it all, but it is also possible that there will be no revolt or indeed that there will be one against everything we have known before, including death itself.

Including death itself? This would be the ultimate incentive for the revolutionary. Mock us, imprison us, even kill us, but we'll be back! I couldn't help but imagine Jesus as the general leading the charge of a zombie army. The Romans and Jews would not have had a word for zombie, but they weren't taking any chances either. Kill Jesus.

So by the end, the guardians are writing their hyped-up Gospels and Mary longs for nothing more than death and reunion with Joseph and her son, were that even possible. A guardian attempts to convince Mary of the ultimate virtue of their and her son's actions for he is the Son of God who by his death has freed all mankind! Her reaction? 'I will say that it was not worth it. It was not worth it.'

I love this version of Mary. Be seeing you.

(I close this section with Martin Amis' The Pregnant Widow, not because it is his best book or even my best written review. It has a warm place in my heart because this is how my Wall of Fame got started, when Amis himself enjoyed the review. We do not write these in order to suck up, but acknowledgement is a very pleasant thing.)

The Pregnant Widow

Martin Amis (Knopf Canada 2010)

The brilliance of an artist can be determined by how well he or she captures and presents The Telling Detail. Is there an architectural point of focus to the building that fixes it as at atmospheric idea? Humphrey Bogart with one drag of a cigarette through a cupped hand applied a lower frame or flesh and smoke underlining so his eyes could speak a thousand cynical words. And as for the writer, he or she must know where and when the story was told.

'What? Shouldn't that be the simplest of all criteria to achieve? Aren't all novels just that - stories?'

Well yes, and I don't thank the Reader for blundering into the middle of my review with questions I was going to answer anyway. Novels are stories all right, but novels are also the stories (plural) of their characters (plural). This is where the art comes in. When was it, where was it and what was it that made these people the way they are? Where was the focal moment lived when fate sat on a teeter totter placed at the tip of a four-sided pyramid. A breeze, a whim, a shuddering of nerve,a coincidence can send the teeter totter and its occupant sliding off to end up wherever it is they end up.

Consider your own life, much as Martin Amis clearly considered his in the writing of *The Pregnant Widow*. Can you look back from the far side of the Hellespont of life that is the sixth decade and say when it was that you were irrefutably cast upon the path that led you to that shore? Can you? Can you really see across the channel of time and find yourself on the opposing beach? From *The Pregnant Widow*:

The Italian summer - that was the only passage in his whole existence that ever felt like a novel. It had chronology and truth (it did happen). But it also boasted the unities of time, place, and action; it aspired to at least partial coherence; it had some shape, some pattern, with its echelons, its bestiaries. Once that was over, all he had was truth and chronology - and, oh yes, the inherently tragic shape (rise, crest, fall), like a mouth on a tragic mask: and this is a face that is common to everyone who doesn't die young.

The Italian summer. It is 1970 and Keith Nearing with his friends, acquaintances and his renewed relationship with his girlfriend Lily are summering in Italy as British youths of a certain background are able to do between sessions of University. Keith is 20 and 1970 marks the time when youth are encountering the freshly conquered territory of the Sexual Revolution. Besides Keith and Lily, the other principals are the impossibly perfect blonde goddess Scheherazade (who does not yet realize she is an impossibly perfect blonde goddess and who Keith lusts for), Gloria Beautyman who has embraced the Revolution and the new sexual equality for women by deciding to lead her life as a Cock, but a Cock that wants status and money before she will settle permanently with anyone, Adriano, a handsome four foot ten inch Italian millionaire who also falls for Scheherazade, and many more. Each is unique. Each is known to us all.

This is the time and these are the people. They play, they plot, they discuss, they read - voluminously through the library in the castle where they stay. *The Pregnant Widow* is a joy for anyone who ever attended a 19th Century English Novel course at university, particularly for fans of Jane Austen as Amis's characters debate over who shagged who in all the novels.

The Pregnant Widow is a novel of genius. I have always admired Martin Amis, and twenty years ago or so I might have described him as my favourite living novelist. He has returned to that place. I bow to the brilliance of his prose, the precision of his words, his damnable ability to capture my own thoughts on my own life's experiences and tell you about them much better than I ever could. Among many excellent books I have read this year, this is the finest. You need to read it.

Essays
&
Others

(Slightly embarrassing I suppose, but this section begins with a bit of a lie. I did in fact go back to Facebook because frankly it is a necessity for business. However, I still believe in every observation and complaint made in the following.)

Why I Left Facebook

As with most acts of rebellion this one had been brewing for some time. And yes, we may as well confront the immediate hypocrisy head on. There is an excellent chance that you are reading this essay because of a link shared to you from Facebook itself. I am going to post it here for two reasons. One, I do not want any of my friends to think they are no longer my friends, subject to the ultimate shaming of being – horrors! - blocked. Also, I actually want them to read this; to actually witness Facebook rather than merely observe it. Therefore I will keep my Facebook account alive until October 21st. After then, no more.

There were several aspects to the Facebook demi-life that had annoyed me without finally pushing me out the door. The interface is no great shakes and never has been, particularly when the nefarious application constantly re-sets itself to Top Stories and away from Most Recent. That of course is done in order to bury any friend who might own a business who has not in turn done business with Facebook. If you don't tip the maitre'd don't expect a table by the window. As well, the application truly enjoys whoring out its users. I was horrified when I received a private message rightfully damning me for 'liking' a racist page from my old hometown in Canada. Because I had at some point (good luck ever finding the origins of these insults) shared some story or another in order to spread the word about these foul people, the Facebook algorithm then splashed it about on people's newsfeeds that I liked the page. Remember that the next time you share anything about a neo-Nazi or even a neo-liberal for you have just given an implied endorsement.

The data collection of course is annoying and more than a little creepy besides. Mention that you have a dog and onwards come the crashing waves of little ads for dog food and canine-crested T-shirts. No, I didn't enjoy that one little bit, however if I don't have the mental strength to resist an impulse buy then I deserve my resultant poverty.

The above of course is the true reason why one cannot 'dislike' anything. Mark Zuckerberg recently said that there is no 'dislike' button because that would be used for public shaming and cyber-abuse. He's right, but if he was truly honest about it he would equally admit that disliking is bad for business. Any salesman learns on his or her first daw of training that it is important, indeed vital, to get the prospect into the habit of saying Yes. Never ask a question that might result in a negative answer. Hence, if one is selling life insurance one asks something like, 'Would you like to protect your family from financial instability in the case of a sudden death?' Yes! And so, all those little 'likes' dotted around the Facebook page are the equivalent of soothing music in a posh clothing store, or the complimentary champagne at a jewelers. We're all friends here! Everything that happens here is positive. Now about that T-shirt with the Border Collie ...

Well, if you're going to go to the beach you have to expect a few clouds across the sun. All of the above were annoyances I would roll my eyes at, yet nothing I couldn't handle. No, what finally got to me was and is how Facebook is an absolutely anti-democratic home of benign division. Allow me to explain, as I am sure you will.

When the internet first truly exploded as a medium twenty years ago, we almost all thought that here was the culmination of the late media philosopher Marshall McLuhan's vision of a true Global Village. Because we could all communicate with one another, we will all communicate with one another. Because we all know some tidbit of information – whether that was how best to peel a banana or how to tax banana growers – we would share it and thus by expanding the concept of Collective Wisdom our little blue ball of Earth would become smarter, egalitarian and better. Utopia in excelsis deo and the face of divinity is our own.

Instead, the world is collectively stupider, more mendacious and hateful than it was pre-internet. Please don't try and argue against that proposition because you will lose the debate. We live in the bizarro universe that flips the lyrics of an old Dean Martin song onto its head by exchanging the verb Love into Everybody Hates Somebody Sometime. Rather than a global truce where we meet on former battlefields to exchange quiet opinions and grow flowers, we have instead wedged ourselves into well-armed sniper's lairs, firing away at anything that moves.

For you see, McLuhan also said that the Medium is the Message. (As a point of trivia, McLuhan by accident mis-pronounced Message as something like Massage, but the old Canadian couldn't be bothered to do a second take of his recorded interview, hence it stuck. But he meant Message.) Our involvement in the Media means that we are involved in the life it projects and so we feel connected to the other users. We then make the unfortunate conclusion that because we want to be involved, want to be connected, therefore whatever is going on during that activity must be justifiable and good. We all watch the shadows on Plato's Cave because, well, everyone else is too.

And this is what I kept increasingly seeing. We share some story, or type in some observation in a silent shouty-voice proclaiming, 'This is what I believe in!' However, there's a problem there. If everyone is a Prophet, then where the hell are the Disciples going to come from?

Ah, you say, but what about those Likes? Aren't those building (ahem) like-minded communities that will in turn expand if their wisdom is correct? No they don't. Frankly, the situation could not be further from that.

I don't think Facebook intended this, although it certainly profits from it, but it is far too easy to ignore (or shame, which is ignoring with hideous laughter added) anyone who disagrees with us. Real conversation, real debate, even if it is just across a pub table requires one to bloody well sit there and listen. Not so Facebook. I can either scroll past you or not 'Like' your post. Hence, you are no longer going to appear as one of those Top Stories because – remember! - Facebook wants its marketplace to be a happy happy place populated only be yes yes people.

Oh, and if I *really* disagree with you, I can block you. To Connacht or to Hell, internet style.

So there's that. The other reason I am walking away from Facebook is that false activism has always made my skin crawl. I have never worn a coloured ribbon or bracelet, dumped a bucket of ice water on my head, or even signed any international petition that was to be sent to a national government. Those are all activities that take the place of effective activism. At worst, these are gigantic acts of hypocrisy, such as the NFL having its players wear pink shoes to show support for women ... while hiring serial domestic abusers and sadistic misogynists as players. Ah.

I have grown tired of the chest-thumping proclamations of leftists and conservatives alike who think that sharing a story from The New Statesman or The National Review means that they are actually doing something. They're not. They are just proving to their sub-community that they are snipers firing in the same direction. The medium may be the message, but a message is a noun and not a verb. It is not action.

Personally, it really hit home to me when I released my book *For Freedom: A Human Rights Reader 1948-2015*. I had worked for close to three years researching and analyzing the work and careers of everyone from Eleanor Roosevelt and Nelson Mandela to Bono and the playwright Robert Patrick. So of course I expected all those good lefties on my Facebook to spread the word. Like like, share share, on to the next item on the scrolling newsfeed and the book sales are dying slowly. I bring this up because that of course is going to be the counter-accusation to my leaving Facebook, that I am leaving it because of hurt feelings and lousy book sales. Well yes, that didn't help. Yet I am thankful for the enlightenment that motivated me to write this essay. Facebook is an insidious place and I do not want it to capture me.

I am free.

Be seeing you.

17th October 2015

In Praise of Older Volumes

I received an unexpected gift today and just for brevity's sake we shall step carefully past the dormant volcano of truth that at my particular stage of life all gifts are indeed unexpected. Just before eleven this morning, the green An Post Eirann van pulled up and the driver dropped a box inside my front door. What with regular deliveries of books and the familiarity born from living in a small Irish village, we don't bother with the familiarities of signing for packges any more; and besides, I never have worked out a decent autograph using that plastic stick on a tiny screen. The result looks more like the trail a snail leaves on a hot sidewalk than any handwriting admissible as evidence.

The package was from an Antiques shop in Cork, with no card or note attached or within after I waved around the green tissue and bubble wrap just to make sure. Instead, bound in a neat bundle with a length of red yarn were five matching paperback books. They were the five volume set, *The Centuries' Poetry* as published by Penguin in 1953. Original price: two shillings. Current price: no idea and I'm not asking as that would be rude. The books had been very gently read with no names written inside the covers, no marginalia, the spines sturdy and the pages well-glued. There is

just a gentle browning at the edges of the soft tawny pages, like
the flattering tan at the end of a well-earned resort vacation. Ah,
someone knows me well, I thought.

It took about an hour to work out who had sent the books; one of
my publishers actually and I only won't identify the name further
as the rest of the contributors may start grumbling as to where's
theirs? My thank you note got me to thinking though, about the
joy of an older book.

I suppose that our first loves in any category establish our tastes.
Apricots still delight me as they were my first baby food and
similarly that must explain my fondness for rice pudding. There
will never be a band to out-rank The Beatles and as for women, ah
I still look for that blonde girl with the laughing blue eyes. (Best
get back to the books.)

I was raised in my grandfather's house as my mother had the
quite good sense to leave my father – a dazzling writer as a
newspaper columnist yet terminal as an alcoholic – while I was, as
it were, three months *en route*. The house was huge and the yard
expansive, but my greatest interest was in one of the smallest
rooms – the Library.

It was just off the short side of the L shaped living room,
separated from the latter by an arch and a heavy gold curtain. It's
funny you know, to this day I don't know what fabric that curtain
was made of, except I hated touching it. In tactility, touching it
raised the same kind of reverse-ASMR response in me as the
touch of balloons does in others. (Oh, are you one of those? Sorry
for bringing it up, but then again my teeth hurt from the memory
of that wretched curtain.) The problem was though I had to touch
it to close it, so I would pull my sleeves down over my fingers and
sort of tug it across the rod with improvised mittens as I needed
the privacy for my own little mountaineering expedition.

Bracketing the ornately filigreed mahogany desk and also on the
opposite wall, separated by a bay window looking out at the two
pear trees in the side yard, were three rows of book shelves above

inset cupboards and drawers. The cupboards were not terrible interesting, mostly papers, folios and bank boxes as well as aging Hansards of Parliamentary debates from my grandfather's work as a Liberal MP. While the drawers held my attention somewhat, with engraved invitations, thick fountain pens and odd items such as plaques, New Year's noisemakers, heavy gold cigarette lighters and swizzle sticks, forgotten in places where they were put in order to be remembered, I was there for the Matterhorn of the book shelves.

That was why the curtain had to be closed as I knew if my mother ever spotted me standing on the narrow, narrow space on that first shelf in order to explore the third, well I didn't want to cause her that kind of stress. She had a good heart, but it was a heart weakened by illness before my birth so I knew – I think it must have been instinctively as I don't recall being told this – it was best to be a quiet little boy. That was fine by me. To this day I prefer a quiet home.

Back again to the books. I enjoyed the old encyclopedias tremendously, particularly in places where they would editorialize about the predicted future once the Second World War had been won, with maps showing places like Trans-Jordan that no longer existed and huge swaths of pink for a British Empire that also no longer existed.

What filled me with shock and horror was when I would pull down a book (I well remember a very heavy grey Survey of English Literature from someone's university days) and find that my aunt or one of my uncles had used its pages as a sketch pad or a place to practice their penmanship, disastrously. Here too, the lessons learned first are the lessons learned last; on the very rare occasions I do write a marginal note for reference when writing a review I feel a sense of guilt equivalent to swiping the cream jug from a tea shop.

My favourites were the classics. They had been delivered from what I suppose was a snootier version of the Book-of-the-Month Club via subscription every month for years before I was born, leather-bound and rough-cut pages in imitation of the Victorian age. Except for The Forsyte Sage, which was quite big on television in the 1970s, I don't think anyone in the house read these classics but me. The poems of John Donne, Keats, Byron, Whitman and Eliot; histories by Churchill and the marvelous H. G. Wells; and novels, novels everywhere! When I saw in a Peanuts cartoon Linus referencing *The Brothers Karamazov* I thought, 'Hey we have that!' and so I dug deeply into Dostoevsky at the age of nine. This is why I have never felt it fair to limit children to children's literature. God knows I loved my *Winnie the Pooh*, the works of Enid Blyton and *The Wind in the Willows* too, but why not let the child explore in books as far as his or her mind leads in curiosity?

I felt and I still feel lives led in books read before me. Sure, sometimes an old newspaper clipping falls out, or there is a library card showing that some poor sod signed the book out repeatedly as one can virtually hear an exasperated teacher wonder where the hell is the damn essay? That is a pleasure found in browsing the used book stores, or ordering on-line from a website like alibris.com. If you have never visited Alibris, oh please do! The old covers alone are a better, more fulfilling browsing experience than many an art gallery.

And so it is that my favourite gift to send to particularly well-loved friends is a used book. Even if ordered on-line, I am giving something that has been touched, that literally carries the dust of souls and metaphysically I like to believe that thoughts may linger within ethereal fingerprints.

And so I received a perfect gift in those five little paperbacks. It is the irony of the reviewer's life that we so have to keep up with the new and newer that we never have the reading time to look back in pleasure. But oh, I shall take some time to read these works that span the near-millenium from Chaucer to Eliot. I shall dip in at random, read, relax and let my thoughts drift, the perfect nostalgia of the written word. Be seeing you.

8th January 2016

How to Read a Book

Yes I know, you probably figure that you mastered the task of reading books years and years ago when you took it upon yourself to open the covers of that little volume on the nightstand next to your first bed because you simply had to know more about that first noble character of heroic fiction, The Little Engine That Cloud. (The craft of spelling was beyond you at that simpler, better time however years of school grade advancement left those kinds of errors behind. We hope.)

There is a difference though between reading to pass the time and reading for total pleasure. Indeed, pleasure should be the only goal when a new – or even a very old – book is read. That too may seem obvious, however schools tend to muddify that objective. I'm afraid that I'm rather harsh on most schools when it comes to how reading great works is taught. For one thing, they either call it literature, which implies that the sentences on a book's pages were intended for people of a higher station than you can ever hope to attain, or English which rather casts in the bin Dostoevsky, Voltaire and Cervantes just to name a few. It is my long held opinion that current sales of poetry are absolutely abysmal because schools suck the life out of it. Someone like Dante Gabriel Rossetti writes a lovely and simple little sonnet, *Without Her*, whose concluding sextet is:

What of the heart without her? Nay, poor heart,
Of thee what word remains ere speech be still?
A wayfarer by barren ways and chill,
Steep ways and weary, without her thou art,
Where the long cloud, the long wood's counterpart,
Sheds doubled in darkness up the labouring hill.

No school has ever recognized the value within the phrase, 'Leave well enough alone.' Instead of allowing those poor adolescent students who are just discovering for themselves that lust exposes the heart to daggers as well as love to just empathize with Rossetti's poor abandoned sod; oh no, one can't grade sentiment!

Instead every meter must be measured, every rhyme schemed, just how steep the gradient of that hill and which are in fact longer – clouds or woods?

Dante Gabriel Rossetti

There are of course exceptions in the form of exceptional teachers and thank heaven for 'em elsewise there would be far fewer writers worth reading in our world. In general though, schools condition us to consume books rather than savour them; they are things to be looked at objectively, not subjectively; to be mined for information rather than gems to be admired and worn as brooches of philosophy.

The ideal method for plunging into the soothing waters of reading for pleasure is by choosing books in a completely random fashion. If you are as lucky as I was and live in a house with a well-stocked personal library, grab one off the shelf and start at page one. Let a cover or a title or even the author's name be enough of a draw. I'm quite sure that I would not have read *The Cherry Orchard* at age ten if Anton Chekhov hadn't shared his last name with that little mop-topped Ensign on the Starship Enterprise. Having then discovered that this Russian chap seems to write pretty well, I went on to Dostoevsky's *The Brothers Karamazov* before running aground on the shoals of *War and Peace*.

No, I don't much care for *War and Peace*. *Moby Dick* is not my bag either. I preferred Defoe's *Moll Flanders* to Fielding's *Tom Jones*, and blasphemy it may be but damn it I get more enjoyment from Thackeray than from Dickens. Your mileage may vary and that is a very important point. You have just as much right to your tastes as does the little girl in the famous Carl Rose cartoon captioned by E.B. White. You know the one, where she says 'I say it's spinach and I say the hell with it.'

No one should ever assume the right of telling you that you are wrong to like something. Suggestions are of course to be encouraged. In books, sticking solely with your favourites means that sooner rather than later you're going to run out of things to read. God knows I mourned the death of Graham Greene, but I've managed to press ahead in life and find other authors.

A further suggestion is to know as little as possible about a book before reading it. Not to sound like one of those dreary judicial nominees at a Senate confirmation hearing, yet that was the framer's intent. Unless a novel or play is an absolute continuation within a series, no writer ever – *ever* – considers how much the reader should know about the story before reading the story unless it's part of a trilogy. Even an historical piece will supply you with whatever details the author thinks you require, much like a good Irish mammy packing a few sandwiches to see you through a long coach ride.

In my particular lucky situation as a reviewer, I quite often know absolutely nothing about a book when it flops through my mail slot and splats on the floor. Even in heavy, non-fiction works on politics or culture I make it a point to not know what the author's left or right tilt may be at his particular windmill. I don't read back covers, fly leafs or the author's bio. The book starts on page one and it ends at The End. Did I laugh along the way? Then I guess it's a comic piece. If I'm frightened it's a thriller, if dragons stalk it's fantasy and if I'm bored speechless I'll put the damn thing away.

Yes, you don't have to finish everything you start. Remember, you're reading for pleasure and not for punishment. Casting a responsible vote in an election requires (or at least should require) one to read through party platforms and the candidates' life experiences; however the fate of your county or country does not depend on your appreciation or lack thereof for the works of Stephen King.

The last piece of advice I have to offer is the best advice I have: make reading a conversation with the book and its author. Read no quicker than a comfortable pace of speech. Writing was first begun as cave paintings and glyphs to pass along experience and learning. Nothing has changed. An author felt something about something and, rather than tuck it away in a private memory, the choice was made to share it with readers. Writers want you to feel feelings, think thoughts, see imagined sights as though they are there before you and hear voices that will intrigue your ear. Allow all that to happen and, just as much as a great book should transport you to another place, even a tourist in a foreign country stops in a street and considers how and why she or he is enjoying the experience. If you love it, brilliant. Learning what it is you love – or not – is the most important lesson there is to be learned in life.

So off you go, find yourself a book, have a personal adventure. Be a bold reader, as limitless as Walt Whitman in his poem *Assurances*:

I do not doubt I am limitless, and that the universes are limitless – in vain I try to think how limitless

Be seeing you.

18th January 2016

How to Write a Book Review

This I suppose is a logical extension of my earlier essay, **How to Read a Book**. Having read a book, you might like to share your opinion of it with other readers. That is actually the first important note: Only share your opinion with other readers as the larger population will think of you as a crashing bore or even worse a pretentious pseud. Pseud you might be – and if so I'll extend an invitation to you for our monthly get-together of absinthe and oysters, as absinthe makes the heart grow fonder – but you're probably better off keeping that one under wraps. Maintain a short list of preferences for Marvel v. DC Comics television series to ensure your continued status as a Regular Joe.

But you know, there are other readers out there and if you have read something terrific that you wish to encourage, or something horrible that makes you want to hammer a warning sign into the book shop floor, it's best to develop a *lingua franca* in order to have your opinions understood. You may even want to write down your assessment and send it off to newspapers, magazines or journals. Well, damn you anyway for muscling your way onto my turf, however so long as you mind your manners I suppose I'll lend you a hand.

Hitch: He knew how to review a book.

The root knowledge you must accept is that ultimately it really doesn't matter what you think, so you may as well be brave in your opinions. After having published well over five hundred book reviews in a wide range of media across North America and Europe, I can honestly say that I have failed to make any author rich, famous or knighted. The most power you have, even amongst your most loyal followers, is you can bump up a writer or title's name recognition from Complete Unknown to the storied heights of Vague Awareness. If the author is already well-known, as when I review novels by Martin Amis or Julian Barnes for example, really you're just one more voice in the chorus, second row from the back.

Now, one of the pleasures you *will* receive is that certain authors and including some very big names will appreciate your efforts and send you a little thank you note. I have my collection framed and hung on either side of the fireplace because, frankly, I'm a big show-off. Besides such home decoration, you will also receive tips from authors as to other books you might like to review. Those tips are one of the two great sources of material.

The other source comes from the finest people in all media: Book publicists. I have dealt with publicists, agents and promoters in every medium – television, movies, comedy, theatre, art, music, you name it – and the book people are the best of the bunch. Whether the publisher they work for is large or small, every one of them will go out of her or his way to suggest books that will appeal to you and get them to you with astonishing speed.

I mention the sources because I truly believe it is vital for any reviewer to keep expanding the range of books read and reviewed. Sticking just to familiar names, or even familiar genres for that matter, leads to a narrowing of consciousness which in turn causes each successive review to be a slight re-write of the hundreds already written. That will make you just as boring and pedantic as (here's where I start to make enemies) most major reviewers.

Oh it's true. It's damn true. When I first started out in this profession, I scoured the book sections of the big national dailies looking for tips, templates, methods of conveying interest to eager readers. There are almost none to be found. Let's take a quick overview of what most Big Name Reviewers do and why I think they are godawful.

Right off the top, they tend to hide themselves behind The Voice of Authority. This involves quoting some *eminence grise*, a noted reviewer or author from the past, who once upon a time stated what the elements of a properly written novel should be. John Updike is a popular source, as is Northrop Frye, Margaret Atwood and several more. I find this a dubious technique for three reasons. One, most of these Voices of Authority are quite dead and therefore cannot read the book you are actually reviewing. Second, quoting someone else to justify your own opinions is timidity bordering on cowardice. And third, John Updike was a goddam bore who saw the world as a Connecticut suburb; yet his acolyte tree of prissy Protestant pontifications still bears branches to this day.

John Updike before he became a complete bore

It can be allowed to quote from other works in your review if the comparisons are truly appropriate. Now at that, the whole thing may come crashing down on your head, so careful now! Just the other week I wrote a review of the Irish author Rob Doyle's new book *this is the ritual*. Doyle included a fictional writer named Killian Turner as a character and I said in my review that I'd eat my hat if Killian Turner wasn't an allusion to Kurt Vonnegut's Kilgore Trout; even the KT initials are the same. All well and good, except when I interviewed the author he told me that he had in fact never heard of Kilgore Trout. Oops.

Now, the other thing that the Big Name Reviewers do that I disapprove of is writing in the third person. To me this is disingenuous bordering on the deceitful. Every review is a personal opinion, no more and no less. Writing a review as through it was an objective piece of reporting – house fires on page one, new poetry on page thirty-eight – is a tin of poppycock. The only art medium that can at all be appraised objectively is architecture, and even then only insofar as do the doors fit the frames and will the bridge stand or collapse?

It is fair to point out that there are newspapers and journals out there whose editorial style policies demand the third person voice. I won't write for those, but that's my choice. Your mileage may vary.

However, whatever voice you write in, please avoid the third admonishment I aim at the Big Time Reviewers: for God's sake stop boring people to death. The same time and effort should go into that five hundred to fifteen hundred word review as was put into any five hundred to fifteen hundred word section of the book under discussion.

Here is a test for you. Read a book review either in a physical newspaper or on-line. Remember the page or leave the tab open in your browser. Go on to the Sport section or check your Facebook for half an hour; walk the dog, you both could stand some exercise. Fine, now that you've returned, before you turn back to the review try and remember any two sentences you read in it. No? Thought as much.

Ultimately my old mucker, you have to write your review with a *voice*. Think of how you express your opinions on anything else in life. How do you describe a great meal, a foul smell, a woman's smile, a rainbow over a hill, or your baby's laugh? If you don't use cautious, balanced terms for any of those, why in hell would you do that with a book? It is just a book after all, not the sceptre of a vengeful Loki risen to dash a reviewer Balder to death.

Dorothy Parker: She never wrote a boring word in her life.

There are reviewers you can learn from, although please don't copy them. Read them for inspiration. For me, there are two I love above all others. Dorothy Parker didn't review for very long, only ten years or so in the decade following the end of the First World War, but oh she left an impact. One of the finest sentences I have ever read concluded her review of a James M. Cain novel: 'He can *write*.' Three words can be superior to three paragraphs of droning on about 'on the one hand.'

Also, there was the late and much-missed Christopher Hitchens. Hitch to me was the perfect reviewer. He was intensely personal, word-perfect in pitch, encyclopedic in knowledge, and unabashed in opinion. When he disagreed with an author's choice, he made sure to tell you exactly why he felt that way. Best of all, Hitch would place a book within a context of literature with the implied message that if you like that sort of thing you will probably like this sort of thing.

So there you have it. Enjoy the conversation you have while reading a book and then tell us about it in colourful terms. You won't get rich from reviewing, unless you consider time spent in the company of art and ideas to be valuable. I'm wagering that you do. Have fun and -

Be seeing you.

26th January 2016

Why You Should Care About Poetry

I'm already re-considering this essay, or at least its title. Although it is clear and perfectly summarizes the intent of the next 1500 words or so, **Why You Should Care About Poetry** is about as catchy as a modern audience-gatherer as its subject. As things stand at present, the great majority of readers or listeners of poetry fall into four groups:

1. The love-smitten searching for evidence that will prove that they are something more than the lout who woke up this morning with his head lolling over the bedside waste basket.

2. Students motivated by stories of Byron or Coleridge who believe that poetry is the source of all passion.

3. Reviewers who have carved out a niche for themselves in a publication and are determined to hold onto it with delicately fierce talons.

4. Other poets.

No, that's not much of an audience and if I'm going to go to all this time and typing I bloody well want one. We shall start over. Pour yourself a beverage. (*Thinks of new title...*)

The Hot, $exy Mess of Poetry!

Yes that's much better. It worked to get you here, now didn't it? And here too, the title is honest and descriptive, for a decent poem is hot, is sexy and is a mess.

Surely though, any art form that is so carefully structured and economical with words cannot truly be described as a mess? We tend to think of poems, when we think of them at all, in personified terms as the cool and silent figure in a dark corner of a busy party, slowly sipping sherry while appraising and judging the goings on before saying the perfect good-bye to the host and hostess, throwing a cloak over slim shoulders and disappearing into the night. Well, you're not wrong; however you're not right either.

The refined structure of a poem is its clothing. The mess is both what's inside and outside that protective layer. Where I am and what I am doing at this precise moment should serve as an explanation and clear up any inscrutability on my part. Through my sitting room window I am observing the multiple personalities of the Irish weather – one second snowing, the next sunny, all throughout windy, and oh look there's a rainbow. Inside, and I mean inside *me* there are collusions and collisions of thoughts like a demolition derby as I look for some sort of narrative sense for this essay. If I wrote down all those random considerations and snatched phrases in the straight order they occurred to me, what you'd be reading would be frankly unreadable. Mess on the outside, mess on the inside, what you get is the refined order of it all.

That refined order should in turn mess you up either a little or a lot. Any worthwhile art should – *should* – unsettle you even while you're being entertained. Metaphorically, the process is like losing your bearings in a large city. You know that your hotel is somewhere to the south, but where exactly is south? To determine that, you maneuver around until find a clear enough area where you can sit down and check the east-to-west movement of the sun. 'Oh! So south is that way! No wonder I'm lost.' (Or, you know, you could just ask directions but where's the fun in that?) And so a walk begun in confidence enters a state of confusion until there is a burst of clarity. Now there's a poem for you.

And actually, here's a poem for you:

(Don Juan, Canto xv. Stanza 99.)

BETWEEN two worlds life hovers like a star,
'Twixt night and morn, upon the horizon's verge.
How little do we know that which we are!
How less what we may be! The eternal surge
Of time and tide rolls on, and bears afar
Our bubbles; as the old burst, new emerge,
Lash'd from the foam of ages; while the graves
Of empires heave but like some passing waves.

Now that's a bit of George Gordon, or Lord Byron to you. Why did I choose this stanza to comment on, other than the fact that it's in the public domain and avoids my having to go through the nuisance of writing to publishers, getting permissions, etc etc etc and life is just too bloody short? For one thing, Byron's poem supports what I wrote above; there is our poet-narrator at night either at sea or on shore, watching the shadowy mass of crashing waves and bubbling foam while above there is an equal mass of dark movement with the scattered stars mimicking the white breakers below. The poet is in the middle, on that horizon's verge with the horizon line determined by the height of his own eyes and he considers that if sky is dark movement with scattered light, and sea is dark movement with scattered light, then is not humanity itself likely to be dark movement with scattered light? We last only slightly longer than sea bubbles and nowhere near as long as stars. Human life, even our collective empires, are but different dots along a timeline, transitional figures. From mess of sky to mess of sea, messy thoughts that coalesce into the order of a poem.

Speaking of transitions, as we segue like a master surfer, that bit of poem also leads us to the Hot and Sexy of our title. What exactly is hot? I take a slightly different view to the notion of a hot medium than does the originator of the term, my fellow Canadian Marshall McLuhan. McLuhan included print as hot media as all necessary information is supplied to the audience, whose members can then merely sit back and receive the intended message. Cool media – such as a cartoon where a human head may only be a brief few drawn lines – require the audience to interpret what is actually going on. The more the medium probes you, the hotter it is; the more you probe or interpret the medium, the colder it is.

Now then, my sense of Hotness is where the audience (in our case here, the poetry reader or listener) becomes a medium his or herself. The poet through the poem sends a complete message to the reader; however that reader by engaging with the poem is also sending a message back. It is immaterial whether or not the poet ever receives it; the transmission itself is a true a definition of a communicative medium. In simple terms, if you were with the late Helen Keller and you said something to her before you remembered she was deaf and blind, you still have communicated a message. You just had to find a different medium to re-communicate it.

Because poems are relatively short when compared to novels, I believe that they lend themselves to the sort of spoken or unspoken conversation I alluded to above. Indeed, that conversation is Quantum Physics in action and it doesn't get any hotter than that. Quantum theory states that the act of observation changes the nature of the object observed. Let's go back to our Byron poem to watch this process in action. First we'll take the point of view of Byron looking at just the sea. Here is what happened:

1. Byron looked at the sea.

2. The sea was impassive, just being a sea.

3. Byron considered the sea as a possibility for metaphor.

4. The sea becomes a sea *and* metaphor.

The sea's very nature has therefore changed. The next point of view is the reader who looks at Stanza 99. Here is that process:

1. The reader looks at the poem.

2. The poem is at first just text.

3. The reader sees meaning in the text.

4. The poem is now text *and* meaning.

Black marks on a page (or a voice at a public reading, same difference) are now much, much more than black marks on a page. But now comes the really interesting part, whereby the reader returns the conversation.

1. The poem observes the reader (or at least does so in the reader's mind).

2. The reader is a passive receptor.

3. The reader has a personal reaction of acceptance or adaptation of the poem's message.

4. The nature of the reader has changed.

The conversation may or may not continue through repeated readings or memory recall, yet each of the two participants has changed because of their actions as media, as message senders, as observers.

Now let's bring sexy back to poetry. Here's another poem for you, from one of my personal favourites, Dante Gabriel Rossetti. This is the first stanza of his poem *Jenny*:

Lazy laughing languid Jenny,
Fond of a kiss and fond of a guinea,
Whose head upon my knee to-night
Rests for a while, as if grown light
With all our dances and the sound
To which the wild tunes spun you round:
Fair Jenny mine, the thoughtless queen

Of kisses which the blush between
Could hardly make much daintier;
Whose eyes are as blue skies, whose hair
Is countless gold incomparable:
Fresh flower, scarce touched with signs that tell
Of Love's exuberant hotbed:—Nay,
Poor flower left torn since yesterday
Until to-morrow leave you bare;
Poor handful of bright spring-water
Flung in the whirlpool's shrieking face;
Poor shameful Jenny, full of grace
Thus with your head upon my knee;—
Whose person or whose purse may be
The lodestar of your reverie?

Now just for a bit of background, Jenny is a prostitute referred to by Shakespeare's recurring character, the vitriolic and harried Mrs. Quickly in *The Merry Wives of Windsor*. Rossetti spends some thirty-two verses considering Jenny, how she became what she became and how it would be to spend a night with her. After all, *This room of yours, my Jenny, looks/ A change from mine so full of books*. What's life for if not a dock from which to launch the ship of fantasy?

Now, before you think I'm stating the drearily obvious, for this section on poetry and sexiness I have not chosen *Jenny* to discuss because of the golden-haired working girl's career. Rather, it is the three-way (heh) among subject/poet/reader that is the true sexiness.

Sexiness is much, much more than mere attraction. Parks, diamonds and cheesecakes are all attractive yet none of them overtly beg for picnickers, jewelers or diners. Such objects are just sort of *there*, make of them what you will. Sexy though, ah! Sexy knows what it wants and it wants you. And what Sexy wants from you is (stand back now, we're going to let fly!) for you two to...

Get mad and crazy touching every cell of skin and hair and mind-melted whose arm is this yours or mine, while our minds fly out of our skulls and into heaven except we might just tilt our wings and see how close we can get to hell without burning ourselves to death, little deaths, they used to call orgasm dying, but we know better for we are never so alive as when we are not just two-backed beasts, oh rather we are gods, goddesses, our temples on the mount as we ourselves mount whether in reality or symbol, the act or shadow or ideas expressed in words and bodies, such beautiful words emerging from our bodies, even when those words are wordless moans and groans – We create our own language!!!

I need a cigarette, how about you?

Yes, Rossetti's Jenny existed for that which we imagine is just as real as the tangible body next to ours. After all, when you dream does not your mind accept the dreamworld as real? No wonder our human bodies never evolved so much that we discarded the need for sleep. We might well have become like the constantly-swimming sharks, yet then we would have lost the capacity to dream at length without interruption, and that would be a backslide rather than an advance in human evolution.

Yes, reading a poem can be as sexy an action as you can do when you become totally immersed in its world of ideas and engage your own desires within it.

Now go read something. Find yourself a hot, sexy mess of a poem. Go meet Jenny on a page somewhere and swim with her in Byron's sea, float on your backs and consider the stars above. It won't hurt a bit.

Be seeing you.

Posted *30th January 2016*

Immodest Proposals: Keep You Doped With Religion and Sex and TV

Inside Television 541

Publication Date: 2-18-11

I haven't written an Immodest Proposals column in, I think, a year or two. For those who don't remember the format, I put forward an idea or three that would make excellent sense in a sane world. They will never happen, for this is not a sane world. Still, it's nice to dream of things that have never been and ask, 'Why not'?

What got me to thinking was a combination of two conversations and one news item. The first conversation was one I held over the phone with Emma Forrest, author of the memoir *Your Voice in My Head*. Forrest, a journalist turned screenwriter (aren't we all?) went through a period of mental illness that included cutting and an attempted suicide. When I asked her why cutting had appeared as a plague affecting adolescent women in the last 15-20 years, she expressed her opinion that it was as a result of the sexualization of very young girls. It starts with the manufacture of the Lindsays and Britneys and carries down into the classrooms and bedrooms of our own neighbourhoods.

The second conversation was with a woman of my acquaintance who sincerely believed and forcefully expressed the opinion that the Muslim people - all of them - had an agenda to kill Christians in order to get to Heaven. Therefore, Canada should lock its immigration doors to Muslims before they 'took over the country.' Being polite (and in shock) at the time I just said, 'No no, they're much too sensible for that.'

And third, there was a radio interview Charlie Sheen gave with Dan Patrick which was repeated on CTV News. Sheen in short said that his drugging and debauching was a periodic thing and the producers of '**Two and a Half Men**' should restart production now while he was reasonably sober and strapped together.

Did I mention that we don't live in a sane world?

Now I have been at this rude sport of covering television a little too long to ever imagine that anything I suggest will ever happen. But I'm rather hoping you might agree and adjust your viewing schedules, or at least your viewing perception accordingly.

Broadly taken, gag orders aren't very popular in North America - they're *de rigueur* in the UK - because those of us on the Western shores of the Atlantic have this silly idea that we have an absolute right to know everything about everything. We are self-accredited experts in solving other people's problems (especially famous people with problems) as it saves all the effort of solving our own. However, I put it to you that a cone of silence above a cloak of invisibility might help in several ways.

I live in a city which is struggling honourably with the development of a drug and intoxication strategy. To me, the issue is a relatively simple one. Should one be arrested for public intoxication in any form. one would then lose the right to purchase or consume any variant of liquor or stimulant that can be quaffed, lit, swallowed or rubbed on the belly for one year. You abuse it, you lose it.

Now what if this was twisted and extended to entertainment and news? Lindsay and Charlie, you aren't doing well and worse than that - for God gives us a perfect right to make fools of ourselves - you are setting the example that it is okay for the kids out there to grow up to be slam partying, abusive slut bags. Um, that really isn't working well for the rest of us.

There is no good reason to incarcerate Charlie Sheen for his addictions - his ritual domestic abuse is another matter - it's expensive and it doesn't work. Rather, let's snuff out the fire by removing the oxygen. No judge can order this; freedom of expression gets in the way. What if the networks and studios dusted off the old 'morals clause' and determined that Charlie's shows (sorry to pick on you old boy, but you are a gold medal pig) can't be seen anywhere for a year, his pictures will not be printed, his interviews will not be requested. For a celebrity, this is Papillon or Dreyfus territory. This would be harsh on a first offence, but if it is established that one is a celebrity Ho, then to no Ho shall celebrity go.

The other item I would like to see suffocated is any reference to religion anywhere in the news. Your mind has immediately focused on the Middle East, as it would, but allow me to explain. One of the basic struggles of that region is usually described as that between Muslims and Jews. That's become a tidy capsule description for correspondents and talking heads who either don't know a Shi'ite from a shirt collar and would never be given the proper time by their producers to do so in the first place. For if that is to be the dominant issue and its resolve a framework for peace, then that issue needs to be re-framed regularly, not just in a 2AM documentary that no one will ever see.

Besides which, it's inaccurate. I was reminded when reading *The Midwife of Venice* by Roberta Rich that around the time of Shakespeare it was the Caliphate based in what we know as Turkey and as Muslim as it gets, that was the sanctuary for Jews fleeing the prejudice of Europe and the press-gang slavery of the Knights of Malta. Those Knights, bored with the end of the Crusades and good Catholic men every won, would capture Jewish traders and hold them for ransom. If the ransom wasn't met, they became slaves. The Turks or Muslims or Arabs took the escapees and protected them.

So if that Middle Eastern struggle is not the result of an intrinsic hatred of a different version of God's opinions on how to lead a model life, then what if analysis took religion right out of the formula? Then stories would be based around subjects, legal subjects, repairable subjects like political repression, loss of human rights, and the distribution of oil wealth. You're never going to completely agree with my sense of who or what God is, any more than you'll ever understand why tears come to my eyes whenever I hear 'You'll Never Walk Alone'. So let's just put religion aside and discuss what we can discuss moving forwards to agreement. And the final benefit is that people won't be hearing snatches of conversation or sound clip exaggerations that leads to half of the Republican Party in the U.S.A. thinking a) that Barack Obama is a Muslim born outside the U.S.A.; and b) that somehow matters. Because even personal religion will be tossed out of the news scripts.

None of this will happen Out There. But in your opinions and perceptions, maybe it can happen In Here. Be seeing you.

(Having spent so many enjoyable years deeply involved in the collective madness of theatre, I had always wanted to tell the story of what life was really like for a working actor – not a star, not a celebrity, no one famous or infamous for who had been slept with – instead tell the story of what that career is. In altered form the following ran as a three-part series of Inside Television columns in the late spring of 2011. That very nearly gave the newspaper heart failure and I was ordered to never again run a multi-part series. Yes of course I ignored that advice. Read on.)

Actress

Lisa Marie DiGiacinto

Lisa Marie DiGiacinto in 2011

Actress. I've never understood why the all-encompassing term Actor ever came into use for both men and women. It has to make life awkward for anglophone women named Jean auditioning in Quebec and francophone men finding similar work in Alberta. I find nothing discriminatory about the word actress; therefore I continue to use it.

This is a story about one actress. You see, we tend to concentrate on the famous ones, those that have made it, or lost it, or are in the position as producers of media products of making it or losing it for other actors. Life looks easy for them when viewed from a distance: pools and pool parties, more champagne darling, and isn't the beach lovely this time of year?

Yet acting is the hardest work, the hardest career you can pick because talent doesn't necessarily rise like cream or champagne bubbles. Actors and actresses work and scrimp and haul tired bodies into empty theatres lit by one bulb so that they can look fresh and sparkly and just what some shadowy face sat at a table is looking for. Except they aren't looking for someone 5'7 with chestnut hair - no, we really want 5'8 and auburn thank you for coming, leave your pictures at the desk.

I'd like to introduce you to a friend of mine that I haven't seen in more than ten years who is right there, right at that moment when the hundredth key has been placed in the lock and turned and - lo and behold - it clicked. She is about to become one of the exalted ones. May we have a round of applause for Lisa DiGiacinto.

Lisa has just secured her first major role, the female lead in Quiver; a feature film that begins shooting in Thunder Bay next month. Lisa is from Thunder Bay originally and it is a splendid irony that she moved first to Calgary and then Vancouver to receive her break in Thunder Bay. But that's acting for you. If you don't have a sense of irony going in, don't worry, it will seek you out.

I want to take you on the path Lisa followed to where she is today. I first met her in 1999. For a very brief time, there was a theatre production group at Lakehead University, where Lisa was a student. I know that theatre group well because I headed it. Dr. Fred Gilbert, the President of LU was kind enough to give me a desk in the basement of the Agora and we put on one show, Anton Chekhov's *The Seagull*. There was no funding, so it all drifted apart like the mists of a Russian dawn, but for a few months it was brilliant.

Lisa played Nina, the female lead. She was twenty then, very pretty and equally unpolished but you could see that she really - really - wanted to act. I remember during rehearsal she broke into tears behind the curtain on the stage right side of the Bora Laskin Auditorium, next to a giant clanking lighting board that looked like a set piece from Wolfgang Petersen's film Das Boot. I don't remember now what I said, but it must have worked.

On opening night she gave a performance that is - yes - my favourite of 105 opening nights I have attended as actor or director or writer. Lisa electrified. In the closing mad scene she was consumed and consumed and fed the audience with all the shock and perfect horror of her character. She became an Actress in that moment.

I wondered over the intervening decade what had become of her, knowing in my heart that if she pursued it, she might breathe the rare air of stardom. Thanks to Facebook, we re-connected.

One of the hard truths of acting that Lisa's story clearly highlights is that no matter how good you might be in Thunder Bay or other hinterland cities, if you want to make it, you have to leave home. Anyone who tries to argue that it is possible to make a living here solely as a creative artist in theatre, film or television either a) has never tried or b) has tried and just hasn't gone broke yet. Small, divided and unsupportive markets will do that to you. Acting is a great hobby in the hinterland; as a profession - no.

The logical place to start for a Canadian actor is Toronto. Lisa looks back today at her fears of Toronto and laughs at them: "There were a few things I was scared of though- the biggest ones being high cost of living and... Apparently I couldn't drive, apparently no one in Toronto had cars?? WTF, coming from Tbay, I didn't understand public transit haha." So, as one of her best friends Harmony had moved to Calgary, which was a growth market for entertainment, she moved there in January 2004.

There survival got in the way of her dreams. Having a degree in Commerce, Lisa worked in a bank for two years and it all might have ended there as it ends for many an actor. But, 'I was...depressed. (or so I thought)... so I did some self analysis, and came to the conclusion that I wasn't happy with my path and something had to change, drastically. So, I did some job personality type tests and what was the #1 career choice for me EVERY TIME???? ACTRESS. I knew in my heart that I would never be happy and fulfilled if I didn't pursue my dreams... the # 2 was broadcasting... so I did both. I started going to acting classes and got a job in promo for a radio station... from there, I started auditioning, and landed my first small one liner role in an indie short called Stolen Horses.' But a credit's a credit and a successful actor knows how to build a mansion starting from one brick.

From that one-liner she continued to get work in Calgary, including a part in a picture directed by her teen years heartthrob Jason Priestley. (He was Brandon in the original Beverly Hills 90210.) But just as you can't go anywhere in Thunder Bay, you can only go so far in Calgary. So in December 2008, Lisa gave herself a Christmas present and moved to the production hotbed of Vancouver. She was leaving on a high, having featured in the stage production of Red Light Winter and been nominated for Best Actress at the Alberta Film and Television Awards for her role in the short film Deadwalkers, available on iTunes.

I've wanted to explain to you the life of the working actress through the story of Lisa's life thus far. What have we established? If I've done my job, you know that she is lovely and talented and ambitious and dedicated and teachable and had established a solid resume in stage, film and radio. So what more do you need? The world's her oyster and pass her the pearl necklace.

Oysters and pearls. A pearl - in case you didn't know or in case you have forgotten - is born of pain. The little oyster is irritated by a grain of sea sand. It hurts. It hurts and the hurt won't go away so the oyster grows this shiny substance that hardens and smooths around the sand hoping it won't hurt any more. We who just see the result thinks the pearl is all prettiness on the half shell. The oyster knows better, but who ever thought to talk to an oyster?

Lisa in 2016

This story called Actress has been in the works for a year now. When I got back in touch Lisa through Facebook I knew that her story was the story every aspiring actor, and every smug audience member who thought that Life is Hard but Acting is Easy needed to know. I asked her last summer what the highs and lows were. She sent me an audio file last August. It was devastating.

We don't have room in a newspaper column to quote from it, so let me summarize the pain. After a year and a half in Vancouver, things were going less than well. Lisa had passed age 30 and that is a dangerous time for an actress. To paraphrase from a play I directed once called Four Dogs and a Bone, and actress gets three lives: Ingenue, Star, and Someone's Maiden Aunt who's dying of cancer. In the ridiculous age standards of Big Entertainment - and they are *our* standards dear friends, for Hollywood gives us what we ask them - Lisa was in her prime time, but where was primetime?

Worse, one has to exist. The old joke that inside every actor is a waiter is true. Also inside every actor is a receptionist, office temp, booth attendant, all manner of jobs where the employer hires you on the understanding that if you have to book off for an audition - no problem! Then you need the time and that is a problem.

And it can get very, very lonely. Working actors are surrounded by bonhomie - good times! Cheers! But the relationships are temporary and often born of a quiet desperation. No one can ever fault an actor for finally saying 'The hell with it.'

But Lisa never said those words. She has overcome. Cast in the feature film Quiver over the internet on Skype, she returns home to Thunder Bay in a few weeks to begin shooting. And, her present day job hits a sweet spot for an actress. She works for a casting agency in Vancouver. They will surely understand an actor's needs.

How does Lisa DiGiacinto summarize her own story? 'I feel that the universe (all my jobs and the industry) is all finally supporting me and that I am extremely excited to see what the near future has to offer me! I just feel that some major successes are just around the corner.. but I needed to go through the tough times to get to where I am now, it was all part of the journey.'

Irony and pain and talent and excitement. That - that is an Actress.

Be seeing you.

(Update: Lisa's career has continued forward. Quiver, the movie mentioned above, is in post-production. She has also had featured roles in among other shows The Flash, Arrow, The Unauthorized Full House Story (as Paula Abdul) and Garage Sale Mystery. But to me she will always be the Nina who blew the roof of a theatre in 1999. Her management is Michelle Gauvin from Performers Management. Michelle and Lisa can be reached at mg@performersmanagement.com)

(Sometimes you get lucky in what you cover. To my knowledge I was the first journalist to review a little song that went to number one around the world, and to this day Carly Rae Jepsen is still one of the nicest people I have ever run across in entertainment.)

Carly Rae Jepsen: A Canadian Idol Success Story

Inside Television 571
Publication Date: 9-23-11

As I start to write this, I'm listening to a peppy little number on YouTube titled Call Me Maybe. It's absolutely infectious in a way that Nick Lowe once termed pure pop for now people. Completely enjoyable in the way that we all do secretly love those happy pop numbers that stick in your head like the phone number you had at university. Released this week on iTunes, Call Me Maybe is the first single off the new album by this week's subject Carly Rae Jepsen.

I'm doubly delighted that the song should be a strong hit as I had already decided to interview Carly Rae before the song was released. You see, after I wrote last week's column on The X Factor, I started to remember the 2007 season of Canadian Idol as the one season of any of the singing contest shows that I truly loved. The final three that year were the epitome of eclecticism. The capped Brian Melo won that year, largely based on a soul-shattering rendition of Radiohead's Karma Police. (That, amazingly is *not* on YouTube.) Second place was a country singer named Jaydee Bixby, who was truly Porter Wagoner or Conway Twitty re-invented into a really cute blonde 17 year old boy whom in his politeness every parent in Canada prayed their daughter would bring home.

Then there was the one I was cheering for - Carly Rae, as you've probably guessed. It's a difficult quality to describe, what her energy is. I've puzzled over the right words for a few minutes, which is unlike me. (I love writing, but I enjoy it more when things are actually completed.) I was thinking of effervesence, but I can be more precise. It was like a mimosa cocktail: the intoxicating nature of champagne - please not sparkling wine, because then you're just pretending to be a healthy drunk - and the goodness and citric sweetness of orange juice. It really all came together for her on Idol when she sang Rickie Lee Jones' Chuck

E's in Love. That someone 21 years old would reach back and find the under-appreciated Jones and then make the song into a smart, sophisticated yet still peppy cabaret performance absolutely sold me.

Because every living and working artist in the world now has a dedicated Facebook page, it was easy to find Carly Rae, to essentially ask, so how's the career going? Is he able to make a living as a singer-songwriter?

'This is my work . This also happens to be my passion, so I got lucky. I write a lot. Lyrics are my constant fascination and I've recently started writing for other artists as well. It's exciting to see what comes next with my new album. I've spent the last year in the studio so I'm dying to crawl out of that cave and start touring again. I can't wait to be honest.'

That does indicate a positive professionalism. For prior to working on what must be a luminescent studio tan, Carly Rae had been touring steadily from her Vancouver base. So naturally I had to ask about the just-released album.

'The album is an exploration of sorts. It's about love. I titled it CURIOSITY for that reason. The grass is always greener. The bad boy is always softer than expected and the heart is ultimately not controllable. I centered the CD around these themes. Ryan Stewart, who produced most of TUG of WAR (**her first album, released 2008**) *was my collaborator and producer once again. Josh Ramsay from Marianas Trench co-wrote and produced Call Me Maybe. Kevvy Mental had his part in Dear Julien and The Store. I'm am altogether very proud with how it turned out. The songs are honest pop. It will be fun to sing these songs live.'*

And of course I had to ask about Idol. What is it like forming this quasi-family with other competitors while still being their, you know, competitor?

'We sincerely liked each other. It was kind of like summer camp in a Mansion. We were all experiencing so many new things. The Mansion itself was intimidating. Indoor pools, basketball courts and movie theaters. Then there were the personal singing coaches, stylists and those

ever looming TV cameras. We sort of clung to each other in the chaos of it all. We were truly sad when someone had to leave.'

Lastly, and after feeling truly happy that a favourite performer was going along well in life, I did the traditional thing that I do. I always offer interview subjects the final word to talk about whatever the heck they want to say about anything. Oftentimes it's just a reiteration of what's been already said,which is why you don't read these a lot. But Carly Rae gives us her personal version of a Fodor's Guide to Vancouver. What would you like to say to the readers? The space is yours. Here is the response:

Bonus round. Haha...ok. I'd like to share with you my favourite places to go in Vancouver . Next time you are here try:
1. Sweet Revenge for the best dessert in town
2. Salt in Blood Alley - they pair great wine and cheese. Heaven.
3. Dream Apparel in Gas Town for some amazing local designs. Her clothes are stunning.
4. Corduroy on Tuesday nights for some great live music. I've discovered some amazing hidden gems there !

I truly enjoyed contacting Carly Rae Jepsen and am pleased to report a good and positive story. It's as refreshing as a mimosa. Be seeing you.

The Passion of Christopher Hitchens

December 16, 2011

For: Herald de Paris, The Chronicle-Journal, et al

There have been precious few regrets in my writing career. The fact that you choose to take the time it takes to read this is indicative of that. There is no real point to writing without an audience - that would be you - and you are as rightfully discriminating as intelligent dogs. You know your taste in treats and if you don't perceive value in what the hand offers you correctly turn your head and look elsewhere.

It was impossible to turn away from Christopher Hitchens, whose death announcement was made public by Vanity Fair late last night. I look back at that sentence and realize I have already been imprecise, which in turn means that I have already proven myself less of a writer than Hitchens. The use of the past tense is entirely incorrect. It is impossible to turn away from Hitchens and will be for, I suspect, a very long time.

I only just realized the meaning of the title of Hitchens' memoir, *Hitch-22*. It was a nice play on words, a nudge to the intelligent who would recognize it as a nod to Joseph Heller's novel Catch-22, the story of the Air Force pilot Yossarian caught up in the madness of war. But I had missed the deeper level until now.

Catch-22 meant that as soon as a pilot reached what was the end of his number of bombing runs and so would be decommissioned, the number was raised by the Air Force. The term of enlistment would never end. The war would never end. There was no going back. It seems so obvious now. Hitchens might turn out a memoir; however his mission would never end.

Now the natural thing to say next is that his mission has now ended, rest in peace, do say hello to God for me. (We will, inevitably, get to God and Hitchens.) The sorrow I feel at his passing - and it is deep, wallowing, misery-spilling sorrow - is that the mission does continue. It continues without his wisdom.

The first anecdote: The first time I remember seeing Hitchens was on CNN at the time of the first Gulf War, which was a War that Hitchens heartily opposed. He was on one half of a split-screen while on the other half was one of those American retired colonels or generals who are on a casting list to be trotted out whenever the guns are fired and bombs are dropped. Hitchens asked this general - let's say it was a general - if he could name the various countries and emirates that bordered the Persian Gulf. Of course the general gaped and spluttered like a freshly-landed trout and was equally as eloquent as that. That was when I knew this Christopher Hitchens was a man to be followed.

Was I, am I, a follower of his? I'd like to think so. The answer to all the important aspects of his life and philosophy is a definite yes.

Regarding Hitchens as a journalist, I note that he is most frequently described as an essayist. That was precisely what made him such a great journalist. You must recall the elements of an acceptable essay as taught to you in school whether you succeeded in the craft or not. An essay is a statement of opinion about a given subject backed up by research and assessment of alternative views. I'm sure it's all coming back to you and sorry if

that is a bad memory. It is that first piece of definition - a statement of opinion - that separated him from the bland pack of journalists, writers and editors both, whose mealy mediocrity has seen papers, magazines and on-line publications turn out the lights and lock the doors in ever-growing numbers.

Hitchens really didn't care who he offended either in print or in person. His best friend of nearly forty years, the novelist Martin Amis, wrote recently in *The Guardian* about Hitchens attacking him from the podium over their differing opinions on the Iraq War. That incident, by the way, speaks well of both men: to be able to disagree viscerally and viciously, yet remain beloved friends afterwards.

The second anecdote: the Pulitzer-Prize winning former New York Times journalist Chris Hedges has written twice about this incident. They were on the same panel arguing about the Iraq War

- Hedges opposed, Hitchens in favour. Hedges had called Hitchens a 'wind-up puppet for the Bush Administration.' Hitchens shouted that Hedges was, 'an apologist for terrorists.' That one actually made Hedges, by his own admission, re-assess not the finality of his opinions but their ramifications. Anyone who can make an equal think has done their job well.

Dear God (yes, we will get to the God question very soon), a lot of people hated Christopher Hitchens. The publisher of one of the publications I write for responded to my email when the news came that Hitchens had died. That publisher dryly noted, 'Sure there are a lot of fundamentalists celebrating.' Sad to say, but I'm sure he's right. Certain people took delight in pointing out the unflattering portrait of Hitchens as 'Peter Fallow' in Tom Wolfe's novel *Bonfire of the Vanities*. He also cameos in bare disguise in Martin Amis' *The Pregnant Widow*. My response is that if you are a big enough character to figure in two of the better novels of the last thirty years, you must be living right.

The fundamentalists though would beg to differ and fundamentalists are not necessarily religious fundamentalists. They exist in politics and philosophy too. Hitchens lost a lot - and I do mean a lot - of, if not friends exactly, at least fond acquaintances and fellow travelers over his support of that Iraq War. It seemed so...inconsistent. It was betrayal!

It was nothing of the sort. On the basics of the war, Hitchens often said that a world without Saddam Hussein was better than a world with Saddam Hussein. And why was that? Because Hitchens had spent significant time amongst the Kurds, had talked, had listened, had observed the effects of the Baath Party atrocities including torture, poison gas and mass execution. George Bush may have gone to war for either oil or Oedipus; that is not why Christopher Hitchens supported him.

The third anecdote: Hitchens volunteered to be water-boarded, to experience torture himself. It was a horrific story to read in Vanity Fair. He did not condone torture. One wonders if Donald Rumsfeld would have been so gung-ho on the subject had he tasted, or been submerged in, his own medicine.

Hitchens stood for freedom against all oppressors. Accused of being anti-Muslim, he would point to the Palestinian lapel pin he always wore at every event. Accused of war-mongering, I note on his behalf that there was no public figure he despised more than Henry Kissinger for his secret war in Cambodia that led to the atrocities of Pol Pot. Accused of being a sell-out to the American Republican Party I invite you to look up a clip on YouTube where Hitchens is asked at an election night party in his own home (he was in the fine glow of a man who understood and appreciated the qualities of single malt Scotch) if there was one incumbent Republican he wished had been defeated. His reply was the Governor of Texas, Rick Perry. Why? Perry had said that in America only Christians should serve in elected office.

Ah yes, the God question. Hitchens was an atheist and I suspect far too many obituaries and memorials are going to dwell on that. He felt that religion was a destructive force that with its reliance on myth and jingoistic superiority had caused far more harm than good over the course of human history. That was one of the points

of his philosophy I used to think I was opposed to. And then, damn or thank him, he made me think. He made me think just as the author (and Israeli-Canadian) David Berlin made me think when we discussed Israel and Berlin shared his final opinion that the only way there could be peace in the Middle East would be by Israel renouncing its Jewish-ness and becoming secular.

You will be reading a lot of opinions about Hitchens - some joking, some serious, some sick - meeting God today. I believe he will, although not as a little be-winged angel meeting (in George Carlin's memorable phrase) a nice old man who lives on a cloud. Much like Catch-22, nothing ever really ends in the universe. Nothing is ever truly destroyed. It just becomes something else. If consciousness exists as a thing, broadly stated, it continues to exist and melds into other consciousness. So Hitchens not just meets God; he becomes part of him. I think that is a delightful way of thinking about it, so I'm sticking to it.

I opened by saying I had few regrets as a writer. Here's one of them. I was scheduled to meet Hitchens for an interview right after Hitch-22 was released. I was going to fly down to Toronto for it. I looked forward to an argument or two, just as an avid golfer would want to play a round with Jack Nicklaus or a poker player sit opposite Phil Ivey. Debater, golfer and poker player all would lose...but what an experience.

The interview never happened because Hitchens was diagnosed with esophageal cancer and so much for the press tour. As I look back on it now, as I recall that voice and that brilliance of grammar that every time I write urges me to want to raise my game to his level, I sadly realize that I probably wouldn't have said what I should have. I will say it now, just for us. Christopher Hitchens, I love you.

The Prisoner:
My Days in Jail

(The following is a true story, occurring on and about New Year's Eve 2013.)

The Prisoner

Life being the carefully arranged set of coincidences and ironies that it is, well beyond the range of the imagination of any video game manufacturer, I see in retrospect that it was inevitable that I would one day become The Prisoner. The Patrick McGoohan series was my favourite of all favourites when I was a boy and yes, even more than Star Trek...

"I am not a number! I am a Free Man!"

"Who is Number One?"

"Be seeing you."

Ah yes, 'Be seeing you.' Let me take a wild stab at a number and no, not Number 6. I would estimate that over the course of my eighteen years as a journalist I've probably written close to 2000 columns, feature stories, reviews etc. and so forth. Of that 2000 I probably have signed off with Be seeing you in 90% of them. I enjoyed the deconstruction of those three simple words, accompanied as they were in the television series by a hand gesture composed of forming a sort of monocle with the thumb and index finger held to the eye followed by the same hand pointing to the recipient.

Be – existence

Seeing – observation

You – the observed

To exist then is to watch and to understand those within our viewing range. And there is also the creepy-crawly underlying warning that this act of observance is constant, perpetual, on-going and never-ending; this some 40 years before the NSA and GCHQ started to monitor every electronic communication we make. You and I – we observe – yet we are also the observed. We are never allowed to be alone; even when we think we are, we are still the observed experiment on the slide beneath an omnipresent microscope.

(An interesting little irony. I just hit Command-S to save the above in OpenOffice, my favourite writing platform. A warning box popped up saying that, 'This document has been edited by others. If you save it, those changes may be lost. Do you wish to continue?' I'm sure that was just an eccentricity of the new version of OpenOffice I recently installed, but under the circumstance of what I had just written...oh my!)

And so it was that near the end of my stay in England, I too briefly became The Prisoner. I wasn't spirited off after being rendered unconscious by a nerve gas to an antique yet modern Village somewhere in the known yet unknown world. No, it was much more mundane than that; but still, as a three-day period where I observed a strange new way of existence more intensely than I had ever observed anything before ... I understood the world of McGoohan's Number 6.

My money had ran out. That much we had established. What with the quest (seemingly simple yet finally proven impossible) of finding a new rental house or flat for my dog Stella and me being blocked at each turn, seven weeks staying at three different Bed and Breakfast houses had made a church mouse seem wealthy as Smaug in comparison to me. Yet, I could see no other option other than to extend my stays at £60 a night, the cheapest I could find, at least until I could move into the YHA Youth Hostel for £10 a night. I was down to waiting for my new Canadian Passport's delivery so I could return to Canada to assist Harald with his plans for an arts centre up the Rideau Valley from Kingston, Ontario. I had given up on living abroad after a only a year.

It is never an easy thing for a man like me who has led for the most part a comfortable upper-middle class existence to admit that one's money has run out, yet I had to. I grant you I could at least truthfully satisfy myself that this was a temporary condition what with the imminent release of my poetry book Random Acts of Love as well as ta contract to write a biography of the director and screenwriter Joss Whedon, I was successful! I just hadn't been paid yet for *being* successful. Knowing money would be coming in allowed me the shred of dignity to ask friends and family for loans, not gifts; investment as I would pay back with interest, not charity. The friends came through. Family? Surely you jest. Still, at least I still had that thin red hair of pride to hold onto.

Until it snapped. Snip! There goes the red hair.

It was New Year's Eve. As noted above, I planned to leave the Cobbled Yard Hotel in two days and at that point I still expected the old family business to come through with a loan sufficient to keep me and Stella alive and sheltered until we could fly back at the end of the month. New Year's Eve 2013 – the end of a year that had begun so happily at Toberbeg Lodge in Ireland, toasting the mysterious Audrey at a distance with champagne at midnight, now ended after an epic romance, victory, defeat and a state of homelessness.

That December 31st morning I thought my biggest concern was whether or not I'd be bored that evening. Oh I'd considered going out to one of the pubs nearby on the High Street and enjoying all the shared revelry and laughter; however I had only been sober a relatively short time, so best not to take the risk of that doomful saying, 'I'll just have one – a red wine for my heart ... or maybe a white wine so I don't have purple lips in case of a random kiss at midnight.' No no no no and uh-uh NO! So instead I went to the Co-Op Foods and picked up two sandwiches, a bag of sausage rolls, a bag of cinnamon doughnuts and a bottle of ginger ale. Graham Norton would be having the cast of Monty Python on his New Year's Eve special and that would be celebration enough. Heck, I'd message Audrey at midnight through Facebook and make a joke of it – 'Last year champagne, this year ginger ale. Oh how the mighty have fallen, eh dear friend? Hugs!' Ah such larks Pip, such larks we had planned!

Then, about five PM there came a rather serious sounding knock on the door. I was in Room 4. It's tempting under the circumstances to say I was in Room 6, just to make The Prisoner motif a little more perfect, but I'm afraid that wasn't the case. There are only five rooms in the whole place. I digress.

The owner of The Cobbled Yard, Linda Miller – a very nice person of whom I have nothing but kind words to say – had wondered why I hadn't paid up my stay after my first extension. (I had thought I could move into the hostel for December 27th, but it was booked solid until January 2nd) She had phoned Meadow Hills Guest House, where I had stayed until December 21st, and discovered I still owed money there. Yes, I had partially paid that bill with an agreement to pay out the rest as soon as possible; nonetheless there was still money owing. Linda worried I would 'crash and dash' and I can't say as I blame her one bit. When I worked at the Comfort Inn in Thunder Bay, we would take the same dubious view of evidently dodgy guests. So, she phoned the Berwick Constabulary to investigate. The knock on the door was followed by information that the police were on their way.

Enter a brief interlude of panic.

I sent out a series of identical Facebook messages to three friends who might maybe, possibly, oh let's throw a Hail Mary pass to the end zone!, have enough room on their credit cards to cover a £660 bill – that's just about exactly $1100 in Canadian or American funds. So as not to leave you in suspense, as I found out later no they couldn't. No matter. Hail Mary Passes only have a success rate of about 7% in the NFL and as we know, credit cards charge at least 17% ... that may be a non sequitir but in the moment my entire life felt like a non sequitir.

In came the police, Sergeant Stephen Crane (did he *have* to have a literary name?) and Constable Susan Aitken. Stella greeted them warmly and I gave her a snack of kibble to keep her occupied. I sat back in the comfy chair – 'No! Not the comfy chair!' - by the window while the officers stood and asked questions.

Q: Do you have the money at present to pay the outstanding bill?

A: No.

Q: Will you have the money to pay the outstanding bill?

A: I have requested a loan to be placed in my account by Thursday.

Q: Will that money be in place by then?

A: I am quite sure it will be. (*Ha! As I later was to discover.*) However, I do not know that for absolute fact.

(In case you're wondering about my memory, yes I actually do talk that formally in high-stress situations. In all truth, from the moment the police arrived right through to the end of this some 72 hour nightmare, I was in a mental state that I'd describe as a genial, benign calm. What had I learnt from all the crises from the time of Kimberly's aneurysm to this? Worry and fear help nothing.)

Q: We would like to ask you to come to the station house voluntarily. You do not have to and you can have a solicitor provided to you. You may also leave at any time unless you are charged.

A: No, I'd like to come with you. As a matter of fact, I'm actually relieved you're here. (*True! I was sick of all this.*) I'm more than happy to answer any and all questions. But one question: What happens to Stella?

Stella was able to come along and I want to stress that the constabulary could not have been better to her – God bless the English and their love of dogs. She would be placed in a kennel, the Berwick Animal Rescue Kennel (B.A.R.K.) where she was beautifully taken care of. That, I must tell you, was my greatest relief. Do what you want with me, but please take care of my dearest furry friend and companion.

So, off we went and yes it really is just like Inspector Morse or Prime Suspect. The interview is recorded on disc, two officers are present and the British version of the Miranda Rights are read and agreed to. I refused a solicitor. All I wanted to do was describe the mess I was in, be clear as to my intent and motivations and let both chips fall and shit smack into fans. Out came all the details of my story of book delays, non-payments, the three house and two flat let agreements having fallen apart, I won't repeat it all here.

Charges were laid. Fraud, or to use its ancient term, Bilking.

My only difference of opinion was that I refused the notion put forward by Sergeant Crane, as indeed is his job, that I intended to defraud the Cobbled Yard. Absolutely not. I always had the intention to pay, much the same as Meadow Hills. In my point of view – and I do realize that this may be a bit of wriggle logic worthy of Bill Clinton – what I had done was no more than what I had to do in order to survive and if Christ himself had said that a man who steals food in order to eat is not a thief, then I was no con artist. I despise owing people ... or rather despised. One of the things I learnt over this year was that sometimes one needs help; and just as I have always helped others without ever looking down on them, why should I think that anyone else is less nobly motivated than I am?

Back to New Year's Eve ...

I was placed in a holding cell in Berwick station. There was a blue mat, in size and thickness exactly the same as a gym mat, on a faux marble bench, a toilet hole (it had running water I hasten to add) cut into the same faux marble, a heavy block glass window, one fluorescent light, a CCTV, a call button and a very heavy door with a peephole and a sliding letter box opening. And you think the decorations at your New Year's Eve Party were disappointing?

Again the police were very kind, offering tea, coffee and sandwiches but honestly all I wanted to do was sleep. I suppose by this time it was around 8PM. One thing I would find maddening is that in none of the three cells I was in was there ever a clock. We spend so much of our days being constantly time-aware that to have it removed is honestly a real sense deprivation. My wristwatch though had been seized and bagged along with my wallet, money (this was to prove important), eyeglasses and belt. And yes, me being me, I did look around these cells with the thought, 'If I was McGyver, how would I break out of here?'

Berwick Police Station

The answer? I'm not McGyver. For that matter, I don't even think McGyver is McGyver. (sorry to crush your hopes Selma Bouvier)

One great knack I have developed somewhere, somehow over the years is the ability to fall asleep virtually anywhere, no matter what external or internal distractions may be about. So I pushed one side of the gym mat about two feet up the wall at one end of the marble bench, and after folding that back into a 'make do' sort of pillow, I curled one arm under my head and nodded off ...

Between hourly slidings open of the letter box door opening as a police officer would ask if I'd like tea, coffee or a sandwich (I told you they were incredibly kind), I found myself dreaming of Ireland. I saw myself back again at Toberbeg Lodge, enjoying the rope swing behind the house, looking out at the blue Wicklow mountains as I rose and fell, rose and fell, rose and fell. Then I was driving again, through those insanely narrow roads, past the fence where my Jaguar had kissed its head lamp farewell, on my way to The Dew Drop Inn in Kill, hoping to see my dearly beloved friend Audrey and tell her all about it.

Constable Aitken opened the letter box and told me there would be a second interview. Ah. So back to the interview room and another CDR loaded in, when I was told that I would be formally charged and moved to a larger facility in Bedlington. I wasn't sure where that was exactly – about 30 miles south of Berwick as it turned out – and I would have a Court appearance in the morning.

On the whole, I looked at this as a good thing. It was a good sort of surprise that there was a Court open for business on New Year's Day ... then again, New Year's Eve was probably one of the peak days for police activity what with having to round up amateur drunks after violent misadventures. I'd actual be curious to know if January 1st is the peak volume for Court imposed fines worldwide. (You can tell someone's a writer when that person is forever trying to find the Larger Context for everything that happens.)

I have no idea what time I was taken in the police van to Bedlington – no clocks anywhere remember – but I was cautioned by the jovial driver that I might wish to prop my feet against the metal box opposite me in the back of the van in the event of sharp corners. You see, I was sat on a metal box as well – no seat belt, no cushioning and yes, I was handcuffed.

A Tip! I was told that the most comfortable, or least uncomfortable way of wearing handcuffs is to turn one wrist up and the other down whilst being cuffed and not the 'arms straight out' popularized on TV dramas.

He was right as it turned out. At a roundabout close to the Bedlington holding cells, I did indeed slide off my white metal box into the channel in the middle of the van floor. I then did a comic impression of a rookie surfer as I attempted to stand and sit whilst handcuffed in a moving vehicle. To be immodest, I doubt if even Charlie Chaplin flopped around to better laugh-inducing effect. What a pity there was no one there to see it, Ho Ho!

I've been wondering where to place an observation and here is as good as any. I saw the same thing everywhere I was over that first 48 hours. Signatures.

> ➔ etched into the pale yellow walls of the holding cell in Berwick

> ➔ into the plasticized glass of the various police vans

> ➔ in the wooden bench at Bedlington

> ➔ every wall, wooden chair, bench, every possible surface that could be drawn on, written on or engraved, all the same thing

There is a compulsion for prisoners to write their names. Given that one is certainly not allowed any sharp objects at any time, not even a belt with its protruding clasp, the only possible tool available would be a hardened thumbnail. In retrospect, I wish now I had tested this out as I can only surmise that it must be bloody difficult; digging block letters into a concrete wall. However, I didn't think to do this experiment until just now – and frankly I don't look forward to further opportunities. Yet it fascinated me.

Why, you ask? Well let's think on this for a second or two. Put yourself in a prisoner's position. There you are – You're under arrest! Cue the music from Law & Order, or if you're of a vintage, from Dragnet. Would not your emotional response, after the first freezing hot wash of fear turns to numbness or in my case a heightened sense of memory absorption, be drawn from a selection of shame, embarrassment and defeat? Let's just use shame for now as it will do nicely for the point I want to make.

What is your first instinct when you've done something you view (or your Mom, your spouse, your boss, your friends...) as shameful? Whether you actually follow through on a Nixon-style Watergate cover-up or not, I believe your initial thought is on the lines of, 'Christ! Don't let anyone find out I broke the Ming Vase/buggered the Anderson Account/didn't walk the dog and now there's shit on the floor!' You want to hide both your boobish act, and yourself in the bargain. Yet prisoners choose to memorialize their names. Why?

As a theory and it is just a theory, what I found from chatting with a dozen or so prisoners in our holding rooms as we went through the stages of incarceration like so many ships traversing the locks of the Great Lakes, is that all but me were repeat offenders. I grant you a dozen is not a large sample, however it *is* a sample. One becomes known as, well, One. Identity is lost behind a prison number or at best a last name. Yes, you are known by your first name to other prisoners, however to the larger system and the world of authority within the walled and razor-wired Known World you now have all the uniqueness of a can of tuna in a warehouse of canned tuna. You are – yes – in the can. The Who even sang about it: *'Eleven hours in a tin can/God there's got to be another way/Who are you?'*

Perhaps I am being overly poetic, not that we poets are incapable of acute conclusions, but what I saw and felt was that this compulsive need by prisoners to indelibly mark their experience was a way of making a statement, a shout, a lesser version of the Sphinx as proof that they actually have walked upon the Earth before disappearing into a grey stone other dimension. *'I am not a number! I am a free man!'* Yes you are a number, and no you're not free any more. Those repeat offenders knew what was coming and – subconsciously anyway – feel a need to grind a last testament of freedom into the grit of concrete or the brown painted wood of a bench. Virtually all the eccentric uniqueness of individuality are about to be taken away, so let us literally make our mark upon the world while we still can.

Of course, it would be a wretched irony if I dehumanized individuals by lumping them all into a one size fits all theory. The prison system does a good enough job of that on its own. These etched names could equally be an act of defiant rebellion; a means of, if you will, owning the environment in which the prisoner is placed; or perhaps just a simple act of boredom with nothing left to do.

Regardless of the individual motivation, I was still left with a sense of wonderment and indeed no small amount of admiration at these men (I saw no women's names interestingly enough) who felt a need to literally make their mark. A simple act of creation, yet creation is indeed the very essence of humanity.

It's interesting you know; I have so often over the years quoted Samuel Johnson's line that the sight of the gallows or the guillotine 'concentrates the mind wonderfully' but he was damn right. No experience in my life - not love, laughter, death or birth - so concentrated my own mind to the point that reliving that experience vividly is as simple and as accurate as flipping through a photo album ... they're just bloody awful pictures to look at though. Take my word for it - please don't try this at home.

At Bedlington, I was led upstairs to the Court room, once more hand-cuffed. Again I refused a solicitor as honestly I did not want to put anyone about and I just wanted to tell my story and answer any questions honestly. And so I did, from the glassed in dock on the left side of the courtroom, before the three magistrate panel.

The courtyard of Durham Prison

The outcome? I was remanded for sentencing the next day back in Berwick which meant that I was transported to Durham to spend the night in Her Majesty's Prison Durham – a penitentiary. It is a Category B prison (there are four categories of A B C and D, with A being reserved for terrorists, bombers and the like) with a prisoner population of about 1000 males. There used to be women inmates, however the suicide rate was too high, so Prison Durham became all-male in 2006. Perhaps an odd thing to say, yet as I remarked to a Guard, it is actually a quite lovely compound, if you don't mind the low arc of the winter sun being blocked off by 30 foot high stone walls casting shadows of the omnipresent razor wire on the buildings within. Yet, I do find a certain joy in the historical solidity of any 200 year old building. It is nice to know that once upon a time, things were built to last. (Think of that the next time you consider your six month old iPhone 'outmoded and old')

Now, to foreshadow events to come, my belongings which had traveled with me in a clear plastic bag, were turned in, listed and signed for. My black trousers had to be exchanged for grey woolen track suit bottoms – black trousers were what the guards wore and one wouldn't want any cases of mistaken identity. I was assigned a pair of blue jeans as well (when asked for my waist size, I said 34 inches ... I'd estimate the jeans were a 28. Darn you, metric measurements!), a shirt, underwear, blue plastic dishes and a cup, a toothbrush, toothpaste and a bed roll consisting of two green sheets, an orange blanket and one firm, green pillow. My other personal clothing and my black walking shoes I could keep with me. Still no belt however. McGyver you know could build a helicopter out of a belt.

It was in the holding rooms – the locks of the Great Lakes I alluded to earlier – between the various stages of admission where I got to know and chat with my fellow prisoners. As you may have guessed, I had no pen or paper to record those thoughts and conversations, so I put my journalist's brain on Record and went to work remembering Everything.

> → Henry Higgins was right. There truly *is* a class distinction based on language and accent. Bearing in mind that I had lived in Ireland, spent significant days in Scotland and Newcastle, and had trained my ear to the unique Scots/English blended accent of Berwick, I nonetheless found most of what the mostly young men around me said to be initially incomprehensible. It is impossible to transcribe unless I use phonetic hieroglyphs that virtually all of you would find unreadable, so let me describe these voices thusly: It was as though all hard consonants were sounded from behind a particularly phlegmy Adam's Apple and all vowels were a variant on the sound 'uh'. Yes, I think that about says it.

> → That truly is a social demarcation. No one with that accent will ever become an MP, a laureate, a banker, or even a call center agent. To be blunt, even if one of these young male

prisoners spent every nominally free hour during their time of incarceration reading the works of Shakespeare, Montesquieu, and Marat-Sade; Adam Smith, Karl Marx and Mein Kampf; the prison writings of Antonio Gramsci, Robert Burns and the Birdman of Alcatraz; Lewis Carroll, A.A. Milne and Maurice Sendak – regardless, if upon release our young parolee attempted to discuss his findings at a literary event he would be shunned as a faker and the silverware counted. Most of the young men had tattoos on their skin; their speech was already marked for life.

→ They all were terrified of the American prison system. I lost count of the number who tried to comfort me as a 'new guy' by saying that (as I became accustomed to their voices) 'It's not so bad in here mate. Not like them American prisons where you get raped and they got drugs and weapons like.' Yes well, *there's* a relief!

→ I met no 'hard men' as it were. The lads were friendly, smiling and in general people you wouldn't mind at all if they sat at the next pub stool beside you. Except of course you would mind once they started drinking. Everyone that told his story to me – and as a journalist, I am damn good at getting people to talk about themselves – had some version of being on the piss then either hitting someone (spouses were, tragically and abhorrently, the most frequent victims), smashing something, or both.

→ All were repeat offenders except me. You'll soon be introduced to my cell mate Artur and he and I talked about it. Artur shook his head as he spoke in his heavily Polish-accented English, 'They come in here, 10 weeks, 20 weeks, then they out 3 weeks, 4 weeks and back again. They drink, they lose their head, they go back to jail.'

A Suggestion: As a Human Rights advocate, I suppose I should be opposed to any form of an identity card. As well, despite my own sobriety, I am broadly in favour of the legalization of anything that brings a smile to the face and a song to the heart. However, I do believe there should be an identity card that must be presented for the purchase of alcohol. If one is convicted of a booze-fueled offence, bye-bye card. Yes, one's friends can always be persuaded to do a run to the Off-License, just as it was when one was under-aged; but still, inconvenience might just deliver a few from repeat incarceration. Anyway, I think it is an idea worth trying.

That metaphor of the Great Lakes locks is a well-chosen one, if I do say so myself. While all the guards, processors and the like were extremely affable – I truly can't over stress just how, well, *cheery* everyone was all through this difficult time – nonetheless as with any bureaucratic process there was a clear order of procedure to be followed and one was ordered and moved about like a piece on some kind of board game. Snakes & Ladders perhaps, not chess as only the back row figures are allowed backwards movements and trust me, there is no more pawn-like existence than that of a prisoner.

So it was that one's papers are checked and personal goods itemized then off to a holding room (Pawn to Her Majesty's Waiting Area 1). Then the change of clothing and a rather embarrassed check of one's person to make sure nothing was attached to the body. The anal search is just done briefly and visually, not a mining procedure by the latex covered finger of doom; thank you God for your small mercy in dignity. Back to the same holding room. (Down goes the Snake! Wheeee!) Next was the assignment of clothes, kit, bed roll and purchase of tobacco at £4.30 for 25 grams of a basic grade plus a sleeve of papers. A new holding room is pointed out to the prisoner, this one the prison chapel. (Climb the Ladder!) A nursing check is the next stage, where one is asked about any health conditions, prescriptions, allergies and such – 'None, none, none and nothing I can think of.' (Back down the Snake to the Chapel ... which just sounds wrong.) Lastly, one is escorted to one's cell – mine was 323 – and meet the Roomie.

Artur was 46 and a Polish emigré who had lived in a suburb of Newcastle with his wife and two children for a decade. As noted, his English was still quite broken, yet one does not need much of a language facility to drive a lorry. He had been remanded for sentencing on a charge of Domestic Abuse, specifically pushing his wife off the front porch and badly bruising her eye socket. He claimed that it was a mistake and a nefarious one – well, he didn't say nefarious. Instead, he mournfully told me that she had taken up with another man – short, bald, but he had money – and then when she had fallen they decided to rid themselves of Artur.

Call me naive and you'd be right more often than not, but I believed him. Artur is a nice, gentle man and I carry his full name and contact info in my wallet. If I can help him in the future, I will.

We rolled our cigarettes – I had been without for close to 24 hours, although here again who knows what time it actually was? Not even the small TV in the cell had a station that included a time signature. He made tea from his daily ration and we talked.

The cell itself frankly wasn't bad as cells go. It was a pale green tall arch with a side washroom consisting of a sink, toilet and a divided cabinet for our washroom kits. A window looked out on... not much frankly. There was the top of a tree above the shadowed stone walls and the local church bells gonged through its opening. They didn't sound the hour either, or they may have, but I did not notice the pattern until the next night at 2AM. More on that shortly.

I took the top bunk, which was a bit of a nightmare to crawl into; I am a writer and not a gymnast. Not too bad once there however. The arched ceiling was tall enough that I could sit erect without mashing my head into the concrete. Just as well, as there was just one chair – a tubular frame wrapped around a thin wood seat and back, the same as a down-at-heels school. Again, every possible surface was inscribed with names.

Word had spread that 'New Guy' – that would be me – had arrived and there were knocks on the door and torn paper slid underneath with a request for New Guy to please share some tobacco, or tobaccy as they called it. Well sure, why not? The odds were good that I might be released the next day and even if not...it is always important to make friends. Although I had been assured by other prisoners that there weren't the stabbings and other violence of American prisons, I ask you, wouldn't you prefer a little insurance?

The evening meal was nutritionally tragic. A bun with the lowest grade tuna mashed into it, two more slices of bread (I turned those down), a mandarin orange, carton of milk, a juice box, and three packages of sweet biscuits plus the daily ration of tea and sugar. Oh yes, there was also a rock hard, literally frozen puck of what might have been a meat pie. I'm not sure of that as it never thawed to an edible temperature. My spirits had not been broken, why should my teeth? There was not a vegetable to be seen and there was much too much sodium, sugar and gluten to ever be considered healthy. I think it's time Chef Jamie Oliver got on the case of prison nutrition.

At last, after Match of the Day and the replay of Graham Norton's New Year's Eve show, with the Monty Python reunion, it was time to sleep, to sleep, perchance to dream ...

Oh I slept hard that night, not even bothering to get out of my clothes or the underwear that I admit was by now giving off a fetid funk of futility. As I drifted off, my last thoughts were of Samantha, Harald, Lawrence and all those Facebook denizens who by now would have known of my arrest and were likely worried about what had happened to me. I hate worrying people. I enjoy worrying *about* people, but the reverse makes me feel like a burden rather than a minor boon to humanity.

And again I dreamt of Ireland. I dreamt of leaving frozen Canada, seeing the fields of snow replaced outside the airplane window by better white fields of clouds. I vividly recall the part of my dream where I sent a Facebook message to Audrey saying I was on my way and *now* would she meet me for lunch at the Dew Drop Inn? That was so vivid that when the Guard slid open the door slot in the morning to tell me to be ready for transport in an hour, I started to search in the blanket for my mobile as I was sure I had sent that message and ... oh ... right ... no of course I hadn't.

I brushed my teeth and told Artur that if in fact I wasn't back by the evening meal, he was welcome to my remaining tobacco (I chain-smoked three tabs – I had learnt the lingo – first), toothpaste and so forth. Then the entire check-in procedure of the previous day was reversed. My coat and trousers were returned – even my belt! - I suppose they did not want any prisoners accidentally dropping trou in front of the magistrates and the rest of the odds and ends that had arrived with me, including my room key from the Cobbled Yard, I thought was packed in a traveling box that would come in the van with me to the Berwick Court. Another visual search (who smuggles things *out* of a a penitentiary?), the same first holding room as the day before along with the others off to various Courts, then I was handcuffed and led out to the van. Moo. Baaaa. Neigh.

Given when the sun rose, I estimated we had left about 7:30AM and finally arrived at Berwick about 9AM. The female officer from the Berwick constabulary who accompanied me on the trip was again thoughtful and kind, just like the others. "Would you like some water?" "No thank you, but kind of you to ask!" "Coffee?" "Yes, that would be great. I would love a coffee." No point in nodding off before the Crown.

This time, when asked, I happily accepted the advice of a Legal Aid solicitor. Although I had considered the possibility of spending a stretch in the penitentiary as something that I would indeed survive, it still was something I wished to avoid if possible. After all, I wanted to pay back my debts and I certainly would have no way of making money from inside a cell. Yes, you've heard of people writing Great Things while in prison, but did any of them ever get published while the authors were still inside? Cervantes had to be released before Don Quixote was printed, Walter Raleigh was executed, and Jean Genet was on the streets again before his work was on the shelves.

I had a great burst of favourable nostalgia when I met my solicitor, Ian O'Rourke. He was the absolute living clone of the finest criminal attorney to ever grace the Courtrooms and black tie dinners of Thunder Bay, one Alfred Petrone. Hawk nosed and thick framed glasses, a thatch of bird's nest for hair and the same habit of lightly sucking on their teeth while thinking, I almost wonder if the late Alfred had perhaps journeyed through North East England on his travels say forty-five years ago or so. I certainly wouldn't put it past him. There is a wonderful story, which I am sure is apocryphal * ahem * that after an assuredly above-board and discrete late night visit to a female – legal business of course! Mais oui! - Alfred's wife Krazy Glued a certain member of his anatomy to his thigh. I think you can guess the details.

It is still so hard to believe that I am actually going back THERE! *(Update: as you know by now, I did not come back to Canada. Ireland became my home again.)* Granted, not Thunder Bay precisely, but even just Canada on general … In recounting that tale of the, shall we say, wounded pride of a prominent attorney it reminded me of why I needed to leave my hometown in the first place. There is absolutely no good reason for me to know the story of the sticky situation, yet I do as do hundreds or thousands of others in Thunder Bay and that is because that is the nature of hometowns – the naked gossiping of bored, lifeless people entertained by the embarrassment of others. No, I prefer to define myself and only reveal that which I choose to be revealed only to those I choose to know it … personal memoir notwithstanding * ahem *.

Ian took down all my details on a legal pad and did an excellent job of persuading the Magistrate panel to give me two weeks to pay off the £660 through a Court pay slip, as well as £85 in prosecution costs. I would be required to stay at the YHA Hostelin Berwick, where I had a reservation made for that day and the next weeks until me new Canadian passport arrived, and finally should I not pay, then the various ports of departure in the UK would be alerted.

Oh it felt good to be a free man again, albeit one deep in debt and still in the shadow of a court order. There was actually a clock in the Berwick station house, so as I was led back to the holding cell pending a fax coming from Durham Prison confirming that I hadn't done anything chargeable the night before – these are the procedures – I could see it was about 11:45AM. So, dear old holding cell One, fluff up the gym mat against the wall and a short nap until my release –

– or a knock and the opening of the letterbox window. The fax had not arrived from Durham, yet of equal importance neither had my wallet with its £80 and my bank card. (The majority of my other belongings were still at the Cobbled Yard where, the police told me, they were being packed up and kept in safe storage pending my release.)

Now this – *THIS* presented a problem! Without any money, how could I check into the YHA, let alone eat or buy cigarettes? How could I even travel to Durham to *get* my money without money? My laptop and mobile were at the Cobbled Yard, so it wasn't like I could even alert anyone as to this plight. In addition, there was and is an oddity with British Rail. You cannot buy a rail ticket for someone else and have them pick it up at the station of departure unless that traveler has in his possession the actual credit or debit card used for making the purchase. The long and the short being – I was stuck.

By this point, it was close to 1PM and once again it was the Berwick Police to the rescue. They asked Durham Prison what time their collection point for prisoners' belongings would be open until (3:30PM was the time, with my belongings kept at the Main Gate), notified the kennel that Stella was at, then they provided me with a travel warrant for a one-way train trip to Durham. The next train left at 2:12 and required a change at Newcastle. Gulp!

I made it to the Berwick train station at 2:05, speed walking through the streets on a chilly, grey day. There was no time to stop at the Cobbled Yard to pick up my mobile phone; that could wait until I got back. The only thing I had with me was the only thing that had come back from Durham; a folio containing my personal papers, which I had brought with me to the Berwick Police Station on my arrest as they required some kind of personal I.D. beyond my Canadian driver's licence. And so, me and that one piece of luggage slumped in a train seat and watched the countryside pass by.

After the change at Newcastle, I made it to Durham Station, high atop a hill overlooking the Cathedral, the Castle and the city itself, at about 3PM. I asked directions of a fellow passenger as to the location of the Royal County Marriott Hotel – I had spotted it just down the street from the prison when the van had left that morning. (Asking someone the directions to a prison, particularly when you are unshowered and in rumpled clothing, is a good way of making people run away from you.) I therefore scurried down the road, then a steep flight of steps, a bridge across the River Wear, down more cobblestone streets and finally made it to the blue doors of the Prison at 3:30 exactly.

There was only one person I met through this whole ordeal who was not completely cooperative or helpful and he was the bald, cynical, smirking guard at the prison reception area.

'I'm here to collect my belongings.'

'Sorry mate, the collection point's closed.'

'The Berwick Police called here and they were told you'd let me get my things up to 3:30.'

'Who did you talk to?', he snorted.

'I didn't talk to anyone. The Berwick Police called here.'

'Well it's closed now. It's all locked up until tomorrow at 9:30.'

'Then what am I going to do? You have my money and my bank card and my train ticket was one day.'

'You'll have to come back at 9:30.' You could tell he was enjoying this.

'Fine then ... what time is your waiting room open until?' There were a few soft chairs, as well as a side room and as I've said, I can sleep anywhere.

'It's closed in about an hour.'

'Then I'm supposed to find a park bench in January?'

Shrug.

And so ... what to do? A cold, mist had started to fall and with that in my face I started the climb back up to the train station where I would hang in there as best I could, hoping that it did not close at night. (*Spoiler Alert! It closes at night.*)

When one gets chilled, stressed, hungry, thirsty and positively craving a cigarette, it is impossible to get warmed up. Realistically, I know that the Durham station had to be kept at a reasonable temperature but I still felt like a head of cabbage stuck in a vegetable crisper. From 4PM until just past midnight, I shuffled back and forth from the waiting room to the washroom; in the latter I would run the tap water as hot as it would get (not very) and soak my hands in it. Even though I didn't have my comb (Durham never did return that) I also soaked my head in the warm water in a feeble attempt at washing my hair and becoming border-line presentable. As I look back on it, thank God they had at least returned my Irish woolen coat. That, my Green Bay Packers sweater and the T-shirt underneath were just enough to keep me warm enough to survive.

Because, when the station started to lock up – I considered hiding in the lift that led up to Platform 2, but I'd been arrested once already and I wasn't looking forward to a second charge being one of illegal trespass – I had to go walking back down into the town. I had eaten, sort of. I remembered how Kimberly's son Bradley used to check all pay phones and vending machines for loose and forgotten change, so I did find two pound coins in one of the train station's phones. That was enough to buy me a bag of Doritos and a Mars bar – Feast! I knew enough about calories and nutrition to know that I had ingested enough calories to keep me alive until morning, but where could I go in this rain, for by now it was a steady drizzle.

There is something beautiful about walking through a completely deserted ancient city, no matter what the circumstances are that lead you there. Cold, wet, aged buildings and steeply winding cobblestone paths are the palette of painters, the paper of poets, and the landscape of existential philosophers all in one. They clear the mind of all thoughts except for the consideration of the streets and buildings themselves. You raise the collar of your coat, eyes peering from above damp cloth and you absorb your life into this city that has seen a hundred generations of lives ... yes ... for you can find beauty anywhere and any time if the time of the land is timeless.

I thought I would head back to the Prison and see if there was a more sympathetic Guard on duty at the main gate. So I crossed the Wear again, feeling slightly dizzy as I always do when walking across a bridge. I have always had a fear of heights, but I have noticed that in the last few years my irrational fear and clammy-handedness at crossing even the widest, most solid bridge has become worse. I find that I cling to railings now like a sloth making his way across a branch.

The lack of clocks was now becoming an absurdity and my curiosity at knowing what time it was an obsession with no satisfaction. I looked in every shop window, including banks, real estate firms, travel agents and restaurants – was it my imagination? Didn't *all* of those have a big circular white clock with black hands and numbers hanging above the counter?

Evidently not, for there was not a clock to be found. Finally, I did hear the Westminster-like chimes of a church clock followed by a single BONNNNNGGGG! Ah. One AM. I had been up for approximately 18 hours and I had another eight and a half hours to, er, kill. (8 1/2 ... just like Fellini, except Durham was not Rome and the fountain was falling from the sky)

I made a wrong turn at the Royal County Hotel and walked past Durham University's buildings and residences. There were also several parkades there that I noted. If worst of worst came, at least I would be dry in one of those. There was a police constabulary opposite the University so I went into there. If the Prison reception area was closed, as a gnawing fear inside me said was likely, perhaps I could just park there for the night? After all, I was technically a free, currently law-abiding citizen. At the least, I hoped they could phone the Berwick Police as my *other* gnawing fear was that as I had not checked into the YHA Hostel as ordered, I certainly did not want anyone thinking I had taken it on the lam.

The station, except for its entranceway, was closed. (Since when do police stations close for the night?) But there was a phone with a sign saying 'Press 3 to talk to an operator.' Well, good enough! The female operator answered:

'Durham Police, how may I assist you?'

'Hi there, may I come in?'

'I'm sorry, we are closed.'

'Ah. Well look, I'm trying to find the Durham Prison and I'm afraid I got a bit lost. Can you direct me?'

She did and after I warmed my hands on the radiator in the foyer, I set out again. The rain had reduced to a mist again, although now the breeze had picked up. I found the prison, walked up the drive to its blue double doors and, as the lack of light inside the windows hinted, it was locked and no there wasn't a door bell. Now what?

There was a nearby church, a Catholic church even, St. Cuthbert's. Although motion sensor lights came on as I walked through its gate and up its path, then more lights as I came to the thick wood door, it too was closed. Oh I know, churches in these sad modern days feel they have to lock up for the night out of fear of theft and vandalism but ... isn't that wrong somehow? What is the point of a church's existence if not to give comfort and shelter to the lone and the fearful?

I checked the various doors of the University buildings. Locked, locked and more locked. I went into a parkade, but that was a flawed fallback position as well. Because of car exhausts, there are cutaway windows throughout these multi-storey buildings and so they really are not of much use for braving the elements. I heard the church chimes ring twice ... it was the church and not the postman. Where the hell do I go? The train station did not re-open until 4:30. I couldn't just walk for another two and a half hours.

I remembered that lovely, warm radiator in the foyer of the police station. Yes, head there. Surely no police officer would charge me with breaking and entering when the outside door was unlocked and God knows these were rather extenuating circumstances! So I slogged up that street again, went into the constabulary, sat down and tried to nod off with my folio as a dim replacement for a pillow.

A police officer did come in through the rear door of the station and when I heard him, I stood up and put on my cheeriest smile. He asked why I was there and I explained, furthermore asking if I might stay inside in their waiting area. No, I couldn't do that (I even asked if there was a cell – a cell would have been as welcome as a suite at this point) because the exits would be locked and should there be a fire, I couldn't get out. Yes, I suppose that did make sense. I was allowed to stay in the foyer and I nodded off again.

I did not hear the second police officer arrive, not until he opened the inner door and said, just like in the movies, 'Hello? What's this about then?' Once more I told the story – Durham – closed – Berwick – property – train – money – and so on. I asked what time it was. It was a quarter past four. Good. By the time I climbed once more back up to the train station, it would be open.

And then ...

Find beauty in the moment. No matter how awful the future may appear as a result of the mishaps of the past, we are always safe in the Now. The only reality is Now; all else is imagination. Live in Now and find beauty in Now.

I made a wrong turn. Instead of walking up the main street rising to the train station, I wound up in winding cobblestoned streets lined with tightly-fitted old Georgian townhouses, dark pubs and uneven sidewalks that had been laid however many centuries before. And then I emerged from the maze and felt a burst of awe and vertigo mixed into one as before me shone the vast edifice of Durham Cathedral.

Durham Cathedral - yes, the Harry Potter movies were shot there

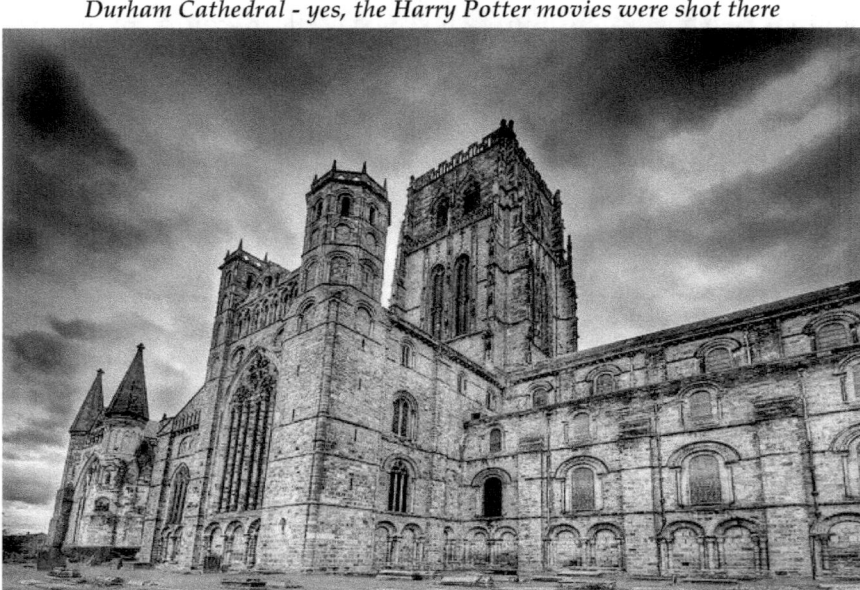

Sure I was over-tired and more than a little stretched emotionally and when you have spent a full day with no company other than the weary desperation of the mind, you are open to exaggerated responses but ... if my knees were still capable of bending, I would have fallen to them. I just stood there in the non-light of a clouded pre-dawn and absorbed this ever so ancient building, begun its construction in 1093, as old as every 'old' building in Canada combined. I beheld the magnificence of man's commitment to God.

There had been times in my life when I had questioned the, I thought madness of building these monumental structures, so thick and so tall, without benefit of truck or crane, just muscle and winch raising massive stones up, up, up over 200 feet in height – and on top of a hill! - for what possible indulgence of a bishop's vanity?

No vanity at all. No, anything but vanity. This Cathedral was a testament to modesty, the required modesty of man. We lead our individual lives in the flap of a hummingbird's wings as measured against time, with all our fears, hopes and raised then broken dreams – and we are nothing. We are nothing except our brevity. But beyond us, there is indeed something noble in the combined purpose of the hummingbird's urgent flapping. When we are measured together into a long chain of civilization, we are then someone, something, some collective cache of ideas worth knowing and passing on. That is why this cathedral and the others like it exist. They remind us of that which is greater than ourselves. We live to make permanent structures – either physical or philosophical - greater than than our individual selves.

From there I found myself walking through an accidentally open gate into Durham Castle and I walked its well-kept, mown grounds and felt the ghosts of history. What plans of war had been made here; what shy or earthy romance had been confessed and consummated in these rooms? What peace there was inside castle walls in the pre-dawn hours of Durham.

And so I struggled back up the steep steps to the train station, as the church chimes announced the hour as six. No more change in the payphones, but at least that day's copy of the free Metro newspaper to sit and read until just after 8AM. Then once more to the prison – the route now so well known to me. I watched Durham awake to another day of work and I hoped pleasure as I walked through those streets once more. What a beautiful city. What a beautiful city after a hellishly long two days.

The prison was open, my belongings (except my comb) returned. I bought my train ticket for £33, a pack of cigarettes for £6.25 and a bacon toastie with coffee for £3.99. I got on the train to Berwick with £36 in my pocket, not a cent in the bank, no idea how to pay my fine and survive until I got back to Canada.

But I was alive, damn it. And I wouldn't have missed this experience for anything.

Theatre

(So if you ask me where in life have I been the happiest, the answer will always be 'in the theatre.' Whether the stage was in Canada, a dinner theatre in Minnesota, or that lovely, leaky old building in Bangor, Northern Ireland there was always a home and a loving family there.

The following is part of a longer work by myself and Ciara Donnelly called One Night at the Poets' Café. This section has been chosen because, well, you see a theatre is a place that encourages love. Play on!)

LES ÉTAGES

Characters:

Michelle (Mickey)

Francis (Fran)

Caitlin (the waitress)

Others in the café take temporary roles as indicated

*(A slim and beautiful woman in her late 30s, **Mickey**, enters the café. She wears a tan raincoat and a slouch hat to protect herself from the rain. When she removes the raincoat, laying it and the hat on a chair at the table she will sit at with **Francis**, she is wearing a vibrant flower-covered blouse and a simple skirt cut just above the knee. She wears a wedding band. Francis, a few years older, wears an open-necked vertically-striped shirt beneath a camel-shaded sportcoat and jeans. Mickey looks around the café, spots Francis sat alone at a table, waves to him and enters brightly. They hug during the following – no kiss.)*

Mickey: Fran!

Francis: Ah Michelle ma belle. You look lovely as always.

Mickey: I'm sorry I'm late. The traffic –

Francis: – that's okay –

Mickey: – and the rain –

Francis: (*sings softly to the tune of 'For He's a Jolly Good Fellow'*)
We're so glad you could join us/We're so glad you could join
us/We're so glad you could joiiiiiin us/We were all here on time.
(*smiles, a half laugh*)

Mickey: Uh oh! Does that mean I have to sing a song or play
Truth or Dare?

Francis: No. I'm too happy to see you. Just wanted to keep up the
old tradition, for old time's sake.

Mickey: Did I keep you waiting? Were you here long?

Francis: Not so long. (*glances at the bottle of red wine on the table*)
Only two glasses in. Come, sit, tell me the news. (*gestures to
Caitlin the waitress*)

Mickey: News? Oh I don't have any news at all. Just the same
Mickey, same as always. But look at you!

Francis: Why? Did I spill something?

Mickey: (*laughs, and when she laughs she laughs brightly*) No! It's
you – you're the one with all the news. When does your plane
leave?

Francis: Day after tomorrow. Seven AM. Then I arrive the next
day, same time actually. Travel sunrise to sunrise. It's going to be
a lonnnng day.

Caitlin: (*interrupts*) Hi, I'm Caitlin, I'll be your waitress. What can I get you?

Francis and Mickey: (*overlap*)

>   **Francis:** – another glass please Caitlin –

>   **Mickey:** – I'll have a coffee please, two sugars no cream –

Francis: No farewell toast?

Mickey: Maybe a sip later. I'm driving and – the rain -

Francis: Bloody rain. It's okay, I understand.

Caitlin: So you're the designated driver? Your coffee's on the house then.

Mickey: Oh I'm not driving – well I mean I am – do you need a ride home?

Francis: Shhh! You just talked yourself out of free coffee! No bother, I'll get it. (*to Caitlin*) I'll pay for the coffee.

Caitlin: Right. Get that straightaway for you. (*leaves table*)

Francis: I'm okay for a ride Mick. I'd planned on taking a cab anyway.

Mickey: I guess you sold your car already.

Francis: Wow, it has been a while since I've seen you. The transmission blew on the Chrysler a good year ago now. It went for scrap – four hundred bucks. I've been a bus guy ever since.

Mickey: I had no idea. Don't you find that inconvenient, getting around?

Francis: It's not so bad. Get a lot of reading done on the bus. I just wish they didn't stop running at eleven o'clock. That's partially why I haven't been out much lately. I work, I read, I ride a bus.

Mickey: When did you leave work?

Francis: Last shift was five days ago. You know I actually felt a bit nostalgic for the hotel when I walked out the door? But I'll be back there again tomorrow night. Me and BooBoo Dog will spend our last night there. Easier. I'll already be packed and she'll have her animal carrier. Good thing we're pet friendly.

Mickey: And then Ireland.

Francis: Eventually.

Mickey: Eventually?

Francis: (*sighs*) Because I'm bringing BooBoo, she has to have a pressurized cabin. So here's our day – leave here at seven (and I'm really hoping this rain doesn't turn to ice) for Toronto. An hour there, then we fly to LaGuardia. From LaGuardia we take a limo to Newark. I check her in at the Pet Terminal – pets get their own terminals, classy – then we fly to Dublin. Nineteen hours traveling until you factor in the time change and that makes it exactly one day.

Caitlin: (*returns with the coffee and two packets of sugar*) One coffee. Two sugars.

Mickey: Thank you! (*Caitlin leaves, Mickey shakes sugar packets and pours them into the coffee, then laughs*)

Francis: What's so funny?

Mickey: Look Fran, they have fortune sugar now. Like fortune cookies but sugar!

Francis: The sugar industry will do anything to grow an addiction.

Mickey: I know I shouldn't. I should be watching my weight.

Francis: Weight? What? You don't mean you, Mick?

Mickey: Yes I mean me! I've put on five pounds since the last time you saw me.

Francis: (*mock serious*) Try to not move around a lot. You might break the chair.

Mickey: Rat.

Francis: Now is that a nice way to say goodbye to an old actor? Never mind. Of all the women on earth, you're one of the last ones who ever needs to worry about her diet. You carry all the weight of a dandelion seed.

Mickey: Aw, you're so sweet.

Francis: Not sweet enough evidently. You still need sugar.

Mickey: (*laughs*) Oh, you always could make me laugh.

Francis: Yeah, I do the funny stuff good. Shall we toast?

Mickey: With coffee?

Francis: Seems appropriate. Coffee and wine, the twin fuels of amateur theatre.

Mickey: Bon voyage Fran.

Francis: Here's looking at you Michelle. (*as they clink glass and cup, the lights shift, moving to a flashback from eleven years earlier. The Director of the play, **Gwenevere**, is addressing a group of three actors sat with legs crossed in front of the stage. Gwenevere and the actor are other people in the café doubling in their roles. Gwenevere is older and, to be polite about it, more than a little spacey and we don't mean Kevin.*)

Gwenevere: It's ten minutes to seven so we shall begin. You already know me, but I will introduce myself anyway because that is how a rehearsal should begin. My name is Gwenevere Revere but don't feel you have to revere me, just obey! (*her laugh is a complete cackle, but without malice*) Ha hahaha HA! I'm just joking! Of course feel perfectly free to *revere* me! Ha hahaha HA! (*abruptly* *becomes deadly serious*) Now then, as to our play, this is a very serious work and it will stretch your senses even as you dredge the silt from the very bottom of long-drowned memories. A man, whose health has been broken by psychological disorder is saved from his own death wish only by his meta-döppelganger. To the ignorant, they are opposites, yet to the perceptive they are both personae of one who creates both, mirrored by the twin love goddesses who seek their own union through sexual coupling with –

An Actor: (*interrupts*) Wait! Isn't The Odd Couple a comedy?

Gwenevere: No!

An Actor: Okey dokey. Just thought I'd ask. (*Mickey and Francis rush towards the stage separately, meeting near to it, presumably at the door to the rehearsal hall. They can be the already established Mickey and Francis, or if the Director wishes younger versions they can be drawn from among the other actors in the café. For clarity, in this flashback their parts are identified as* **Mickey-a** *and* **Francis-a**)

Francis-a: Hi.

Mickey-a: Hi.

Francis-a: You're here for –

Mickey-a: –The Odd Couple. You?

Francis-a: Yes.

Mickey-a: Felix?

Francis-a: Francis.

Mickey-a: Francis?

Francis-a: My name.

Mickey-a: Ahh. Oscar?

Francis: No. Murray.

Mickey-a: Murray?

Francis-a: Cop.

Mickey-a: Ahh.

Francis-a: Your name?

Mickey-a: Mickey, short for Michelle.

Francis-a: Pigeon sister?

Mickey-a: Stage manager.

Francis-a: Ahh.

Mickey-a: Are we late?

Francis-a: Don't you know?

Mickey-a: I'm new.

Francis-a: So am I. (*Gwenevere storms off the stage and forms a triangle between them.*)

Gwenevere: You two are late!

Francis-a, Mickey-a: Ahhhh! (*light shift and back to present. The other actors fade back into the café.*)

Francis: Any idea whatever became of Gwenevere?

Mickey: No, not really. The last thing I heard she went away to a reservation to teach Japanese paper folding to the natives. Or no, wait! That wasn't it.

Francis: Well that's a relief.

Mickey: No, on second thought, that was it. She was always very good at applying for Arts Council grants.

Francis: A true artist's ninja for our times. We should send her to the Middle East as a peace negotiator.

Mickey: Doesn't the Middle East have enough problems without Gwenevere Revere?

Francis: That would be the genius of it. Arab and Jew would be united trying to sort out what in hell Gwenevere Revere was carrying on about.

Mickey: Sort out, Fran?

Francis: (*slightly confused*) Yeah?

Mickey: You sound like you're there already, in Ireland.

Francis: Oh, that. (*slightly embarrassed*) Yeah well, I've been doing a lot of reading. And I met a friend over the internet. She's Irish, and, she's been teaching me a lot of things.

Mickey: A she? Okay, spill, I want to know all the details. What's her name? How'd you meet?

Francis: Her name is spelled A-O-I-F-E.

Mickey: That's unusual. And pretty!

Francis: I think so. I had to go onto Google to figure out how to pronounce it. A-O-I-F-E.

Mickey: Owf?

Francis: Yeah, that was my first run at it too, Mick. It's actually pronounced Aoife. I'm slightly embarrassed to admit that we met on a dating site.

Mickey: Noooo! You? You went on a dating site Fran?

Francis: Did I ever tell you that you're the only person in the world that calls me Fran?

Mickey: No changing the subject.

Francis: I wasn't changing the subject.

Mickey: (*coughs theatrically*)

Francis: Okay, so I was changing the subject. But I've always meant to mention that and this is, well, this is probably my last chance to do that. (*A breath of a pause.*) Anyway, as I don't know a soul in Ireland outside of my future landlord, I thought 'Oh what the hell' so I found a free site one night and logged on. There was a martini or two involved.

Mickey: I'd guessed that already.

Francis: You did?

Mickey: I've known you a long time now.

Francis: That you have.

Mickey: Six shows together.

Francis: Is that all it was?

Mickey: That's quite a few.

Francis: Too bad there wasn't more.

Mickey: Well, we were busy people. Busy getting engaged, busy getting married, busy getting divorced – do you ever hear from Louisa?

Francis: When the phone rings I quote Dorothy Parker: 'What fresh hell is this?'

Mickey: Same as me and Stan. He moved in with the bimbo. Now he and bimbo have a baby. Poor thing. She'll have to watch a lot of television and read a lot of books because there's certainly no role model living in my – in their house.

Francis: That was a great house.

Mickey: Great house, bad husband.

Francis: You kept the painting I hope?

Mickey: The one of me from the set of that play? Oh yeah.

Francis: Good.

Mickey: Back to Aoife.

Francis: Right, back to Aoife. Well let's see, she works in theatre in Ireland ironically enough.

Mickey: Actress?

Francis: No, a set decorator. Say, do you have time still for one more coffee? (*She checks her watch, frowns.*) If not ...

Mickey: No, I'm okay for time. Sure, one more. But I'll get this one.

Francis: The hell you will. (*Gestures to Caitlyn when he catches her eye, points a 'one more' at Mickey's cup.*) But yeah, she's a set decorator. She's our age, or your age to be specific. (*The following description can be tweaked as Francis – whether he realizes it or not is open to debate – describes Mickey to the nth degree.*) She's very slim, almost bird-like in structure with wavy dark brown hair, shoulder length. It's the eyes of course that get you. Huge. Big as lily pads. Violet, which is rare. Like, well like yours. (*a breath of a pause*) You know.

Mickey: So are you in love with her?

Francis: Oh Jaysus – sorry, practicing my Irish again – can anyone be in love with someone you haven't met?

Mickey: If anyone could, it would be you.

Francis: Oh really now? Is that a compliment or should I be offended?

Mickey: Either, both or neither. It's just who you are. As long as I've known you, you've always been either falling in love with someone or in love with someone.

Francis: You know me that well. (*Caitlin arrives with the fresh coffee*) Thank you. (*Back to the conversation*) Yeah true. I always have been in love with someone. (*Pause, thinking. Mickey shakes sugar packets, stops*)

Mickey: (*holds out the two sugar packets*) Draw.

Francis: Pick a fortune?

Mickey: Yup.

Francis: Sure. But if it says, 'A wise man tips generously' I smell a rat. (*draws. They each look at their sugar packet and smile to themselves.*) What'd you get?

Mickey: 'Look at your past for your path to happiness.'

Francis: Sensible I guess. Mine's almost the same. 'All you desire is ahead of you.' (*They look at each other for a moment. Quite important*)

Mickey: Good for Ireland!

Francis: Ireland? Oh right! That's what's ahead of me. Of course of course. Good. Wouldn't want to change my itinerary now.

Mickey: Do you think you'll get back into theatre when you're there?

Francis: I don't know. I'd like to, for sure. Aiofe can introduce me and as we both know the fastest way of meeting a bunch of good people all at once is by joining a community theatre. From what I've researched there's scarcely a town or village over there without one. Theatre was hugely important in the independence movement. Yeats and Synge, O'Casey and this remarkable woman name Lady Gregory really pushed for Irish drama in order to renew pride in an Irish identity back at the turn of the twentieth century. And what about you? When will the formidable Michelle Rousseau once again trod the boards?

Mickey: I'm not sure. Next season at the soonest. It'll be after the wedding anyway.

Francis: Which is when?

Mickey: In June.

Francis: You old traditionalist you!

Mickey: I'm sorry you won't be there.

Francis: Ah well, fair play to that – more Irish. You weren't at mine either.

Mickey: I'm sorry.

Francis: Don't be. As an old reviewer once said, 'The curtain rose sharply at eight thirty and fell with a thud at eleven.' Never ever marry the Stage Manager.

Mickey: Dave's a salesman, so I guess I'm lucky.

Francis: You're in luck. What's he sell?

Mickey: Industrial paint.

Francis: Good for covering up the cracks.

Mickey: He has a big territory to cover so he's on the road a lot.

Francis: You won't be too lonely?

Mickey: He'll be home most weekends. Besides, I know how to be lonely. I was married remember. (*thinks*) So who are Stage Managers supposed to marry?

Francis: How should I know?

Mickey: Well you said 'Never marry a Stage Manager' but Stage Managers should and do get married, so who should they marry or who should marry them?

Francis: Martyrs in training. Sorry, that was mean and I promised myself I wouldn't be mean about this. Look, I do hope that Louisa finds someone eventually and not just because that means I can stop the alimony payments. Although that does enter into it.

Mickey: I remember your telling me you were having problems. After I told you about how Stan and I were getting a divorce. During Opening Knights.

Francis: Ah, now *that* was a play! (*laughs*) We had to sneak around to rehearse in private so Louisa wouldn't kill us both!

Mickey: I can't believe she was sooo jealous of everyone you acted with. You never cheated on her did you?

Francis: I could never cheat on someone I truly loved.

Mickey: I didn't think so.

Francis: So the answer is yes. Don't think badly of me – or do, it's your choice, your critic's choice.

Mickey: Fran!!! Who? When? Or wait, sorry, you don't have to tell me.

Francis: I won't give the name. I'm not a heel, but you're bright, so you could probably guess. She was nineteen, it was one night, two weeks after the wedding. We were together nearly seven years. Never ever slept together. Had sex maybe twenty times in seven years. I was terrified she might become pregnant. She could never, ever be a mother. That's why I needed theatre so badly. It was the only place I could touch other people, feel loved even in that temporary way.

Mickey: You deserve happiness.

Francis: Well, nice of you to say, but I'm not so sure I deserve anything beyond whatever happens. But ... even all that said, I had some good times. I was so glad for Opening Knights. Only time I ever got to be on stage with my favourite actress. That would be you.

(*Lights shift as either Mickey and Francis or substitutes here referred to as **Mickey-b and Francis-b** move to the small stage area. Flashback. First a song by **Felicia**[1].*)

Should I Have Kept a Secret?

I ask myself
In the security
Of quiet, silent rooms
Should I have told you
Anyway
About thoughts of brides and grooms?

As I open
The closed fire curtains
Of who we almost were
Should I still tell you
About
The mists, the myths, the myrrh?

They say morality is given
A place at God's feast table
But I still respond
That it's not food for which I'm asking.
I'd still replace it
For a space in your bed
Where I'd hold and softly kiss
Your tousled head.

1

    Felicia is the entertainer at the Poets Café. Music by Ciara Donnelly.

Should I have kept
A secret, if it was?
Did you know all along

The guile behind my smile?
And if you did
Know it, so then
What secrets don't you say?

When you hear me in dreams
What questions do you ask?
Do we share a fantasy
Of who we might have been?
If I never said
A thing
Would we still be thinking the same?

Would we still be thinking the same?

(*Lights up on the small stage. Mickey-b and Francis-b are in rehearsal for Opening Knights. Francis-b is seated on the edge of the stage, head in hands, quite glum. Mickey-b is standing and much more confident.*)

Francis-b: You know what I hate? I hate doing stupid things.

Mickey-b: Look, just stop beating yourself up about it and let's rehearse. We're here, we have a show to do, we have the whole theatre to ourselves, let's rehearse.

Francis-b: Kind of hard to do when your lame ass acting partner forgets his script at home and brings the wrong one. The Actor's Nightmare. Did it *have* to be so ironic?

Mickey-b: Then let's do what we can. We can explore our roles and our relationships, do blocking. Hey! We can do improv!

Francis-b: (*brightening*) Oh. Oh? Oh! Yeah yeah yeah, we can do that can't we?

Mickey-b: Good! Let's get going then.

Francis-b: But Mick -

Mickey-b: - No buts! Let's get on with this.

Francis-b: We will – promise – but I do apologize for dragging you out tonight. Tell Stan I'm sorry too.

Mickey-b: Oh sure. Don't worry about Stan. He doesn't understand about acting and theatre. That's my thing. His thing is hockey. My thing is theatre. We have our things. Let's do this.

Francis-b: Right then. (*stands*) Where do you want to start, seeing as we can't run lines?

Mickey-b: Let's do our third scene together. I'm pretty sure I know that one anyway. It's early evening, your wife has left to go to the opening without you and you're drunk.

Francis-b: Right. Sure. Yeah. Yeah, I know that one too. So I've called my ex-wife, you, to come over.

Mickey-b: And you're drunk.

Francis-b: Yes.

Mickey-b: How drunk are you?

Francis-b: Hmph. Yeah. That's a decision. That's one to decide. Ummm ... um. Um. Um. Let's go from where you come in and I'll keep going up the scales, as it were and we'll pick a level.

Mickey-b: That sounds good. Do you answer the door or do I just walk in?

Francis-b: Well that'll be up to Don to decide, but for now let's say I answer, so I can move around a bit. Feel how much the floor moves, like that.

Mickey-b: Okay good. I'll go outside to the hall. (*heads far stage right*)

Francis-b: And I'm slouched over at my desk. (*heads far left*)

Mickey-b: (*mimes knocking on a door while stomping one foot to do the* *knocking sound. Calls out*) Hello Arthur!

Francis-b: (*not in character*) Wait. I don't have a doorbell?

Mickey-b: Do you want to be an asshole or do you want to rehearse? The scene's not about doorbells!

Francis-b: Sorry! Okay, start over.

Mickey-b: Fine. (*action as before*) Hello Arthur! (*He rises proudly and moves with only the slightest weave across the stage. His drunkenness is only marked by the slightest of slurring and a very fixed eye focus on every move Mickey makes.*)

Francis-b: Diana, thank God you're here.

Mickey-b: (*looks around at the apartment, for she used to live there*) Oh what a horror! What on earth has Lolita -

Francis-b: - Lisa -

Mickey-b: - done to this apartment? All these things and things and (*picks up an imaginary small piece of pottery*) yucky yucky things.

Francis-b: I know.

Mickey-b: And why are there all these ... what are all these ... who are all these *clowns* hanging there?

Francis-b: Red Skelton painted them. There was a charity auction and Lisa bought them all. It was for rescue dogs.

Mickey-b: It would have been better to have brought home a dog.

Francis-b: She was worried about widdles on the carpet.

Mickey-b: So instead she put shit on the walls.

Francis-b: Ha ha! Oh Diana, thank you for being here. You look wonderful my darling. (*they come together. Both break character and the coming kiss is an air kiss that doesn't come within a foot of each* *other's cheek*) And kiss kiss.

Mickey-b: Kiss kiss. Okay. Let's do it again. You'll be drunker?

Francis-b: Yes. That was strutting drunk. Now I'll move to stumbling drunk. Glad I know this bit. Back to the desk.

Mickey-b: Back to the hallway. (*they separate. This time through the slurring is more pronounced and Francis/Arthur has to lean on walls and steers himself along the back of an imaginary couch. The actual slurring is not suggested in the text. All other action is as before unless noted otherwise.*) Hello Arthur! (*He reacts more slowly and Mickey knocks again. He ushers her in with an exaggerated sweep of his arm that nearly topples him over.*)

Francis-b: Diana, thank *God* you're here.

Mickey-b: Oh what a horror! What on earth has Lolita -

Francis-b: - Liiiiiisa -

Mickey-b: - done to this apartment? All these things and things and yucky yucky things.

Francis-b: (*laughs a bit too heartily*) I know! (*burps*)

Mickey-b: (*breaks character*) Oh Fran, that's just gross.

Francis-b: Agreed. Too much. Carry on. (*they resume acting*)

Mickey-b: And why are there all these ... what are all these ... who are all these *clowns* hanging there?

Francis-b: Red Skelton painted them. There was a charity auction and Liiiiiisa bought them all. It was. For. Rescue *dogs*.

Mickey-b: It would have been better to have brought home a dog.

Francis-b: She was worried about widdlies on the carpet.

Mickey-b: So instead she put shit on the walls.

Francis-b: Ha ha ha ha HA! Oh Diana, thank you for being here. You look ... wonderful my darling. (*despite his being much more*

lecherous, the kiss is still snap sober and no contact is made) Kiss kiss.

Mickey-b: And kiss kiss. Want to work on that level?

Francis-b: I have one more. Hunter S. Thompson described drunkenness as having three stages: strutting drunk, stumbling drunk and crawling drunk. I haven't tried crawling yet.

Mickey-b: Not literally?

Francis-b: No, the scene would take forever. But pretty close to actual crawling.

Mickey-b: Okay then. Oh. How am I doing, by the way?

Francis-b: Perfect as always Mick.

Mickey-b: (*laughs, rather delighted at the compliment, but pretends otherwise*) Oh hardly, but let's take care of you first. (*pats him on the cheek*) Back to the bottle dear.

Francis-b: Get out of my sight my darling. (*They return to their separate corners. This time Francis/Arthur will be massively drunk. As a hint to actors, the character is at a state of drunkenness where he overly enunciates every word, trying mightily in an attempt to make every syllable sound sober.*)

Mickey-b: (*knocks and*) Hello Arthur!

Francis-b: (*This is literally a case of three steps forward, one step back, then a very long step forward as though making up for the lost ground, followed by skittering small steps smacking him into the – imaginary or not depending on the stage layout – wall next to the door, which he then opens, clinging to the knob for balance.*) Diana, thank God you're here. (*He does the theatrical wave into the room as before, but this time when she sweeps past he falls straight to the floor. From here he will crawl on his knees – not hands and knees, just knees – over to her.*)

Mickey-b: Oh what a horror! What on earth has Lolita -

Francis-b: - Liiiiiiiiiiiiiiiisaaaaa -

Mickey-b: (*overlaps his bleated Liiisaaa*) - done to this apartment? All these things and things and yucky yucky things.

Francis-b: I know!

Mickey-b: And why are there all these ... what are all these ... who are all these *clowns* hanging there?

Francis-b: (*He has nearly reached her on his knees, but stops to speak*) Red Skelton painted them. There was a charity auction and Liiiiiisssssa bought them all. It was.... For..... Rescue ... *dogs.*

Mickey-b: It would have been better to have brought home a dog.

Francis-b: (*he has resumed creeping up on her, but again stops to speak*) She was worried about widdlies on the carpet. (*he makes up the last few feet in a quick knee crawl*)

Mickey-b: (*turns to face him, sees him below her, so she kneels to deliver her line face to face*) So instead she put shit on the walls.

Francis-b: (*they stare at each other for a moment – in character or not? You decide – and then he speaks*) Ha ha! Oh Diana, thank you for being here. You look ... wonderful my darling. (*they move to kiss but he misses and fails face first*)

Francis-b: (*NOT in character*) Ow.

Mickey-b: Oh Fran! Did that hurt?

Francis-b: (*still face down*) Oh yeah. Yeah, that is hurting. Uh huh. (*rolls onto his back, looking up at Mickey who is still on her knees*) You know, you're much taller than I remember. (*They adjust and sit beside one another, legs crossed*)

Mickey-b: So.

Francis-b: So. How was that?

Mickey-b: I liked the first one. And the second. The third one was good too, but ...

Francis-b: Too big?

Mickey-b: Yeah maybe. Or maybe not. Here's the problem I have Fran. Would Diana stay if Francis was that drunk?

Francis-b: You mean Arthur.

Mickey-b: What? (*she realizes her error*) Oh shit! Yes of course I mean Arthur. Would any woman stay if a man was that drunk? Even her ex-husband. *Especially* her ex-husband! He might be abusive or she could even be, you know ...

Francis-b: I know. Although we do end up in bed together. Presumably.

Mickey-b: Presumably, although we never really know. The script doesn't directly say that.

Francis-b: No, true enough. Although they do enough rolling around on the floor in this scene.

Mickey-b: Which we'll have to work on. (*very slight pause*) So you don't get injured again.

Francis-b: Yeah. Klutz-r-Us. Or Klutz-r-Me. I shouldn't include you in that.

Mickey-b: Oh I do klutz. I locked myself out of the house the other day, you know? And the keys were upstairs in the bedroom, so I went into the garage, pulled out Stan's twelve-foot ladder, went up the ladder to the window and of course I couldn't open it, so I sat on the roof to think. Then Rufus wanted to know what I was doing, so he puts his paws on the ladder and knocks it over.

Francis-b: What the hell did you do Mick?

Mickey-b: I laid on the roof and watched the clouds – it was a nice day – and the sunset. And the moon rise. And then I counted all the stars you can see inside the bucket of the Big Dipper. Fifty-four. I remember because that's what time Stan got home. Five to four. He wasn't impressed.

Francis-b: *He* wasn't impressed? Why was he out until four in the morning?

Mickey-b: He was working a side job. They gave him a new washing machine as a payment.

Francis-b: Jesus. Well, I'm glad you're okay. (*hugs her with one arm. Pause*) So why do you think they split up, Arthur and Diana?

Mickey-b: Well she is a bitch after all.

Francis-b: Not necessarily. Arthur couldn't have been any treat to live with. He's supposed to be an arrogant jerk.

Mickey-b: What makes you say that?

Francis-b: Have you *read* the play? The man's a puffed-up know-it-all.

Mickey-b: But he can be sweet.

Francis-b: Well the show is a comedy.

Mickey-b: He's by far the smartest character in the show.

Francis-b: Diana's no slouch in the brains department. She certainly has a better sense of home decor than Lolita.

Mickey-b: Lisa.

Francis-b: Wait, that's my line.

Mickey-b: How would you know? You forgot your script. (*pokes him in the side, then merrily*) Gotch-aaaa!

Francis-b: May I say, I love finally acting with you.

Mickey-b: I know. Me too. After all the Tuesday night classes, and you directing, or me stage managing. We made it! (*they high five*)

Francis-b: So what do you really think of Diana?

Mickey-b: Truth?

Francis-b: No, lie to me. Of course truth.

Mickey-b: Can't stand her. No one I'd ever be friends with or want to be friends with. She's not ... of the earth, earthy.

Francis-b: Elvira, Blithe Spirit.

Mickey-b: Exactly. She's more of a Ruth.

Francis-b: Ruth's not a bad person.

Mickey-b: You directed that show. You wouldn't answer me when I asked you then, so now's your chance: Who would you rather be with, Ruth or Elvira?

Francis-b: Oh Elvira, beyond a shadow of a doubt.

Mickey-b: (*very smugly, almost childishly satisfied. It is obvious she played Elvira.*) Thank youuuu!

Francis-b: (*disconsolate, grumpy*) I married a Ruth.

Mickey-b: That's what I'm saying! That's what caused the divorce! (*Francis stares blankly*) In the play!

Francis-b: Yes! Yes! In the play ... oh God, we hate the people we have to become and we have to love them. This ain't gonna be easy Mick.

Mickey-b: Here, let's help each other. This is something I learned at university. Improv exercise. Character development. Scrunch around and sit facing me. Knees touching. Good. Now you lay your right hand on my left hand palm and I do the same to you. Good. Now I'll go first. You close your eyes and I'm going to tell you as Diana everything I ever loved about you. But you can't interrupt. Close your eyes!

Francis-b: Okay. (*does so*)

Mickey-b: Arthur Barrington, did you ever wonder why I never re-married after our divorce? I may yet someday, if I get old enough, bored enough, or horny enough although it's easy enough to satisfy horny enough until you're old enough to be too old enough. Enough. Of all the men I have and ever will meet you're the only one someone like me could ever really love. I love how you think you're so inscrutable, hiding behind the plays you write and all their characters. You think sometimes when you make little side comments that you're the only one who gets their meaning, but I get every one and I love them. Oh I never gave that away. Why ruin your fun? If I ruined your fun, I'd ruin you. Because even though on the outside you might be all vinegar and violets, I know why you do that. Deep down inside, behind those dancing saucer blue eyes of yours, and the cause of that little smile you have when you watch something sweet, I know there's an innocent boy there that never quite grew up because you've never wanted to let him slip behind into your past. But I became greedy and that's why I lost you. Just once I wanted to talk to the boy that speaks within you and I grew frustrated when you always thought he's be laughed at if his voice was ever heard. I love you Arthur. (*pause. She squeezes his hands, closes her eyes*) Your turn.

Francis-b: Diana Barrington, if I might borrow from the Brownings, you have touched me in so many different ways. The first touch was through my eyes. When I first saw you, I was entranced by that incredible skin, how you moved like an ice dancer, the way your whole body could speak without need of a voice. And then when you did speak, you touched my ears. Sometimes you tickled them with your wit. If it's not too prideful to say, yours is the only mind I have ever met that could fence with me joke to joke, quip to quip, dry view to dry view. And then I did touch you, flesh to flesh. A confession – I actually felt afraid to touch you Those bones like birds' wings ... I was afraid I would crush you, yet with our first kiss .. and second ... and third ... and thousandth I felt the power of your goddess sensuality. And so it was you touched my heart. A second confession. Years and years ago I was hurt. Wretchedly, awfully when life turned on me like a simple candle become Vesuvius burying me in thick, grey ash. Though all about me was burnt, within the insulated safety of my heart I allowed a shard of ice to form around love itself and I vowed nothing, no one, no one ever would be allowed to melt that ice. Your touch formed love and made the ice turn to soft and gentle water. When you rejected me, began to grow apart, that ice re-formed and I could not speak of my feelings for fear of ... well, for fear of. I love you Diana because only you have ever touched me. (*squeezes her hands. She opens her eyes*) Hi.

Mickey-b: Hi Arthur. Thank you for sharing.

Francis-b: You too. That was kinda beautiful Mick.

Mickey-b: Yeah, yes, that exercise works. Now what do we do?

Francis-b: Well, not sure if this is the time for it, or maybe it's the perfect time for it, but one thing we have to rehearse is the, uh ... (*he kisses the air*)

Mickey-b: The (*kisses the air*)?

Francis-b: Yeah. Do you feel as shy as I do?

Mickey-b: (*gestures him even closer*) Know what?

Francis-b: Huh? (*she kisses him quickly*)

Mickey-b: There! We've lost out virgi-kissity. Now we can rehearse it.

(*The lights shift again. Now, depending as to whether the Director's choice is to use the original Francis and Mickey for the flashback scene, or two others in the overall play as a Francis-b and Mickey-b, the staging of the following can vary. In either circumstance, the two head towards the table, hand in hand and speaking softly, where Francis and Mickey were sat. This conversation is the never-spoken fantasy of both, existing only within their minds. Therefore, if substitutes are used, the 'real' Francis and Mickey do not hear a word of it, as it all has existed in but a*) *moment's thought simultaneously in their minds. If it is the real Francis and Mickey who executed the flashback scene, this fantasy conversation happens totally while they are standing. Once they sit, it ends immediately and abruptly.)*

Francis-b: Those were the greatest kisses of my life.

Mickey-b: On stage you mean.

Francis-b: Did I say on stage? I mean anywhere. Remember? (*They kiss long and deeply.*)

Mickey-b: I dunno. I'm a girl who tends to forget things. You better refresh my memory.

Francis-b: I think you're turning into Lauren Bacall.

Mickey-b: Any objections?

Francis-b: None. (*a second long kiss*) We never talked about it. Why?

Mickey-b: Did we need to?

Francis-b: I think we did. Fourteen shows. Thirteen wonderful kisses.

Mickey-b: Thirteen only?

Francis-b: Thirteen out of fpurteen were wonderful. Plus the ones 'for good luck' behind the sets, in the wings ...

Mickey-b: I felt awkward the night Stan came to see the show.

Francis-b: Oh, I could tell. The audience couldn't, but I could. That night we were acting.

Mickey-b: Weren't we always?

Francis-b: Never in the theatre, only outside it.

Mickey-b: I wasn't sure about, you know, if it was a show thing or something else.

Francis-b: That's why I've never said anything either. That and ...

Mickey-b: Go on.

Francis-b: Your marriage to Stan was ending. So was mine to Louisa, even before yours, but I didn't have the guts to pull the pin. Not yet. And if what you felt really was a show thing then – ah hell Mick, I was afraid of getting hurt again.

Mickey-b: That's what I thought. That's what I thought you thought. And what I thought about myself. I wonder what would have happened if we had fallen in love?

Francis-b: Oh we fell in love all right. You know that as well as I do.

Mickey-b: Really?

Francis-b: Yeahhhh. I mean, why else could it be, what else would have stopped us from never having this exact conversation? Out loud. Except only in our heads where it's safe.

Mickey-b: (*they hug, right next to the table*) You know something Fran?

Francis-b: What, Mick?

Mickey-b: We're two pretty damn good actors.

Francis-b: Yeah, we ain't so bad.

Mickey-b: We just have one flaw. Same one, both of us.

Francis-b: Oh yeah? What's that?

Mickey-b: Our timing sucks.

Francis-b: (*absolutely howls with laughter, as does Mickey*) You are brilliant. (*big, affectionate kiss*) Cheers Mick.

Mickey-b: Cheers Fran. Have a great time in Ireland. Stay in touch.

Francis-b: That my love you can take to the bank. (*If substitutes, they return to their original seats. If it has been the same Mickey and Francis all along, they sit back at the table. Did that past scene actually happen or was it just in their fantasies? Does it matter?*)

Francis: So, think you'll ever come and visit me in Ireland? Fine place for a honeymoon you know, or to get away from one when the honeymoon's over. I'm kidding.

Mickey: Oh I'd love to, but I have a real problem. I have this huge fear of flying.

Francis: They have courses for that. Hypnosis. Booze. Happy floaty cloud drugs. And in the worst cases – boats. (*Felicia has gone to the keyboard and started picking out a slow swing song*)

Mickey: We'll see. You never know, I may surprise me.

Francis: Then one last thing, because I know you have to leave.

Mickey: What?

Francis: You're the last friend I'll see before I leave this town. And I'm glad it was you. So if this is the final curtain, ya know Michelle, we gotta do us a curtain call song.

Mickey: But I don't sing!

Francis: Neither do I, but these people won't know that until it's too late! (*He takes her hand and they go on the stage and sing the following:*)

Curtain Time

(*it swings, singers alternate*)

Right from your opening speech
I wanted what you preach

But you were out of reach
Until curtain time

I saw you in the wings
Your eyes like diamond rings
I hear the choirs sing
At curtain time

I take your hand so firm in mine
As we stand in the bowing line
It feels so fine ,so fine next to you

Because it's curtains
We close those curtains
What goes on can never been seen

I tell you all the secrets there
In our own private secret lair
I touch your hair and everywhere it all starts there

It's just a special time
That makes its own romantic rhyme
When it's my curtain time
With you

(together)

It's just a special time
That makes its own romantic rhyme
When it's my curtain time
With you

fin.

Music

(My becoming a music writer was an extension of the old movie actor's rule: Never turn down a part. If they ask you if you can roller skate off a cliff and do a perfect pike dive into a tea cup, always say yes. Once you're there, if they find out you can't, they'll get a stunt person to do it.

As for music, my editor at the newspaper called me one day and said, 'You know all about the Blues, right? I need you to cover a concert.' Thus began days of research and years of enjoyable writing. Here for your enjoyment, some of my favourite music writing.)

Dana Fuchs: The Force of Nature

For: American Blues Scene, Match 2013

Yes, it is the Janis Joplin comparison that is hung around singers' necks like the chains wrapped about Jacob Marley's ghost. It demeans the artist – both the living and the dead frankly – as to be considered an artist one must be uniquely creating art that is true to one's own soul. The worst of it is that a perpetually lazy press corps, seeing the attractively impassioned rock n' blues singer, makes the Janis Comparative and stops there. On the other hand, while using a bit of Janis Joplin to describe one part of Dana Fuchs to you, there are many more facets to this force of nature projected as music.

Ah yes, Dana Fuchs. Dana Fuchs is indeed one of the great singers, as in Now or Ever. Her voice is unmatched for the combination of maximum power, maximum passion and masterful control. How strong is that voice? When chatting in her trailer after a performance, her guitar player and song collaborator, the great and under-rated Jon Diamond came in bearing the remains of a top quality wireless microphone that had imploded from her singing. The only other artists that come to mindf doing that was Tom Jones in his much younger days, or James Cotton with his Blues harp.

So if the Janis Jopin comparison is an unfair one, what would be fair? Let's go with this – if Dana Fuchs and Robert Plant exchanged souls from birth across time, sex and experience it is highly likely they would have grown up to be much as we see them now. The blending would occur naturally. Each well-grounded in the Blues; each equally capable of rocking out; each capable of the soft notes that can hold a room with a whisper.

Volume isn't everything, you know. There's a wonderful line in Chekhov's The Seagull where the local lawyer says (depending on which translation), 'My voice is very loud, but unfortunately not pleasant to listen to.' Fuchs has all the other qualities of the great singers. Let's face it, there are as many gravelly-voiced girl singers as there are cheeseburgers in a MacDonald's; what Dana Fuchs has is a mixture of clarity, passion and the astonishing ability to break into a softened tone with no audible corrosion from the gravel.

Beyond that of course is the physicality. Dana Fuchs is an incredibly sexual performer. It is absolutely no wonder that when Baz Luhrmann was casting the part of the Earth mother Sexy Sadie for Across the Universe that Fuchs was the chosen one, despite zero acting experience on her part. There is a certain design that stands as an ideal in North American male sexual ideals and Fuchs fits as comfortably into one of those ideal figures as you do in *those* jeans; those jeans that have become so accommodated to every ripple, drop and curl of your torso that like an invisible tailor they can make even you look good.

Dana Fuchs can grab any old pair of extra talls off the rack at Sam's Club and wear them like gold. She is the great blue jean girl and the image that summons in your mind is absolutely correct. The blue jean girl: not the cocktail party girl or the library girl or the club girl or the smart and smouldering lawyer girl. No, the blue jean girl who lopes more than she walks, who talks with a sincerity that never allows a doubted thought to enter the listener's mind, who clearly is not overly concerned with the latest offerings on the hair products aisle, for she knows that little wicked angels will toss the long dark blonde waves and curls into a pleasing form. Plus she can probably drink your sorry ass under a table and drop your sorry drunken butt on your Momma's lawn while she drives away yelling Wooooo! That's the blue jean girl.

Yet there is another dimension. There is also the soul-fed, soul-feeding aura of love she speaks to and projects. For there is a truth about the Blues and even the electrified Earth sounds that rock-blues fusions create: that sound is either one of two things for the artist – it is either a style or an ethos.

Dana Fuchs is utterly real both on-stage and in conversation. That implied persona is not visible. Her desire to feel and create love with her audience is equally sincere whether expressed over the microphone or over a casual glass of wine in her trailer.

On first meeting, at the Thunder Bay Blues Festival in 2011, there were hundreds of people lined up at the merch tent for Dana Fuchs' autograph time and each and every one had to be served.

Not just served with a scrawl and a smile; rather an actual moment of individual conversation. There was actual listening and involvement going on and trust me, that's rare. It was like watching Arnold Palmer in his prime. Someone who genuinely appreciates their audience.

So there was an hour and a half wait for the interview, allowing every day pass fan to have their moment. It was admirable and a proper placement of priorities.

The first thing I said to her when she came behind the large tent stage into the protective circled wagon train of artists' trailers, volunteer mini-vans and Port-a-Potties was, 'You know, if you're tired we don't have to do this.' This was true. A daily newspaper article from the Festival had already been posted, besides which the decision was already made that Dana would be named the Performer of the Year barring God dropping down from Heaven playing Green Onions on a Hammond. Which, in case you hadn't heard, didn't happen. The remaining fascination was finding out if the wrenching and celebratory truth I had witnessed on-stage was real.

Oh it's real. It's damn real. She was asked her feelings for the audience: 'I want the audience to feel what I'm feeling – shout and cry and laugh and stomp. That's why I get down on my knees. I'm tall anyway and in these big shoes so I don't want to be above them.'

From there the discussion ranged about, well, most of everything. Life, health, the then-recent death of her brother, love and passion and the whole damn thing.

What most told the story of Dana Fuchs was her discussion of the immediate post-Across the Universe period. 'Every agent in Hollywood – every agent told me the same thing. "Stay in L.A."' She was movie-hot then. A tall beautiful blonde who could act and sing? It is fair judgment to say that she would have been certainly in the running for a major part in any multi-gajillion dollar budget musical made in the last decade. Her opinion though? 'Well the "terms" were pretty simple: quit touring, leave New York and come to LA for at least a year and do nothing but audition for films. Pretty much a no brainer!'

Dana Fuchs lives life on her terms and does what she loves and where she loves it. Perhaps equally or even more popular in Europe and particularly Norway as in the U.S., as touring dates turned out she was booked into Norway within weeks of the senseless slaughter at Utoya Island where a useless little racist freak named Anders Breivik killed 59 people, mostly youths, after killing 8 people from a car bomb in Oslo. The nation was in shock and grieving. Because Dana stays in touch with her fans – not just 'sign up for my newsletter' touch, but real touch, she was one of the first to hear of the tragedy. 'Wow. Many memories. Mostly getting the breaking news as it happened on BBC, then getting into the van and getting a text from my dear Norwegian friend, Oda, who lost 3 friends in the youth camp. All about 17 years old just like her. Went to the site and a memorial. Felt all too familiar since I lived only blocks away from the WTC on 9/11. '

So what, Dana, what if any differences are found between the North American audiences and European:

'I always imagined there would be but honestly no! People come to shows I think hoping to get a little respite from the life's trials and tribulations. It's our job as performers to give it to them. If we do, they respond no matter where they're from!'

She is currently back in the studio making her new album, Bliss Avenue. So Dana, tell us about the album…

'Well, the new CD is definitely going back to some of my bluesy, southern rock roots! After interviewing several producers, Jon and I decided our own vision for producing was going to give us a more sincere and authentic representation of our music. It's a calculated risk that we had to take to stay true to ourselves and hopefully the listeners of this album will agree! I am carefully measuring my growth as an artist on this effort and hence taking more of a leadership role in producing than I ever have before. I assembled an incredible band with Shawn Pelton on drums, Jack Daley on bass, Glenn Patscha on keys, of course Jon playing his ass off on guitar. We added Tabitha Fair and Nicki Richards on background vocals and we have Tim Hatfield engineering again and co-producing with me and Jon.

'I feel like the writing is perhaps a little more mature and definitely a bit darker lyrically. Lots about addiction and religion – and all of the temporary relief we try to get from suffering in a samsaric world! (Hence, the title "Bliss Ave."). It's not meant to be a depressing album – just a starkly honest one that I felt I had to make. Of course, with dark there is light, so I'm hoping people will understand the redemption in the pain and by no means is the music all dark and depressing…quite the contrary as often in the blues the joy forces it's way out in the music and melody often redeems the darkness of the lyrics and song. I'm in the studio mixing all week and putting the finishing touches on this album has me excited and cautiously optimistic about delivering a piece of work that will transcend. I hope that helps frame up where I'm coming from!'

As always in an interview, the last word goes to the artist; What would she like to say to the readers?:

'I feel so grateful to the people who enable me to do what I love and need to do most. I am honored to get the opportunity to bring joy to people all over the world and want to be sure that everyone who comes to a show or listens to my music knows that they are a part of me. We are ALL in this f**king boat called life together! Let's lean on each other. Music can be our holy common ground!'

(I have both interviewed and reviewed the work of wrestler turned country rocker Mickie James. This was the first piece I did on her, back in 2010.)

Mickie James

Inside Television 521

Publication date: 10-01-10

This is a story that I hope turns into a continuing story for two reasons. The first reason - selfishly - is that it will fill many a column inch tracking a television show right from its absolute genesis as an idea. The second reason - unselfishly - is that I think the prospective star is someone that I think has earned her shot at possibly become a very big, very wealthy, star. Allow me to introduce you to Mickie James. And this is much more than a wrestling story.

Mickie James is a young woman who first came into televised view as a WWE Diva wrestler from 2005 until her release from that company earlier this year. I well remember her debut. Mickie played an unbelievably perky obsessed fan of Toronto's own Trish Stratus. Mickie would run out to happy happy joy joy music, waving pompoms and cheering for Trish. She liked Trish. She liked Trish a whole lot. She liked Trish more than the increasingly-nervous Trish liked her. Complications arose. And for once a women's wrestling angle was allowed to play out for more than, oh, about three weeks of Raw and three minutes of wrestling. We'll get back to that.

It helped that among the WWE Divas, Mickie and Trish could actually wrestle. You might think that would be a prerequisite before being signed to Vince McMahon's gigantic promotion, but you'd be wrong. Very wrong. Vince casts his Divas for their swimsuit appeal, not for their ability to recreate the best moves of Lou Thesz.

But for five years, Mickie was the best of both worlds - cute as a button with a massive army of loyal fans, good matches with any other Diva who could tell an armbar from a crowbar, and was rewarded as a five-time Champion. Being anointed as a Champion by WWE (or any other company) really does mean something - it means Vince thinks you're a star and can earn Vince money. Simple as that. And great as long as Vince likes you.

As sports commentator Jim Rome once said, 'There's no doubt about it. Vince McMahon is the bad seed.' When Vince dislikes or grows bored with a wrestler, before the release inevitably containing the words 'We wish (insert name) all the best in (his/her) future endeavors', he attempts to destroy the wrestler's appeal. What if they started earning money for TNA, or WCW back in the day? Can't be having that! Vince would then appear to be - egad! - wrong. Vince doesn't do wrong well.

So, the wrestler might be turned heel, so he or she won't be welcomed by another promotion's fans as a conquering hero. Or, they might be jobbed out - put on a long losing string so they lose their athletic appeal. Or Vince might just make fun of you in as demeaning a fashion as possible. That's what he did to Mickie James. He had other Divas on Smackdown repeatedly say that Mickie was -

Fat.

Piggy James. Fat fat ickity ick. Now, I do invite the reader to look at the young woman in the accompanying picture. If that is fat, then I'm the Mighty Mouse balloon in the Macy's Parade. So what Vince was doing made no sense, but in his mind the absolute cruelest thing he could happen to a woman was to be accused of losing her sex appeal. Margaret Thatcher, Golda Meir and Queen Elizabeth the First might beg to differ, but none of them were wrestlers. Margaret Thatcher would have made one heck of a manager of a heel faction however. Eric Bischoff and Vince Russo might have saved WCW if they'd put Thatcher in the N.W.O. My apologies if this is getting too inside. We're done with the wrestling part mostly.

Mickie had and has a second talent. She is a country singer and songwriter, mostly of the hard-playin' James Gang style. Just after her release from WWE she released an album called *Strangers & Angels*, available on iTunes. So, as the late Stan Rogers used to say, it was time 'to hit the highways and the byways, singing the songs of our land.'
As any musician will tell you (and tell you and tell you) life on the road is not easy - bars, fairs and shopping mall openings. Mickie being a known quantity with a fan base has an edge, but it's an edge that is only as good as a letter of introduction. After that, it's up to the singer and the songs to sell themselves.

Sounds like a reality series to me, as it does to Mickie and her manager. She still takes the occasional independent wrestling gig, has name recognition, a traveling story, and most importantly she has the character to draw a smile. People like to smile.
The idea is going to be pitched to various networks and I'm going to track it for you. Until then - Be seeing you.

(Update: Now happily married and with a baby daughter, Mickie still occasionally appears on the wrestling circuit. Her newest album is Somebody's Gonna Pay.)

(Ciara Donnelly and I have also teamed up as music reviewers on occasion. This is our review of one of the best albums of 2015.)

Florence and the Machine:

How Big How Blue How Beautiful

For: Hispanic News Online, May 2015

(I am delighted to be joined in reviewing with the wonderfully talented Ciara Donnelly, known professionally throughout Ireland and the UK as Yellowbridge. She brings the kind of insight into recording and performances that only a professional musician can have. Her comments throughout these reviews will be in *bold italics*. Now on with the review!)

Unblinking. On the cover of her third album **How Big How Blue How Beautiful** Florence Welch stares out straight ahead, slightly hunched, a poker player daring you to call, one hand poised to take the chips. Or is this a look that the brilliant British singer-songwriter has given herself, looking hard into the mirror?

How Big How Blue How Beautiful is a richly formed song cycle that in its honest telling of one woman's journey from false security and resultant danger towards self-realization and peace makes it the aural equivalent of a thematically similar novel, Margaret Atwood's **Surfacing**. Best of all in this dubious time of singles and shuffle-play, Florence and the Machine have released an album that actually is an *album*. Of course each song carries its own rewards and beauty, yet **How Big How Blue How Beautiful** requests the listener to play it in its entirety, start to finish and to do so repeatedly. This very review is being drafted while **How Big How Blue How Beautiful** is playing on the iTunes screen behind the OpenOffice page for the sixth time in slightly under twenty-four hours. Now that hasn't happened with any record in a very, very long time (the last was probably Dana Fuchs' 2013 release **Bliss Avenue**). Further, to use a cliché as old as the first phonograph, this album gets better and better with each listening. It comes across like the soundtrack of a better movie than anything you'll see this year.

How Big How Blue How Beautiful plays out as a narrative and therefore deserves to be reviewed as such. When we first meet the narrator/central figure (we'll call her Florence although whether or not the story parallels Florence Welch's own is not of the slightest concern to us) she is not in a good place at all. Ship to Wreck finds Florence dreaming of a great white shark swimming in her bed and asking herself the question, 'Did I build this ship to wreck?' What Kind of Man, chosen by Island Records as the first single from the album, defines the present issue:

Florence is in a lousy relationship, but should she stay or should she go? The stresses and changing feelings are directly placed forward in colliding themes and abrupt tempo shifts. All accentuate what the lyrics state succinctly, 'Sometimes I'm half in and I'm half out cause you never close the door.' In other words, the decision-making power is being left to the man. Clearly, that is a problem. Why is an unsatisfactory lover allowed the power to decide? Ciara Donnelly noted about What Kind of Man: *A surprise use of structure make this track a grower, yet ultimately like any good grower it has longevity and an air of quiet confidence.*

Florence then enters into a series of explorations, seeking to make herself whole and av oid destruction. The first version of the title track defines what she wants and needs, except Florence is doubtful as to its becoming reality. Instead, let's mask our troubles! The rather ominously titled Delilah, with its implications of infidelity and abuse (Samson and Delilah + the old Tom Jones song = a nasty situation indeed) finds Florence tossing back 'a handful of pills to pass the time'. That doesn't work well as she still must admit, 'I can't let go.' She wonders if salvation might come from Mother, in the track of the same title, or heck let's try that old-time religion in the song Saint Jude. What's lost of course isn't something as mundane as car keys; rather it is Florence herself, the 'original lifeline' mentioned in the two renditions of **How Big How Blue How Beautiful**'s key song, the luminous and buoyantly New Gospel number Third Eye. Eventually Florence does discover that the only savior is the savior we are born as and her world like her soul itself is big, blue and beautiful.

Now, lest anyone think that this is all heavy fare, a weepy chick flick or chick lit of po' po' pitiful me fare, **How Big**

How Blue How Beautiful is first of all a cracking good rock record. There are many subtleties contained within the over-all urgency of Florence and the Machine's songs, a sonic wave that Welch's voice does not so much surf as float just above, like some great sea bird skimming the surroundings looking where to land. Or as Ciara puts it, *Retro pumping and chugging guitars counteract her delicate falsetto but fall perfectly in line rhythmically once her signature falsetto soars through the record. Also, the technical skills in the multi-track vocals are as powerful as ever. They truly are her signature.*

Whether it is the Sgt Pepper-like horn section in the first version on the title track, suggesting an idyllic land to be sought with a coda of sad strings following as a shrugged pessimism, or the maraca beat in Mother that so echoes U2's She Moves in Mysterious Ways (no accidental reference that), each song's structure and production reinforces the truths of the lyric content. That's the way records are meant to be made.

Ciara Donnelly noticed several aspects of the album's sound that mark a shift in style for Florence and the Machine. *The use of the retro acoustic guitar strums and tambourine combo throughout the whole record gives it a humble Americana feel, that naturally stems from the production by Markus Davis (Arcade Fire). Florence's new best friend now is not the harp but the brass section that works exceptionally well on the title track, along with old school rolling organs, major uplifting notes and a huge orchestral finish that demands its place on the big screen of the song. The bass is really prevalent in this record, something Florence hasn't done before, yet incredibly melodic.*

And then of course there is Florence Welch herself. There was an observation made of Eric Clapton some years ago, that he looks slightly different in every photograph so one is never quite sure if there is one Clapton or is there an odd factory somewhere turning out Slowhands to order. The

same sort of different-similarity can be applied to Welch as
a singer and a songwriter as well. She clearly owes to that
now long-ago age when Grace Slick or Chrissie Hynde
were brave, tough women who belted out a number and if
you don't like it, lump it Charlie. Yet, Welch also has a
subtlety of phrasing that treats every word and syllable as
morsels that have unique tastes and deserve their own
reaction. The great Joni Mitchell had that same phrasing at
her dynastic peak and it is an absolute joy to hear it again –
a voice with all the flexibility and dynamics of a piano.

Where does **How Big How Blue How Beautiful** rank?
Frankly it is as good as music gets in 2015. It has been six
years since Florence and the Machine's first album **Lungs**
was released and six years is an interesting marking point
for an act in the rock era. It was roughly at the six year
point when The Beatles released the aforementioned Sgt
Pepper, The Beach Boys' **Pet Sounds**, The Who's **Tommy**
and, well you get the idea. A group and its songwriters
either take that great leap forward or fade away. **How Big
How Blue How Beautiful** is a great leap forward. Ciara
has the last word on the subject – *This record is a
soundtrack to Florence Welch's bruised heart, this is
expressed through all-powerful roaring banshee breaths
and delicate whispering chorals. How Big How Blue How
Beautiful is not quite as experimental or theatrical as
Lungs, but it is amazing*

Hubert O'Hearn's Score: 9.7/10

Ciara Donnelly's Score: 9.0/10

Beady Eye

O2ABC Club

300 Sauchiehall Street

Glasgow, Scotland
22 June 2013

Photos By: Miranda Huckle

The first stop on this series of great club rooms in the UK is the O2 ABC Club in Glasgow. A former music hall known as the Hippodrome and later a movie theatre, it was converted into a two tier showroom by the O2 mobile phone/broadband company twenty years ago. It is a glorious old barn, although it presents a serious challenge for sound engineers given its wooden, triangular ceiling that equally bounces and absorbs sound.

Seating is severely limited; for all intents and purposes the main showroom holding some 800 people may as well be termed Standing Room Only. Still, for a big, noisy, energy-filled band the effect is that of an indoor festival. Drinks are reasonably priced and easily accessible with long bars and side lounges at every turn. The stage measures approximately 60' by 30' depth and is well-rigged for both show and bar band lighting. Excellent venue, give it a 4 out of 5 star rating.

One of the first lessons I ever learned in the entertainment industry is just two words – Pro shows. To expand a bit on that concept, a real pro knows how to give an audience exactly what they want, how to stage it, present it and put it over in a way that sends the working stiff feeling that he received full value for his entertainment purchase. Liam Gallagher's post-Oasis band Beady Eye were ultimate pros on Saturday night on June 22nd in Glasgow, the night we visited the O2 ABC Club.

Wait?, one asks, isn't Beady Eye a rock group? What on earth does it have to do with the Blues? Quite a bit actually..

The easy, received wisdom is that Beady Eye is equal parts 'Son of Oasis' and a bit of an up yours to Noel Gallagher who split from his brother and their immensely successful band in August of 2009. Liam re-assembled various parts of Oasis (guitarists Gem Archer and Andy Bell, rounded by drummer Chris Sharrock) and has since released two albums. Is Beady Eye as successful as Oasis? Not yet. Going from stadiums to show rooms is a commercial decline. However, they deserve more.

The Gallagher brothers are not clones of one another. Whereas Noel tends to write the dreamier, more orchestral pieces as in the underrated album The Master Plan; Liam is more raw and roots oriented. As such, his latest single Flick of the Finger with its blasting horns and synched drum and bass beneath would fit perfectly within the Stax Records era of Rufus Thomas or Booker T and the M.G.'s.

Seen live, Beady Eye is a straight-ahead rock band which contains the delightful surprise that Liam is just as good as Noel in crafting song hooks that get feet stomping, hands clapping and voices singing along. When he sang the old Oasis hit I'm A Rock n' Roll

Star, that was not so much a tribute to that 'other' band as it was a way of saying to the enjoyably crazed audience, 'See? This fits in rather than stands out.'

Liam Gallagher has had some vocal issues in recent years, as one might expect from someone who once sang a song called 'Cigarettes and Alcohol', however, his reedy voice was in fine form on Saturday. And the man knows how to work a crowd. When some eejit threw a beer at him within seconds of the band starting their first song (why does someone spend money for the honour of being kicked out of a bar?), Liam milked the moment for all it was worth, cleaning and drying ever square inch of his clothing before saying...well, you can guess what he he said and the second word was indeed 'off'.

This was top drawer rock n' roll. I urge readers to – if not to forget Oasis exactly – enjoy its prodigal son on Beady Eye's own merits.

Beth Hart Thanks You for Your Company

For: American Blues Scene

February, 2013

'It sounds selfish to say, but honestly I so much want people to have a reaction – a beautiful reaction – so that I don't feel alone, you know? I've been through my ups and downs, so I often feel I'm just crazy and alone in the world.'

What? This is Beth Hart we're talking about. Beth Hart as in ten albums, the huge and lasting hit 'L.A. Song', world tours, Star Search winner, blow the roof off the Kennedy Center Honors performance Beth Hart; if she feels lonely where's the hope for the rest of us?

She elaborates, 'But once I get to come and perform for that audience, or they buy that record, and I see them connecting with it, it's like I'm part of their family and I'm not alone in my life and in my head. So that's what's really important.'

Family members tend to give gifts to loved ones, and Beth Hart's latest release is a fantastic jewelry box of an album called Bang bang Boom Boom whose every track is a surprise, each successive song just a little bit different in tone, style or subject from the one before it. Take for instance the song Swing That Thing Back Around which has all the feel of an old Ella Fitzgerald number with a swing band back-up.

'Yeah! I just love that song! That was one of the first songs I wrote and it's a style I'd never, ever approached before on the piano. But it's stuff that I'd loved hearing from Big Band stuff from Billie Holiday to Big Band stuff from Joe Turner. I love that kind of stuff but I never, ever thought I would ever write it. I didn't know I could. I didn't know how to do those changes on the piano and what not, but that was so much fun.'

Bang Bang Boom Boom was produced by Kevin Shirley, who has engineered or produced Iron Maiden, Rush, Aerosmith, Led Zeppelin and Joe Bonamassa, the last of which features on guitar on Beth Hart's most recent albums. His tremendous knowledge of music lends Boom Boom Bang Bang a tremendous richness and indeed a wit in the arrangements that make it one of the best-*sounding* albums in years. When asked how they collaborated to make this depth and variety happen, Beth Hart explained:

'One of the ways I just fell madly in love with him about was when I worked on the record Don't Explain (*her 2011 release – Ed.*), how he does it is: I'm going to play piano and sing and do it simultaneously together with the band. Everybody always plays the simultaneously, together. I just fell in love with that. I've always loved live performance so much, but I didn't really care so much for the studio. It's just something I didn't have the attention span for it – layering and getting drum sounds and oboe and getting this together. It just never did it for me. But working with Kevin, it's like the old days! In the old days, they'd just come in and sing right!'

Of course, in discussing Beth Hart one cannot overlook her voice – it growls, it roars, it purrs, it displays the full dynamic range and often within the space of one song. How does she take care of that magnificent instrument? What advice would she offer?

'Yeah, number one, go to a good vocal coach who will teach you how to get up there on those highs and all that fun stuff; how to do proper placement and have proper air. I think all that's really important, especially if you want to have a long career and not ruin your voice as you get older, I think it's really important to have a good, steady coach and someone you go to check in with regularly.

'But some of the tricks that I do – I don't scream a lot on stage. I have *moments* and the reason why, not only to take care of my voice but it's also to take care of the audience! I find if you do too much hollerin' and gookin', they get bored. It's like it's no more fun thing; and really the focus should be on the lyric, talking to the audience, moving your body, getting them involved, giving them those stories and really, trusting your band! They're working their ass off to set down a great groove.

'So not make it all about *you*. I think that's really important, because then the pressure goes off and when you don't have pressure, you relax and then your voice – you can sing so much better without hurting yourself. When you're all tense, and filled with pressure, you can really hurt it.

'And then the last thing I do, is I really try and not talk during the day, so I just use my voice for work. I do my sound check before the show and then I'm quiet.'

It is always interesting to ask an artist what he or she would like to say about the media, the judges that sit behind keyboards and microphones passing judgment on a work. What are Beth Hart's feelings on that?

'Well, it's been a great dream of mine for so many years now, to come back to the United States, releasing an album of original material and getting to meet the press again. I haven't talked to the press here in so many years and I'm glad to get a relationship going with those guys again. I find that helps you to grow a lot. You get a lot of constructive criticism and I think that's a good thing. Being in this business, you can get narcissistic. It's very easy, you can make it all about you. I think that's one of the cool things about the press is – the press can be very kind and the press can be very tough on you. I think that's a good practice in being able to grow instead of being suspended.'

Beth Hart – coming to a room or Festival near you. You're part of her family.

Be seeing you.

Human Rights

(The following is a speech delivered in 2013)

Embracing Racial Diversity

I have been asked today to speak to you on the subject of Racial Diversity and how it can be embraced within a modern culture. There are certainly lighter topics in the world. For some reason no one ever asks me to come and speak about the movies of Frank Capra, or show slides from weddings and birthday parties I have attended. That is still an option by the way? (PAUSE) No? All right then.

Let us therefore begin here. A quote for you:

Their families segregated themselves from the native-born population, adhered to religious and cultural beliefs that were at odds with the dominant culture, kept customs and traditions that seemed centuries behind the times, and expanded their numbers at an astonishing rate. At that point they were using the neighborhood as a base to plot a wave of terrorist attacks that, by the end of the 1880s, had killed more people and caused more political alarm than the jihadist attacks that began the twenty-first century would.

Well who were these murderous, dangerous people wreaking havoc on a peaceful country and why did that country ever have such low standards of acceptance that it allowed entry to this vile lot?

I suspect that several of you in this room are direct or indirect descendants or relatives of them. This segregated community was the Irish who had fled the Great Famine of the 1840s and 1850s, coming to North America by the tens of thousands. Yes, Irish Catholics were seen with as much fear, dread and prejudice in the nineteenth century as Arab Muslims are in our ever so advanced twenty-first century.

The quotation by the way is from Doug Saunders' recent and excellent book *The Myth of the Muslim Tide*. It truly is an excellent piece of journalistic research as it absolutely destroys the notion that Muslim immigrants are somehow bent on the destruction of Western civilization ... whatever that is.

I say, 'whatever that is' not to be flippant or sarcastic; rather it is a very real question. A civilization, a culture, an ethic, a sense of 'This is the way things are and this is how we want them to stay' is in many ways at the root of racism.

We don't much like change. Not really. A new shirt or a new car can be one thing, but basically we want things to stay as we know them for that is much less scary. It's the reason why people go on foreign vacations to see different places, but do so by staying in a North American style hotel that looks exactly like a hotel in Boston, Toronto, or Orlando and then when the adventurous tourist becomes hungry, he immediately looks for the nearest McDonald's or Burger King. Stick with what you know, after all 'THEIR' food might make us sick. And for God's sake don't drink the water! Any water! Anywhere! Stick with Budweiser. In Bud We Trust.

Let me share a deep-seated observation of mine that I hold as a truth. Emotions can delight and invigorate us, no matter what random pointy-eared Vulcans say, however there is one extremely dangerous emotion and that is nostalgia. Marcel Proust certainly knew it. The novel we know as *Remembrance of Things Past*, has a more accurate translation as In Search of Lost Time, for its original French title was *À la Reserche du Temps Perdu*. Seven volumes emerging from a man named Swann eating a single cookie – a madeline – that sends him off into a reverie of memory, preferring his mind to occupy the past that was known rather than the present that is uncertain or the future which is absolutely terrifying to contemplate. One quick observation, which I include only because it is such a wonderful line. The late, great A.J. Liebling, boxing writer and food critic at The New Yorker said of that famous madeline and Proust, "given a better appetite, he might have written a masterpiece."

I digress. Nostalgia is dangerous because it is so bloody powerful. It surrounds us, engages us, seduces us so completely it would make Casanova shuffle out of the room, head hanging in shame. Christmas is the perfect example – all those greeting cards with horse-drawn sleighs bought by couples who drive SUV's; a Santa Claus drawn in the style of Winslow Homer slugging down a Coke, or outdoor lighting designed to look like dripping icicles as there were before Dad lined the eaves with electric cable to fry any fallen leaf to a crispy crunch and send any snow into steam sent to heaven. It's very smart marketing. Cast the mind back to the days when Mom and Dad, or Grandpa and Grandma were young and strong, so you'll buy a new Smartphone to replace the one you gave one year ago because, by gosh, that's what they did in the Good Old Days.

Nostalgia makes an otherwise rational man, married to a fine woman who he loves, go creeping on Facebook for old girlfriends who were well rid of him twenty years before. He looks in the bathroom mirror and the swirl of fallen hair on the shower floor and realizes time is passing so as The Beatles' sang, it's time to Get Back, Get Back, Get Back to Where You Once Belonged. You do remember The Beatles don't you? Or am I being a silly old fuddy duddy stuck in the past? There you see, it happens even to the best or least of us.

Where nostalgia gets truly creepy and dangerous is when it enters into politics and its manipulation of the fear of change. 'What?', you likely just thought, 'Fear of change? Aren't all successful campaigns built on change? What about all that "change we can believe in" business that Barack Obama won with?'

Well no, not really. Whether it was the references to Bill Clinton's economic policies, the selected quotes from John F. Kennedy, the suggestion of a Hundred Days to rival that of Franklin Roosevelt and selected images of Dr Martin Luther King, the implication was that the young, modern black man Barack Obama was just the guy to bring back all those great things the electorate knew and loved. Oh, and in 2008 the possible future based on the then-present past was a terrible idea. Most of that campaign was based on a strong suggestion that, 'I, Barack Obama, am not George W. Bush.' The whole thing was change based upon pulling a favourite old sweater out of a closet and wearing it proudly again after many hours spent in the gym working off the fat.

Nostalgia is everything and it can kill. Oh yes, it can kill. Another quotation for you:

The individuals I have been accused of illegally executing are all category A and B traitors. They are supporters of the anti-European hate ideology known as multiculturalism, an ideology that facilitates Islamisation and Islamic demographic warfare. The category A and B traitors I executed were killed in self defence through a pre-emptive strike. They have been found guilty of high treason and condemned to death.

And so on. The entire document that nauseating paragraph comes from runs 1,518 pages and is called *2083: A European Declaration of Independence*. And who were these traitors? 69 people, some as young as 14 on Utoya Island, Norway. The author was Anders Breivik. After first letting off a car bomb in Oslo in order to create a distraction, Breivik then headed to Utoya armed with automatic rifles and explosives. I believe you know the deadly outcome.

Now what leads clearly diseased minds like Breivik – although to the Norwegian Court's credit he was deemed to fit to stand trial as that nation sought to understand what the source was for this act of carnage – what leads someone like Breivik to quite literally attack something like multiculturalism? Well, he had lots of help.

As Jean-Marie Le Pen said, "An ancient dictum says that when Zeus wanted to destroy someone, he would first drive him mad." You remember Le Pen don't you? He was the founder of the neo-Fascist Front National in France and another of his memorable lines was, "When Joan D' Arc was asked by her judges why as a Christian she did not love the British, she answered that she did love them, but she loved British in their country. In the same way, we do not hate the Turks, we love them, but in their country." The Front National is currently led by Jean-Marie's daughter, Marine Le Pen and she in turn garnered 17.9% of the first ballot vote in the 2012 Presidential elections. That is a fairly large percentage, less that one percent under what Canada's Liberal Party received in the 2011 Federal Election. When better than one in six voting citizens – never mind the lazy, the disaffected or those who so hate a democratic system they do not even bother to vote – when better than one in six think the best solution is a closing of the immigration doors and an ethnic cleansing in whatever soothing terms, that constitutes a national problem.

Ah well, that's Europe for you. All those countries, all those borders, all those continental wars. Good thing we aren't like that over here in North America, now isn't it? As George and Ira Gershwin wrote, It ain't necessarily so.

Here's a lovely statement by a supposedly serious man:

I believe Shariah is a mortal threat to the survival of freedom in the United States and in the world as we know it. I think it's that straightforward and it's real.

This is the theory of 'stealth Jihad', whereby Muslim immigration and a secret and separate culture will somehow take over the Congress, Presidency, Supreme Court and unravel the Constitution. Just the same way those starving Irish in the 1850s turned the United States into potato-eating, Vatican-loving, fiddle-playing rustics who wandered about with a pig under their arm and saying 'Faith and begorrah' to everyone they meet. (Incidentally, if you're ever in Ireland, never say 'Faith and begorrah.' You'll be marked as an idiot.) The very idea is utter nonsense, based on the notion that because of higher birthrates, Muslim immigrants will eventually out-number the 'real Americans', 'real french', 'real Germans', etecetera and so forth. The fact of the matter is, and again I quote Doug Saunders' research, is that by the time of the second generation of immigration, Muslim birthrates are 2.1 per couple, same as the rest of us.

So who was the fool who refused the facts and chose instead to spread the fear? That last quote was by Newt Gingrich in 2010, as in former Speaker of the House Newt Gingrich and, for a time the likely Republican Presidential nominee in 2012 Newt Gingrich. It is not at all beyond the realm of possibility that if a few – and a very few – events had turned like poker cards slightly differently, a believer in Islamic stealth jihad might have been inaugurated as President this past January.

But that's the Americans! For heaven's sake, they even took Sarah Palin so seriously they couldn't tell the difference between her and Tina Fey. Palin, you know, never said she could see Russia from her house. That was Tina Fey. Anyway, surely no Canadian would never come out with anything so incredibly insane. We're the polite country, the cultural mosaic country, the country populated mostly by immigrants and their sons and daughters. Well now, yet another direct quote:

The major threat is still Islamicism. There are other threats out there, but that is the one that I can tell you occupies the security apparatus most regularly in terms of actual terrorist threats.

That was our Prime Minister, Stephen Harper, speaking to Peter Mansbridge in the fall of 2011, and inventing the word Islamicism. And yes, Islamicism would be something the government would be, quote, 'keeping an eye on' and Harper went on to promise that 'keeping an eye on' such homeland threats would include bringing back expired laws such as allowing a judge to compel a witness to testify in secret about past associations or perhaps pending acts under penalty of going to jail if the witness didn't comply. Franz Kafka would be proud and Anders Breivik would be inspired. Yes, I have made an extremely harsh association there, but when leaders of parties, senior government officers and Prime Ministers say dangerous things, they must be called on them.

The obvious reaction to such depraved ravings and actions is that rash speech by pandering politicians, can lead to horrid actions by diseased minds. Actions may speak louder than words; however actions are the outcome of words. And therefore, when rights compete we must never lose sight of the fact that human rights legislation is in place to protect the dignity of all.

And this – this – is at the nut of it all. Both the nostalgia and the naked pandering to fear is based on an absolutely false assumption, which is that there was ever an extended period of time when a culture was in an amiable stasis. Ronald Reagan made a career of it, that once upon a time there was an America where all neighbourhoods were safe, all were treated with respect, you didn't have to lock your door, your kids weren't addicted to drugs and sex and everyone around you looked and acted just like you. It was and is a vision of a country or culture about as accurate as a theme park.

There would actually be something to be said about that, you know. Before I continue and risk the friendship of absolutely every friend I have, let me say that I am being utterly facetious here. But a certain *reductio ad absurdum* or if you'd prefer Swiftian satire can bring a point forward. After all, if you want someone to take you seriously, make them laugh.

Why not run nations like theme parks? Decide on a national identity and stick with it, allowing absolutely no variation? In France, upon birth one would be assigned a beret and a baguette, men would grow little mustaches upon late adolescence and keep them there, while all wives would tolerate their husband's affairs. All Italians would be compelled to watch the films of Federico Fellini, smoulder like Marcello Mastroianni in his prime and frolic in fountains with Anita Exberg look-alikes (Anita Ekberg being the kind of immigrant we approve of). The Irish would get drunk and smile a lot, the English must all be ironic, and the Americans would drive to a properly Protestant church ever Sunday in Chevrolets with all the kids in the back seat earing Mickey Mouse ears. Wouldn't life be ever so much easier?

But life is not like that. Not at all. Oh, there are mustachioed Frenchmen, smouldering Italians and happy, drunk Irishmen but no country and no culture has never been a majority of any of those bad joke stereotypes. Yet, we cling to them and we are taught by nostalgia and the fear panderers to cling to them as an ideal that can never, ever, ever be reached.

To combat racism, the very first and overwhelming principle that must be realized is: the only constant is change. That is a massive psychological shift, a rejection of a fear of change that is so innate one wonders if it is actually genetic in make-up. Don't step out of the cave, young Fred Flintstone, for out there a saber-toothed tiger may be waiting to eat you. Stay with what you know, for what you know has enabled you to survive this far; whereas what you don't know might eat you.

So that is the thing. To embrace diversity, first and above all, you must accept reality. Find me any culture in any land in the last 500 years which for any 50 year period has had no substantial cultural change and no immigration for say half a century and if you aren't looking at the quote enquote lost tribes of Papua-New Guinea I am going to tell you that you are absolutely wrong. Everything. Changes. And everything changes all the time.

Quite likely, within the lifespans of some of you in this room, there were no black men in major league baseball, no French language on corn flakes boxes, possibly no Asians or Arabs in your hometown. Yet here we are, in Canada, post-Jackie Robinson, post-Pierre Trudeau's Official Languages Act, and post-Dr David Suzuki. Look past the hedge of your own front yard and see the kaleidoscope of the world.

And yet...and yet responsibility and indeed embrace requires two sets of arms in order to be accomplished. I don't know how many of you are familiar with the writing of Caitlin Moran, who is a columnist for The Times of London. If you aren't, please pick up one of her books. She is very funny and as I say, if you want to be taken seriously, make someone laugh. We have had, in North America and also in Europe, no end of court and tribunal cases regarding whether or not women should be allowed to wear burqas or hijab, the veil used to cover the faces of conservatively devout Islamic women. In simplest terms, you can't wear a mask when walking into a liquor store in case you hold it up and is not a burqa a mask? Similarly, the question has arisen that if an Islamic woman is called to testify at a trial, she should not be allowed to wear the hijab, as that in turns hides facial expression.

That in turns begs the question, can the blind serve on a jury, if the Sherlock Holemes-esque interpretation of dodgy facial language is so important? Well, in most countries of the world, including Canada, the UK and Australia, yes they can. So where exactly is the argument? With the rarity of the liquor store hold-up?

This is where I enjoy Caitlin Moran's take on the situation. Sit back and enjoy as I read a selection from one of her columns, after France had passed a law banning the burqa:

In the case of the French government against burqas, who is really telling them what to wear here? Well, I have a rule for working out if the root problem of something is, in fact, sexism. And it is this: asking `` are the boys doing it? Are the boys having to worry about this stuff? Are the boys the subject of a gigantic global debate on this subject?

And this is the basis on which I finally decided I was against both the French legislation, and women wearing burqas. France was the last European country to give women the vote, the French Senate is 76.5 % male, and it's never passed a law on which men can wear. Not even deck shoes; or alarming all-in-one ski-suits in bright pink nylon. Do there's clearly some sexism going on there.

Etcetera and so forth.

This is the tar baby of racism. If on the one hand, a person wishes to obey a cultural directive, they should have the freedom to do so, provided it does no harm. On the other hand, should that cultural directive interfere with the norms and established legal standards of the host nation, then one is left with the gigantic ethical dilemma of: Which has the higher standing – the rights of the individual, possibly a recent immigrant, or the established rights and freedoms of the larger host nation?

And it on this issue that I will fail you as a speaker for I cannot give you a simple take-away solution. Although at that, there are a few. Any decision based on the colour of one's skin is a decision based on the opinion of an idiot. Canada has more than a few of those in its past, whether it is the internment of citizens – citizens mind you – of Japanese ancestry, including Dr Suzuki and his parents during World War Two, or the refusal of entry of the refugee ship Komagata Maru of Sikhs fleeing danger in British India in 1914.

Can a foreign culture take over an established national culture, such as are the fears of the Le Pens and Gingriches of the world, cautioning against a stealth jihad? No, that is naked pandering to the fearful. Yet, is there something to be said for say the injection of government funds into established cultural institutions at the expense – given limited resources – of say supporting the development of new cultural institutions? Then yes. But then again, what is established and what isn't? There is not – and one cannot pretend there is – an easy answer.

If there is a clue or a path to a solution, perhaps it begins with the words of Elie Wiesel, 'No human race is superior; no religious faith is inferior. All collective judgments are wrong. Only racists make them.' And indeed, as the Austrian economist and sociologist Friedrich Otto Hertz once noted, 'At the heart of racism is the religious assertion that God made a creative mistake when He brought some people into being.'

The path to the elimination of racism is one followed by the individual and how the individual perceives other individuals. The basic unit of a society, nation, culture or group is the individual. Every one of us in this room is every 'one' of us. And each of us from birth have the same basic desires: peace, food, air, water, happiness and above all love.

Within our recent history there have been many great men and women who have fought the good fight against racism and bigotry: Nelson Mandela, Eleanor Roosevelt, Robert Kennedy and so, so many others. Perhaps the greatest and the most eloquent of them all was the late Dr Martin Luther King Jr. Dr King chose his weapon wisely in fighting for equality in an American society split by racial tension since the days of slavery until, sadly, our own sad days. He said, 'I refuse to accept the view that mankind is so tragically bound to the starless midnight of racism and war that the bright daybreak of peace and brotherhood can never become a reality.... I believe that unarmed truth and unconditional love will have the final word.'

If we can possibly see each other as individuals with the same needs as ourselves, rather than as white, black, Christian, Muslim, Scots, French or Chinese – all these rather silly labels that become imposed on babies as labels of fear and misunderstanding – if we can see each other as individuals, then we might be able to follow that path out of the dark forest of fear into the clearing of equality.

Of course there is much government can do; courts, tribunals and the United Nations can do. Hate speech must be enforced as a crime. Discrimination in employment and opportunity must be eliminated. No language should be seen as superior to another; no faith, culture or nationality was created to dominate another. We must respect our individual cultures and preserve them, certainly; for it is from those historic roots that all the beauty of civilization has emerged and cultural integrity must be honoured. Yet culture must be used as a book or a harp, and not as a sword or a gun.

However, no matter what government legislates it cannot and indeed should not micro-manage every single human interaction. Therefore, just as the path to equality begins with the recognition of the individual, so too then is it a path that must be walked by each of us as individuals. When we hear a racial slur, do we stand up against it or choose to wait for better time that never comes? When we hear of a tragedy somewhere in the world, do we make a blanket judgment and say, 'Oh that must be the work of "them"'? When we hear someone pray, or indeed choose not to pray in a way different from our own perception of God and the universe, do we think that person, 'got it wrong'?

I began this talk today – and I truly appreciate this time and the attention you have given me – by mentioning that there is no 'frozen moment' of time. Cultures and societies develop, change, alter themselves constantly. Twas ever thus, and so it shall always be. And it is a good thing. Just as those frightened, starving Irish immigrants a century and a half ago brought North America families whose descendants became authors, Presidents, scholars and musicians; just as those wrongfully transported slaves gave birth to generations of authors, scholars, musicians and eventually a President; so too will each immigrant have the potential to enrich our lives and the lives of future generations with their wisdom...if we give them half a chance.

And if we fail? If we fail now, what will the future – assuming humanity's survival – what will it think of us? I close with a poem that you may well have read in school but truly speaks to the heart of the matter – Percy Bysshe Shelley's Ozymandias:

I met a traveller from an antique land
Who said: "Two vast and trunkless legs of stone
Stand in the desert. Near them on the sand,
Half sunk, a shattered visage lies, whose frown
And wrinkled lip and sneer of cold command
Tell that its sculptor well those passions read
Which yet survive, stamped on these lifeless things,
The hand that mocked them and the heart that fed.
And on the pedestal these words appear:
`My name is Ozymandias, King of Kings:
Look on my works, ye mighty, and despair!'
Nothing beside remains. Round the decay
Of that colossal wreck, boundless and bare,
The lone and level sands stretch far away".

Let us be travelers, my friends, and walk the same path towards the light. Thank you.

(From my book **For Freedom: A Human Rights Reader 1948-2015)**

Nelson Mandela and the Struggle Against Apartheid

An excerpt from *Conversations with Myself,* by Nelson Mandela; specifically a conversation recorded with Richard Stengel:

STENGEL: I'd like to explain the whole process of how the decision to form MK [Umkhonto we Sizwe] (the paramilitary wing of the African National Congress – Ed.) *was made, At the Rivonia Trial you explain it in a general way. You said at the end, the second half of 1960, you and some collwgaues reached the conclusion that violence was going to be inevitable. How did this whole process happen? Did you talk first privately with people and then there was the decision of the Working Committee? Was there a build-up to the decision?*

MANDELA: No, what actually happened was I discussed the matter with Comrade Walter [Sisulu]. We discussed it because when Comrade Walter was going overseas, in 1953, I them said to him, 'When you reach the People's Republic of China, you must tell them, as them, that we want to start an armed struggle and get arms,' and then I made that speech in Sophiatown (where Mandela said the time for passive resistance had ended – Ed.). *I was pulled up for this but I remained convinced that this was the correct strategy for us. And then when I was underground I then discussed the matter with Comrade Walter and we decided to raise it at a meeting of the Working Committee. We raised the matter but, as I told you, I was dismissed very cheaply, because [Moses] Kotane – the secretary of the Party and of course a member of the Working Committee and the National Executive – his argument was the time had not come for that: 'Because of the severe measures taken by the government you are unable to continue in the old way. The difficulties have paralysed you and you now want to talk a revolutionary language and talk about armed struggle, when in fact there is still room for the old method that we are using if we are imaginative and determined enough.*

*You just want to expose people, you see, to massacres by the enemy. Yiu
have not even thought very carefully about this.' So he dismissed me like
that and he was quick to speak and everybody supported him. I
discussed the matter with Walter afterwards...The opposition was so
heavy that Walter did not even dare to say a word.* [laughs] *But he has
always been a very diplomatic chap, you know, but* reliable, *you know,
when you take a decision with hum. Very reliable. And so we reviewed
the matter, and he has always been resourceful, and he says, 'No, call
him alone; discuss it with him. I'll arrange for him to come and see you'
because I was already underground. So Kotane came and we spent the
whole day together. This time I was* very frank *and I said, 'You are
doing precisely what the Communist Party in Cuba did – they said the
conditions for a revolution had not yet arrived. Following the old
methods, you see, which were advocated by Stalin – how a revolutionary
situation can be identified, that is, by Lenin and Stalin. Here we have to
decide from our own situation. The situation in this country is that it is
time for us to consider a revolution, an armed struggle, because people
are already forming military units in order to start acts of violence. And
if we don't do so, they are going to continue.They haven't got the
resources, they haven't got the experience, they haven't got the political
machinery to carry out that decision. The only organisation that can do
so is the African National Congress which commands the masses of the
people. And you must be creative and* change *your attitude because
your attitude really is the attitude of a man who is leading a movement
in the old way when we were legal, who is not considering leading now
in terms of the illegal conditions under which we are operating.' So I
was able to be blunt in order to challenge him, you know ... I was able to
challenge him. So he says, 'Well, I'm not going to promise anything, but
raise it again.' So I went and raised it and he said, 'Well I'm still not
convinced, but let's give him a chance. Let him go and put these ideas to
the Executive, with our support.' So we then went down and everyone
· agreed. We went down to Durban at a meeting of the National Executive
of the ANC, Then Chief [Albert Luthuli], Yengwa and others opposed
this very strongly. So we knew of course that we were going to get a
proposition from the Chief, because he* believed *in non-violence as a*
principle, *whereas we believed in it as a* tactic, *although we couldn't
say so to court ... To the court, that is [during] the Treason Trial, we*

said we believe in non-violence as a principle, because if we had said [we believe in it] as a tactic it would give a loophole to the crown, to the state,

to say that at any time, when it suited us, we would use violence, and that in fact, that is what we had been doing. So we avoided that, but only *for that reason. We have always believed in non-violence as a tactic,* Where *the conditions demanded that we should depart from non-violence we would do so. So, but we knew that Chief was ... would oppose this,* and *he opposed it* very *well, but we persuaded him ...*

There is much to be admired about Nelson Mandela and his long, victorious struggle to end the apartheid policy in South Africa. That the transition to majority rule with a minimum of the chaos and corruption that rained down the majority of other post-colonial African republics is perhaps an even greater accomplishment than the end of apartheid itself. Mandela's Presidency should not be outweighed in history by the 27 years spent imprisoned on Robben Island.

—

Yet, a man is a man, a revolutionary a revolutionary; and myth should never overwhelm reality. Granted, Mandela was never quite so cold in public discourse as Mao Zedong who said, '*A revolution is not a dinner party, or writing an essay, or painting a picture, or doing embroidery; it cannot be so refined, so leisurely and gentle, so temperate, kind, courteous, restrained and magnanimous. A revolution is an insurrection, an act of violence by which one class overthrows another.'* Or at least, Mandela could not have said any such thing at the time. As the above interview clearly states, the non-violence for which he is so admired was a tactic and not a principle, but that was certainly not anything that one would want the government, courts or police to know. Had the African National Congress (ANC) been open about the formation of its MK paramilitary wing, there is an excellent chance that what we would be discussing here is a hope that apartheid might end in the future, rather than a brief analysis of how it was eliminated essentially upon Mandela and the ANC's victory in the 1994 elections.

It is always a wonder how it is that a regime with absolute power ever chooses to relinquish it. The clearest example may be the successful suffragette movements in the UK and US. Women had no vote (obviously enough), little or no economic power and were minimal – albeit individually powerful – voices in the print media of the early twentieth century. Yet they succeeded in securing equality at the ballot box with the passage of the 19th Amendment to the US Constitution in 1920 and in the UK with first the still-limited Representation of the People Act of 1918 then full equality with men in 1928. In both nations, as well as others around the world, essentially these were lobbying efforts with persuasive powers overcoming resistance.

However, even with the suffragettes there was a certain amount of violent conduct involved. In February 1913, the home of the future Prime Minister David Lloyd George was burnt to the ground by members of the Women's Social and Protective Union; this despite the fact that Lloyd George was a supporter of the women's suffrage movement. Prior to that, on November 18, 1910 (known as Black Friday) 200 women protestors were viciously assaulted and arrested by the police, also resulting in two deaths amongst the protestors. In the United States, a march by 5,000 suffragists in Washington was met by hostile crowds, police indifference, the arrival of the cavalry and 100 women hospitalized.

The point really is that even the most peaceful social changes are not always all that peaceful. Even Mohandas K. Gandhi with his benevolent theory of the use of Satyagraha (roughly translatable as soul-force) was arguably not opposed to roughing it up with the opposition. In much the same way as the women's rights activists essentially invited upon themselves the – obviously reprehensible and unjustified – police and mob brutality through their protest marches, the Gandhi-led campaigns of civil disobedience had predictable results. The British Arm massacred 400 of his followers in 1920, the national strike in India led to two dozen police officers being killed (Gandhi admitted he had blundered) and the Dharasana Satyagraha or Salt March of 1930 resulted in beatings to 320 or more non-violent protestors. That

Gandhi did not order or even ask his followers to perform violent acts is one thing; to suggest that he would not be aware that civil disobedience would cause massive personal injuries and arrests among those followers is to accuse him of naivete and no one can seriously argue he was that. To paraphrase Mandela, non-violence may have been his principle, but it was also a tactic to invite violence in the hopes of shocking the world.

To segue from Gandhi to Mandela, this highly acidic quote from Christopher Hitchens' 2011 essay, 'The Real Mahatma Gandhi':

And it is not disputable that Gandhi himself regarded his own versions of ahimsa and satyagraha as universally applicable. By 1939, he was announcing that, if adopted by "a single Jew standing up and refusing to bow to Hitler's decrees," such methods might suffice to "melt Hitler's heart." This may read like mere foolishness, but a personal letter to the Führer in the same year began with the words, My friend and went on, ingratiatingly, to ask: "Will you listen to the appeal of one who has deliberately shunned the method of war not without considerable success?" Apart from its conceit, this would appear to be suggesting that Hitler, too, might hope to get more of what he wanted by adopting a more herbivorous approach. Gandhi also instructed a Chinese visitor to "shame some Japanese" by passivity in the face of invasion, and found time to lecture a member of the South African National Congress about the vices of Western apparel. "You must not ... feel ashamed of carrying an assagai, or of going around with only a tiny clout round your loins." (One tries to picture Nelson Mandela taking this homespun counsel, which draws upon the most clichéd impression of African dress and tradition.)

As for Mandela and South Africa, although both he and Oliver Tambo (Secretary general of the ANC after Walter Sisulu was banned by the South African government in 1955) certainly had peaceful resistance in the ANC's Program of Action when the National Party removed all voting rights from blacks and the odiously termed 'coloreds', there was also to be found the phrase, 'such other means as may bring about the accomplishment and realization of our aspirations'. Presumably that meant something a little more forceful than writing a pleasant letter or two to John Vorster (the Minister of Justice who oversaw Mandela's trial and later South Africa's intransigent, utterly racist Prime Minister).

So if strikes, sit-ins and the support of brave journalists such as Doris Lessing were not going to do the trick, then the anti-apartheid revolution had to turn to violence. Between 1961 and 1963, the MK para-military wing of the ANC carried out 134 attacks against the apartheid regime. Generally these were attacks against such static objects as hydro-electric towers, remote from population bases to ensure that any loss of life was unlikely.

By 1965, with Mandela already in solitary confinement on Robben Island, MK moved to a higher level, with up to 800 members receiving military training at bases in Tanzania, Czechoslovakia, the Soviet Union and China. The principal difficulty these guerrilla trops faced was how to get back into South Africa itself. The neighbouring states of Mozambique and Rhodesia (sic) were not only of no help, they actively tipped off the South African government as to troop movements throughout the 1960s.

The attempt by MK to force military pressure on the South African government cannot in any real sense be deemed a successful one, although it did have one curious outcome. It has always been debatable just how much of an impact international sanctions actually have on any nation's internal politics; however, short of an actual armed intervention, they at least do put some muscle behind any diplomacy performed bu the greater global community. The scholar Alexander Laverty notes the following:

Talk in the 1960s of the use of sanctions to force a policy change were looked at with skepticism based on their predicted effectiveness. In fact one writer believed that only a world wide sanctions movement, coupled with a naval blockade would have the intended effect. For this to happen the UN would have to be willing to send in an invasion force to reinstall stability in the country after it had fallen into disarray following a world-wide boycott. The belief was that if South Africa was able to promote an appearance of stability then the Western powers would not have the resolve or justification for economic sanctions. Proponents of the sanctions movement in the 1960s believed that white South Africans would abandon the National Party in great numbers because many South Africans only supported white supremacy because of the high standard of living that the National Party gave them. This does not recognize that many whites were in fact Nationalists and would prove inflexible to outside pressure.

With the passing of Resolution 418 by the UN Security Council in 1977, international efforts to hurt the apartheid government turned to the form of an arms embargo. This resolution stemmed from the international attention created by the 1976 Soweto movement. This was revolt in a Johannesburg suburb that erupted against the apartheid government over a plan to hold instruction of maths and sciences in public schools in Afrikaans. The South African government in turn began to develop and produce more of their arms in country, but sophisticated systems such as high-performance aircraft, helicopters, and naval vessels were not so easily produced at home. However, self-sufficiency did come in the production of ammunition, military vehicles and communications equipment.

In short, by virtue of limiting sanctions to an armaments used against an unsuccessful guerrilla campaign, the effect was to propagate a homemade armament industry. This in turn has led to South Africa, even since the arrival of the ANC into government, becoming a major arms exporter, with sales reaching above $US 5 billion (in 1990 constant dollar terms) annually during the 1980s' embargo' and cracking US$18 billion by 2008, abeit having subsided since to a level clost to the level of 1980s activity.The biggest buyer, incidentally, was and is the United States. No wonder the US Congress had to override President Ronald Reagan's veto of greater sanctions in 1985. To the latter, Nobel Peace Prize Laureate Archbishop Desmond Tutu commented, 'In my view, the Reagan administration's support and collaboration with it is equally immoral, evil, and totally un-Christian. . . . You are either for or against apartheid and not by rhetoric. You are either in favor of evil or you are in favor of good. You are either on the side of the oppressed or on the side of the oppressor. You can't be neutral.' Indeed not; having an under-the-table partner in the apartheid regime willing to supply the various dirty wars of the US made the Reagan Administration (and those preceding and following him) anything but neutral. Being publicly opposed to apartheid was a tactic, not a principle.

Ultimately, the internal pressures in South Africa did cause the National Party government of President F.W. de Klerk to relent, free Mandela and return to one citizen/one vote. De Klerk, as quoted in an article by Ivan Fallon of the UK's The Independent said of his decision (which make no mistake, came as a shock to his own National Party) to end the voting restrictions on the day of Mandela's release:

"For many years I supported the concept of separate states," he says now. "I believed it could bring justice for everyone, including the blacks who would determine their own lives inside their own states. But by the early 1980s I had concluded this would not work and was leading to injustice and that the system had to change. I still believed in 1990 that the independent states had a place, but in the end the ANC had put so much pressure on them that they didn't want to go on. Had we offered Buthelezi a Zululand with Richards Bay harbour, he would have accepted that. But the whites wanted to hang on to as much as they could and were too greedy."

He had, he says, "long come to the realisation that we were involved in a downward spiral of increasing violence and we could not hang on indefinitely. We were involved in an armed struggle where there would be no winners. The key decision I had to take now, for myself, was whether to make a paradigm shift."

The lessons of Mandela, of the ANC, of South Africa itself are eloquent to anyone wishing to create a revolution of Human Rights in any country. One must be willing to take whatever route, or more to the point routes, that are necessary for the advance of freedom. To close this chapter, reproduced here are teh concluding paragraphs Mandela's famed Speech from the Dock during the Rivonia Trial at which he was sentenced to those 27 years on Robben island, years spent when for many of them he was allowed one visitor annually. Please note the final five words:

The lack of human dignity experienced by Africans is the direct result of the policy of white supremacy. White supremacy implies black inferiority. Legislation designed to preserve white supremacy entrenches this notion. Menial tasks in South Africa are invariably performed by Africans. When anything has to be carried or cleaned the white man will look around for an African to do it for him, whether the African is employed by him or not. Because of this sort of attitude, whites tend to regard Africans as a separate breed. They do not look upon them as people with families of their own; they do not realize that they have emotions - that they fall in love like white people do; that they want to be with their wives and children like white people want to be with theirs; that they want to earn enough money to support their families properly, to feed and clothe them and send them to school. And what 'house-boy' or 'garden-boy' or laborer can ever hope to do this?

Pass laws, which to the Africans are among the most hated bits of legislation in South Africa, render any African liable to police surveillance at any time. I doubt whether there is a single African male in South Africa who has not at some stage had a brush with the police over his pass. Hundreds and thousands of Africans are thrown into jail each year under pass laws. Even worse than this is the fact that pass laws keep husband and wife apart and lead to the breakdown of family life.

Poverty and the breakdown of family life have secondary effects. Children wander about the streets of the townships because they have no schools to go to, or no money to enable them to go to school, or no parents at home to see that they go to school, because both parents (if there be two) have to work to keep the family alive. This leads to a breakdown in moral standards, to an alarming rise in illegitimacy, and to growing violence which erupts not only politically, but everywhere. Life in the townships is dangerous. There is not a day that goes by without somebody being stabbed or assaulted. And violence is carried out of the townships in the white living areas. People are afraid to walk alone in the streets after dark. Housebreakings and robberies are increasing, despite the fact that the death sentence can now be imposed for such offences. Death sentences cannot cure the festering sore.

Africans want to be paid a living wage. Africans want to perform work which they are capable of doing, and not work which the Government declares them to be capable of. Africans want to be allowed to live where they obtain work, and not be endorsed out of an area because they were not born there. Africans want to be allowed to own land in places where they work, and not to be obliged to live in rented houses which they can never call their own. Africans want to be part of the general population, and not confined to living in their own ghettoes. African men want to have their wives and children to live with them where they work, and not be forced into an unnatural existence in men's hostels. African women want to be with their menfolk and not be left permanently widowed in the Reserves. Africans want to be allowed out after eleven o'clock at night and not to be confined to their rooms like little children. Africans want to be allowed to travel in their own country and to seek work where they want to and not where the Labor Bureau tells them to. Africans want a just share in the whole of South Africa; they want security and a stake in society.

Above all, we want equal political rights, because without them our disabilities will be permanent. I know this sounds revolutionary to the whites in this country, because the majority of voters will be Africans. This makes the white man fear democracy.

But this fear cannot be allowed to stand in the way of the only solution which will guarantee racial harmony and freedom for all. It is not true that the enfranchisement of all will result in racial domination. Political division, based on color, is entirely artificial and, when it disappears, so will the domination of one color group by another. The ANC has spent half a century fighting against racialism. When it triumphs it will not change that policy.

This then is what the ANC is fighting. Their struggle is a truly national one. It is a struggle of the African people, inspired by their own suffering and their own experience. It is a struggle for the right to live.

During my lifetime I have dedicated myself to this struggle of the African people. I have fought against white domination, and I have fought against black domination. I have cherished the ideal of a democratic and free society in which all persons live together in harmony and with equal opportunities. It is an ideal which I hope to live for and to achieve. But if needs be, it is an ideal for which I am prepared to die.

Kimberly

(Two lives were destroyed on February 7, 2010. My fiancée Kimberly McInnis had a brain aneurysm burst as we were standing in our kitchen one ordinary Sunday afternoon. As a result, she lost all short-term memory. At the request of her parents, I have never released in book form the harrowing months of emergency surgery and false and failed therapy. I do however share the following chapters with you. They have been copied here with only the lightest of editing, written as I felt within weeks of the events described. That event and what followed made me who I am today, occasionally foe better, yet often for worst.)

Chapter Four: February 7, 2010

I have been slow in writing this chapter. Oddly, because most of it is already written. Having begun writing the narrative of what happened on a normal humdrum February Sunday quite soon after - you do forget details, but on the other hand you need some time to find any rhythm, rhyme or meaning to it - I haven't wanted to go back and look at those notes.

I am optimistic about the outcome, as I write this 78 days later. For one thing you have to be. For another, I see no reason not to be. I have infinite faith in the marvel that is the human brain to re-generate and repair. Along among human organs it can re-route and re-wire. Imagine if the spinal cord could do that.

But still, tomorrow will be the first major assessment since our return to Thunder Bay. A gathering of all the therapists, the overseeing doctor, John, Marie, Amanda and me. We get to ask our questions. Or to be truthful, we get to express our fears in the form of questions. Welcome to medical Jeopardy where our only category today is The Future.

So we will come closer to knowing the outcome. I read a wonderful line in a recent novel called The Waterfront Bible. It said that we humans don't get it. There are no happy or sad endings. It just depends on where you end the story. I loved the line at the time and was putting it into my shared philosophy. Now I think it's bullshit. There are happy endings and there are sad endings and I want to know how this story comes out.

And therefore a return to that time and place 78 days ago is not a mental voyage I have looked forward to boarding. But I began this as a narrative of hope and thoughts and open feelings. To do that we must go back. And so we will.

I'm going to directly copy in the first organized version of my notes. the style may vary from the rest, but my mind was different then too. I'll italicize this portion.

Looking back on it, it is a bizarre series of randomly lucky decisions that kept Kimberly alive. I'll be sure to introduce you properly to her after I describe the events of that February day. My apologies to my favourite English Professor from Queen's University - George Clark - but Chaucer had it wrong. April isn't the cruelest month; February is. It's a miserable month usually. Most sensible northern mammals sleep through it. For the rest of us it is the month of cruel dashed hopes of an early spring buried in the cold white barfing of a Hudson's Bay front. It is separated far enough from Christmas and New Year's that its winter is about as welcome as the pine needles still being vacuumed up from the rug in February. And it also features Valentine's Day which trumps the Ides of March because February 14th has the dual power of being able to either bless or break your heart: and if it's really on its game the fates of St. Valentine can do both simultaneously. If things in your life are going to go weird, there is an excellent chance they're going weird in February. Our lives did.

But here are the lucky decisions:

1) It was a Sunday morning. I was coming off the first day off after six straight nights working as the Night Auditor at

the Comfort Inn in Thunder Bay. And yes, this is the life of a relatively successful writer in Canada. But the job is fine, the guests amusing usually and the hours conducive to long stretches of uninterrupted reading and writing. This in turn is important, as we'll get to later.

The point for now is that I was in "clothes at the end of the bed" mode, hadn't showered or shaved yet and felt a bit of a cold coming in. At the time, say up until 11:48 that morning, I was the pitiable one. That changed and changed so fast and hard it would give an owl whiplash.

I'd been watching Arsenal v. Chelsea on the upstairs flat screen TV in my Mother's sitting room. Mom had moved in with us at the age of 84 in October for both health and financial reasons. I had dreaded the coming of that day as do, in our most whispered confidences of the heart, the majority of you who have to take in a parent. The adolescent dream is to escape the parent - the middle-aged reality is adopting the parent. But there it was and it had become (pleasant) ritual for me to bring up waffles and sausages and coffee Sunday morning and watch a bit of the footie on The Score. Harmless fun and appropriate too. My Mom had made me a sports fan - raising an only child as a single Mom in the 1960s meant that things needed to be done to insure her son had manly influences. My biological father was a deceased Ontario syndicated political columnist named Don O'Hearn. My spiritual father was Vince Lombardi.

So football (real football) being the precisely timed game that it is had halftime fall at 11:45 AM or just after. I can down to our kitchen to get more coffee. Had halftime begun five minutes later or ended five minutes earlier, Kimberly would not be alive.

2) But halftime was when halftime was and I came into the kitchen where Kimberly was drying her hair in the adjoining bathroom. She has beautiful hair by the way. Long and blonde and healthy, it is the hair of a shade and texture that other women spend serious money in attempting to imitate but all they end up with is imitation itself. Because that beautiful hair had taken a bit longer to dry than usual, Kimberly made a crucial decision. Sunday

was going to be grocery day. Because I was a bit under the weather, she was going to go herself. Because the second of our two cars had bit the dust transmission-wise three months before, we were now bus people. That is not a disreputable term by the way and public transit becomes a sub-theme of this narrative. For now it's a digression.

She made the decision that instead of taking the bus that left in eight minutes from just down the block from our tall, skinny white house she would take the bus that left in 48 minutes. If she had taken the bus that left in eight minutes she would have collapsed on the snow and ice covered sidewalk and who's to say how long it would have taken for someone to notice and even at that how long would it have taken for someone to have actually done something like called 911? As you'll see, every delayed second could have killed her.

3) Because of the later bus Kimberly poured herself a second coffee. She pours great huge vat mugs of coffee then drinks about a third of the cup. That's her pattern...and I just found myself wondering if that will still be her pattern. The road to recovery has the same winding paths and blinding lights of Oasis's Wonderwall. And that was our song when we'd met a scarce five years before. I'll get to the history bit too.

But by virtue of her pouring that coffee because of the bus because of the hair, I had to make a fresh pot in order to bring two cups back upstairs. Kimberly I should mention tolerated footie as at least being better than hockey or North American football. But as you may have inferred, she wasn't a huge fan either. Still, she never minded when I would slip off to watch a game or hit the last channel button to a match when we were otherwise watching American Idol or a movie.

So waiting for that pot to brew meant I was in the kitchen when all hell broke loose

4) She was brushing her teeth. Kimberly brushes and cleans her teeth like George Barris buffing a hot rod. Care would be taken to the point that eventually one of the nurses in Toronto Western Hospital four days later would say, "She

really has lovely teeth." And at the time they were covered in God only knows What kind of post-operative mucus. But then, standing in front of the refrigerator that is covered in pictures of and by children, that leeks a bit from the freezer side and we really have to look at replacing that after we get the car and after we get the new stove - standing in front of that refrigerator she froze - stopped brushing - bent slightly over and said, "Oh my God."

"What?"

"I just got the worst pain in the back of my head. Oh my God."

"Here Love sit," I said pushing over a kitchen chair. The cordless phone was right where it shouldn't have been - on the kitchen table and not in the charger in the living room. "Is this a hospital thing? Should I be calling an ambulance?" I was already reaching for the phone.

"I don't know," she said. In Kimberly-speak, that meant to me, "I don't want the reason for this pain to be what it potentially might be so I don't want to say yes. But dear God get me medical help now."And to think we used to debate whether I was good at picking up signals. Turns out I'm not bad at it. Otherwise I might have taken "I don't know" as a suggestion to rest a bit and see what happens next. Maybe it'll pass. Portions of our graveyards are freshly turned every day because of people who say, 'Maybe it'll pass.'

I dialed 911. It connected.

5)   This was hugely important.

6)   Right after the call to 911 connected, Kimberly said, "No, wait." I pressed the red stop button on the phone.

"Why?"

"Maybe we should take a cab to the hospital."

"No, it's an ambulance." I re-dialed 911.

As I spoke to 911, explaining that I thought that Kimberly was having a stroke or an aneurysm, she said in a loud yet not screaming elementally surprised voice that "Oh my God! Now it feels like my whole head is going to explode." And one second later she fell off the kitchen chair face first on to the floor, where her left arm began to twitch in an irregular spasm, white foam began to flow from one corner of her mouth and she stopped breathing. I described the symptoms as quickly as I could to the 911 dispatcher, I said "Please hurry." And hung up.

Because I had hung up on that initial 911 call an immediate trace went out on it and the Thunder Bay Police were required to respond with the urgency of an emergency assignment - such as anyone being mugged, murdered or in cardiac arrest might just have done - called 911 with the last gasp. But because of that, there was a Thunder Bay Police Officer at the door within 20 seconds of Kimberly hitting the floor. It was so fast i literally had not even had time to touch her. That Officer began CPR. I do not know CPR. Without that Officer, Kimberly would not be alive today.

As it turned out, the ambulance and paramedics arrived within three minutes. While they were performing the initial triage assessment, I felt I should tell someone what was going on. I phoned Kimberly's daughter Amanda, who had moved out in October with our two year old grandson Logan.

I will pick up the story again. But next I think should be the results of the assessment. Peace.

Chapter Six: How are Skis and Philosophy Related?

Answer: Both benefit from regular waxing. In the next chapter we'll resume the medical narrative, but the thunderbolts of emotion and reflection had begun as soon as I got off the phone with Kimberly's 19 year old daughter Amanda -

"You need to know this. Mom's collapsed in the kitchen, but the ambulance is here and we're on our way to the hospital."

"What do you mean, 'collapsed'?"

"That has not yet been determined. It appears that she has suffered either an aneurysm or a stroke."

That has not yet been determined? Who talks like that? Why am I talking like that? I started wondering about this while I was grabbing Kimberly's prescriptions out of the cupboard above the stove (Yeah, lousy place, but remember there's a two year old grandson and a six month old border collie sniffing around.); and racing up and down the stairs twice to tell my eighty-four year old Mom what was going on and phoning my friends Kim Hansen and Paul Ruebsam to please come over to the house to keep an eye on her; and getting together all the Health Cards, Social Insurance Cards, Credit Cards and every other darn thing that could be stuffed in a pocket because I was already thinking this might mean hopping an air ambulance and there wasn't going to be time to pack.

But who talks like that? Then I remembered. That's who I am, that's what I do. There have been five or six moments of Maximum Stress Overdrive in my life - why is there not a band named Maximum Stress Overdrive? - not the least of which being open heart surgery - and my emotional reaction to all of them has been to Go Vulcan. That isn't just some cheesy Star Trek metaphor designed to give this story Geek Appeal. I literally start channeling Spock, stand with my hands clasped behind my back and say things like, 'That has not yet been determined.'

True Story: When I woke up in the Intensive Care Unit at the Hamilton Hospital after my quadruple bypass and Kimberly was allowed in to see me, she asked me how I was. I replied, "It was fun." So sometimes you need a little Captain Kirk mixed in with the Spock. And yes, Kimberly hates when I tell that story. I had never thought of it before now, but I guess it could be somewhat demeaning to the emotional trauma she must have been going through when I grin a little William Shatner grin and say, "It was fun." I'm sorry dear. I look forward to your reading this. I get it now.

I get it now. Yes, that is the thing, the nut inside the shell split from a long fall from a high branch on a tall tree. I always liked and quoted Samuel Johnson's line about an impending hanging concentrates the mind wonderfully. Compared to literally not knowing second by second if a vasal spasm or a seizure was going to snap away the life of the woman I adored more than anything, snap it away like a broken fishing line, gone into cold depths of water and mystery...compared to that, I'll go with the hanging.

This time, this completely focused reality, it is so hard to describe but it has to be described. You hear the cliches about time moving fast or time moving slow, but neither of those are right, not in our case. Time moved very smoothly - activity, then wait - activity, then wait - activity, then wait - but what was different about the time and how it blended with the atmosphere, the bundling grey clouds of fate kneading themselves in the imaginary air was how both sight and insight sharpened their image. It was as though everything for weeks was being filmed by Gregg Toland in his Citizen Kane pomp. Things that on an ordinary day might not even be noticed but now they were in vivid detail because you never know ... I never knew what might be importanta nd what might prove to have meaning during this time of madness that required absolute calm in response. Otherwise it all might have been an emotional shipwreck and the last thing Kimberly needed was for me to be in Helpless Castaway mindset.

And I just had this eerie sense that I've mentioned several times already that Kimberly was not going to die. I don't know why, but I was relaxed about it as soon as the ambulance arrived. 'Relaxed' may be too strong a word. I'm man enough to admit to a good possibility of having gone into shock. But - shock or no, the confidence was still there. Maybe it was faith, maybe it was that I'd lived through two 'deaths' already - on the operating table for bowel surgery, and the quadruple bypass. I was very glad for the knowledge of that bypass, by the way, as we'll get to when we arrive at Toronto Western Hospital and the surgical options were presented to me.

So all that, and there is never any *one* reason for anyone's thoughts or actions. Humans tend to be complex crystals. Yet, there was a significant part of me - the writer and reviewer part of me - that just felt that in terms of narrative there was no way Kimberly's life was going to play out this way. Two divorces, two kids, on-going custody and support battles, house fires, a man in her life (me) who emotionally went off the rails when his financial practice collapsed, house fires, Amanda leaving the house, and we were just getting past all that. There was light at the end of the tunnel. I had beaten my demons ... if I am going to honestly write this book I have to write this book honestly ... I was clearly an alcoholic for a year and a half. I'd totally quit drinking - cold turkey - four months before all this happened. Thank God. I was finally back on my game. I needed to be, to put it mildly.

But Kimberly's life was not meant to end here. I like to think that God has a pretty good sense of story - He's quite good at character development - and I didn't buy that this would be the last chapter. We have medical knowledge. People survive strokes. People survive aneurysms. So long as a breath can be drawn, there is hope.

I thought of two sports figures during those minutes after I had called Amanda and before the stretcher was placed in the ambulance. I've mentioned Bret 'The Hitman' Hart. He'd survived a massive stroke and was healthy physically and mentally. And then there was the late basketball coach of the North Carolina State Wolfpack, Jim Valvano. Jimmy V. Valvano had died of cancer at a young age, but before he did, he gave one of the great triumphant speeches of courage ever made. You can watch it on YouTube. Don't give up. Don't ever give up.

It is indeed the one great virtue that grows as a result of being a sports fan. You see so many examples of courage, of trust, of faith and of seemingly impossible things that become possible. You never give up.

But now I had been told that there was no room for me in the ambulance and I had to start considering bus routes or could we afford a cab? Things were at an interesting point financially, as I'll get to explaining shortly. But the police officer who had initiated CPR on Kimberly offered to give me a lift. I went to get in the back of his cruiser, but he said, "Uh, I'd rather you didn't sit back there sir. It's not exactly hygienic." Ah yes. It was a Sunday morning after a Saturday night. Good times. This was just the right point to inject some levity and the right point to end this chapter.

Chapter Seven: A Great Day to be a Saint

There was business to be attended to while I was being driven to the hospital. Thank God for that Vulcan state of mind. And by the way, I would have paid serious money to have heard the late Johnny Cash sing a mournful country song titled That Vulcan State of Mind. Not to go out on a limb or anything, but it appeared unlikely I'd be able to work that night. So I called the Comfort Inn on the cell phone and said that Kimberly had suffered an aneurysm or stroke and I wouldn't be in at eleven. My colleague Amanda Moore took care of everything from there and so began a time of tremendous support from everyone at the hotel and the entire Comfort Inn and Clarion chain. You need help to survive a crisis and as you'll keep seeing, my employers did it in spades.

So that was taken care of. There was still the matter of my Mom. Aileen O'Hearn is for all intents and purposes a shut-in. She was active and vigorous and healthy and had such an iron will that she would quite smoking for two years - cold turkey - then re-start 'because I was bored' for a few years then quit cold turkey again.

Then she had a brain injury as the result of a virus and after that along with several broken bones and joints later she is as she is. On the night I moved her to our house I told her that she could only smoke outside and she sat out on the front lawn in a white plastic folding deck chair trying to decide if the sacrifice was worth it. She begrudgingly admitted that it was and she's been with us ever since. And will I have to put her in a home for the aged?

To move to the present, briefly, that is a worry. Will I possibly be able to handle two invalids at home while also working a midnight shift? I may be good, but am I *that* good? There's enough Ric Flair meets Pierre Trudeau swagger and arrogance in me to say, 'Oh hell yeah.' Actually, if you'll indulge me while I get something out of my system, I'm going to let off steam and write the wrestling promo of my life right now. Feel free to skip forwards to the squad car following it.

FLAIR: (*enters ring in expensive suit and sunglasses while Thus Spake Zarathustra plays - removes sunglasses, places them in handkerchief pocket of suit jacket, stares down his large, masked opponent Aneurysm who responds by gesturing for as fight while looking quickly from side to side, checking for the nearest escape route. He then lifts the microphone and speaks.*) Do you have any idea who's standing in front of you? WELL DO YOU? I want to hear you say MY NAME! Say it!

ANEURYSM: (mumbling) I'm not playing games here -

FLAIR: Say it!

ANEURYSM: What in hell do you want? Are you crazy or something?

FLAIR: Crazy? Crazy? CRAZY? You think I'm crazy? W000-oooo! You're damn right I'm crazy! And you want to know why I'm crazy? Because of - YOU! I have been living with you in my space, in my ring, in my house, in my family for TOO LONG! The first day was TOO LONG! One month was TOO LONG! Two months was TOO LONG! Now four months - TIME'S UP! But before I beat you to death right here, in this ring, tonight, I want to be sure you know the name behind the last face you're ever going to see. Now ... what's ... my ... name?

ANEURYSM: You're Ric Flair.

FLAIR: WHO?

ANEURYSM: You're Hubert O'Hearn.

FLAIR: WHO?

ANEURYSM: You know who you are!

FLAIR: You're damn right I know who I am! I am the one person, the one man, the only jet flying (*waits for crowd pop*) limousine riding, styling and profiling son of a gun! - who's not afraid of you. I'M NOT AFRAID OF YOU! Why should I be? WHY IN HELL SHOULD I BE? I've been beating punks like you for TWENTY YEARS! One of 'em ripped my bowels apart. I beat him! One of them tried to stop my heart! I beat him! I've taken on all your crew - Failure! Debt! Illness! Booze! - and everyone of 'em is lying in a big blue box in a back alley because I BEAT 'EM ALL!

ANEURYSM: I know you've got a great record Flair. Hey I respect you man -

FLAIR: NO YOU DON'T! You DON'T respect me! You FEAR ME! That's why you wouldn't go after me because you knew I'd beat you down. You attacked my wife instead ... you attacked the kindest person on Earth because you thought you could beat her. Well guess what ... you ain't going to beat her either. Because (*slowly prods on finger into Aneurysm's chest*) you didn't just attack Kimberly Mc Innis ... I got a surprise for you ... you attacked THE NATURE GIRL! And she's every bit as tough as The Nature Boy! (*slaps Aneurysm across the face, Irish whip into the corner followed by hard chops to Aneurysm's chest, the brawl broken up by security guards, road agents, the N.W.O. and hey look, isn't that Dallas Page?*)

Yes, well, when the emotions are bottled for too long, sometimes the cork opens with force. While in the squad car I talked on the cell phone to Paul Ruebsam. Paul is a Personal Support Worker and one of my absolute dearest friends. He had been giving Mom her weekly showers for the past three years and I knew that he could explain to her what was going on. It also occurred to me that this was Super Bowl Sunday and I had invited him over to the house to watch it. There had been a simmering difference of opinions between Paul and Kim Hansen (who I had called to move into the house) for several months, so I guessed that they would either kill each other or figuratively kiss and make up. Thank God it was the latter. And thank God it was figurative.

I've always played silly little mind games with myself - if this happens (the bus arrives in the next minute, say) that will happen (a review will be accepted by a paper). They make time pass. The beloved New Orleans Saints, representing the hard-luck city of the century thus far were underdogs to the jet fuel offence of the Indianapolis Colts. I've always been an NFC guy anyway and although the Saints had beaten Brett Favre's Vikings two weeks earlier I wanted the Saints to win. So I played a silly mind game. If the Saints win the Super Bowl then Kimberly will come out of all this okay. If the Saints lost, I'd dismiss the result as unconnected to our crisis - illogical, captain. But if the Saints won, it would be a sign. 'Damn it Spock, it doesn't have to make sense! It's a song!' Or a sign.

Kimberly's Dad called me as I was walking in to the hospital emergency room. I could hear her Mom crying in the background. They were on their way to Thunder Bay, as were Deanna with Kayla and Maija. As was Amanda. And Amanda had called Bradley's father to arrange for him to come as well.

Hell of a place for a Super Bowl party ...

Chapter Eight: The Long, Long Night Begins

It would have been around 12:30PM when I arrived at the hospital. For those unfamiliar with Thunder Bay Regional Health Sciences Centre (what you or I would call a Hospital), it is a work of art more than it is a work of efficiency. It sprawls like a pride of lions across a hilltop - not the most advantageous spot when the parking for Emergency lies at the bottom of a steep, 50 foot slope - just what you want when you might be pulling up with a wife in labour, a heart attack or a severed limb. Granted, one can always damn the signs and drive up to the Emergency Room door and work out the parking later, but we are Canadians and we obey the printed rules. But the examination rooms and patient rooms are as spacious as the hospital sets on The Young and the Restless. (Kimberly's favourite soap and I admit to a man-crush on Victor Newman. That is the way a man is meant to age.) A troop of boy scouts could easily bivouac by the bedside.

All this money spent on design - lots of curvy wooden things and happy forest creatures frolicking in patterns set in the floor tiles - meant that there would be shortages elsewhere. Forgive me for dripping melting sarcasm all over the page but I'm so pleased that cost cutting was only on unimportant things like the ability to perform a heart bypass or brain surgery. Much later, when we had returned to Thunder Bay, a Doctor at Thunder Bay Regional told me that they had the human resources, the doctors with the skills, to perform the surgery that eventually saved Kimberly's life. They just didn't have the money to purchase the additional equipment they would need. It's a pricing problem. This is why, although I am not a red flag waving socialist, the one industry I would support a government takeover of is the medical industry - pharmaceuticals and equipment manufacturers alike. I absolutely am skeptical of the Adam Smith or Milton Friedman argument that only a private company in a competitive market will press the

research and innovation to stay ahead in the market. The
competition in a government-run system would be in the form of

the research grants doled out to successfully competing bidders.
Furthermore, the actual manufacture of pills or machines would
also be contracted out. the difference would be that the
government, as principal buyer through the hospital system and
subsidized drug plans, would also set the most advantageous
price for itself while still achieving a result expectation of
excellence.

That may have been quite a digression but it leads to a narrative
point. Dr. Haq performed the initial examination and MRI and
informed me that there were two and a half brain aneurysms
spotted, one of which had burst. As a result, cranial fluid was
spilling out into the narrow liquid shock absorption space
between the brain and the skull, with the further risk that the
'escape valve' for the fluid might become plugged, meaning
pressure would continue to build up with an extreme risk of
seizure (stroke) or rampant death among the brain cells. As you
might have guessed, surgery was recommended. Surgery that
could not be done in Thunder Bay. An air ambulance was being
diverted to Thunder Bay and now it was a time of waiting while
Dr. Haq called around various hospitals to find out who had
space for emergency brain surgery.

Haq: "I am going to see if they have space in Toronto. Otherwise,
you might be going to Ottawa, London ... or maybe Winnipeg."

He said 'Winnipeg' with the same mood and tone of a diner who
has just tasted a badly made soup. I instantly despised Winnipeg,
a city I'd previously liked. I secretly sent out a telepathic message
to flocks of pigeons to feed heartily then congregate and defecate
on the Golden Boy's head.

It would have been around 3:30 when the word came that it
would be Toronto Western Hospital. I didn't know it then but I
soon would that we had won the air ambulance lottery. Besides

being acknowledged the finest neurological research hospital in Canada, one could make fair argument that it might even have that standing in all of North America. And yes, I have thought many, many times - what results if it had been somewhere else ... even Winnipeg.

By now the family had begun to congregate, first in the large and comfortably padded Intensive Care waiting room. Later, we had enough room to go into Kimberly's ICU room - as I said, the place is nothing if not spacious. We were all there - John and Marie, Deanna, our nieces Kayla and Maija, and later Bradley, Amanda, and her new boyfriend Tyler. This by the way was the first time Kimberly and I had met Tyler. It certainly avoids any awkward pauses in the conversation.

Kimberly was of course sedated, but not too heavily for obvious reasons. One of the things I would marvel at was how precisely sedation could be measured. In Toronto, when they wanted to wake Kimberly up for testing, a mere twist of a dial and seconds later she would be awake. To tell an anecdote here that possibly should have been saved for later, when I had to return to Thunder Bay from Toronto for a week in order to (I thought at the time) arrange for Employment Insurance, talk to work about the situation and make sure Kim Hansen hadn't killed my Mom and our dog in the mean time), the last words a very friendly and completely informative nurse said to me before I headed out to the streetcar was, "Don't worry, she's just on a happy little cloud. She's on the same stuff Michael Jackson was on."

And of course that worked out so well the last time ...

Chapter Nine: The Flight

The scene at the hospital while waiting to leave Thunder Bay seems to move so slowly in memory. Because the air ambulance had to be diverted to Thunder Bay and there was a shift change at 7PM, it wasn't until after 9PM when the ambulance finally took

Kimberly and me to the airport. The two hour drive from
Atikokan had I think allowed a certain numbness to take over the
family's initial shock. I shall never, ever forget our two nieces
though. Kayla, the eldest and the prospective writer I admire, was
the one person free enough to start crying. I promised her I would
bring her Auntie Kim back safe and sound. (Thank God I was able
to keep my word.) And Maija gave me a bracelet from her wrist.
You know those rubber bracelets everyone wears? This was a
black one with little white footprints on it - footprints in the sand.
I never took it off until, sadly, some time after we came back to
Thunder Bay it had to have broken and was lost. I wasn't able to
keep my promise on that one. I'd said that I'd wear in until Auntie
Kim was home - not just Thunder Bay - home. Maybe the bracelet
will re-appear before then. I'll be sure and let you know.

There remains one curiousity. Some eight weeks after we were
given a copy of the official medical report, which alludes to
Kimberly suffering two seizures during the ambulance trip. It
does not state whether that was ground or air transport, but
except for the short time when we were separated for the ride
from our house to the hospital, I was with her every step of the
way and I saw no seizure.A minor point certainly, but still one of
curiousity.

We boarded the ambulance to the airport early in the third quarter
of the Super Bowl. The Saints, who looked rocky early, were
starting to rise in confidence and looked a good bet to knock off
the favoured Colts. Well, I'd just have to read the papers the next
day.

That - by the way - was a minor blessing in winning the medical
lottery and ending up in Toronto. Thank God for a city with four
vibrant daily newspapers, as you can imagine how many hours
were spent sitting and reading.

And as we boarded the spanking new Orange Air ambulance, I
knew two things. One, this would be the most dangerous time of
all. One hour and forty five minutes in the air, where, if anything
went wrong the odds were deeply against us surviving.

Paramedics are wonderful practitioners and all the telemetry was being sent directly to Toronto Western, but still ... if Kimberly had taken a stroke that likely would have been it. I would find out a few hours later that she was at an 80% risk of having a stroke for the first seventy-two hours after the aneurysm burst. Well, in all the good sports movies, the underdog wins anyway.

It was tense, no doubt of it. I believe my stress levels were emitting enough particle energy to power a small apartment building. But I couldn't help still feeling calm and confident. This was going to be an extraordinary time in our lives, but we were going to survive it. As I've said before - that's what a good writer would do, and God is an excellent plot writer.

I was also so damn glad and relieved we were going to Toronto. A) and of course because we were going to the best medical care in Canada; yet also B) I knew that I could survive in Toronto for an extended stay. There was my semi-sister Martha (Dad had complicated relationships with women.) and I knew that I could get a cheap hotel if need be. I was certainly at the right point in life in terms of working for a hotel chain and getting an employee discount.

I'd lived there. I'd loved living there. Toronto and I got along very well, like a couple of old friends who only see one another once every couple of years. I've never found it un-friendly or snooty. Dad did. Hated it for every one of the thirty years he lived there. I was of the opinion that if you have to live in an asylum, it might as well have cultural attractions and cheap restaurants. Toronto qualified.

And then we landed at the Toronto Island Airport and took the short ambulance ride up Bathurst to Toronto Western.

Letter to Kimberly

January 7, 2012

Dear Love of My Life -

It's hard to believe that in another month and a day it will be two years since you had the brain aneurysm. You don't know what I'm talking about. 'What brain aneurysm?', you're thinking or even saying out loud. I know you don't remember it and that's why I'm writing you this letter. You still won't remember much or any of it; however you'll at least have reference material. heh

Now I'm calling this a letter, except it's a whole lot more than that. I want to write down everything I can - what our lives were like before the aneurysm, what it was like while you were right on the edge between life and death and what it's been like during these long, long months of recuperation.

I have to tell you, it hasn't been easy. I never had any doubt - not a bit of it - that you were going to survive a little blood vessel in your brain going Pop!, no matter how dangerous that was. From the moment the ambulance arrived, I was blissfully confident that the doctors would get you through the crisis. Blissfully confident, or I was in shock, In retrospect, it might have been more of the latter. Either way, that part was right. You're here and alive and able to read this.

The hard part for me is not being able to take care of you. Now, you may think that you don't need much taking care of - as you used to say, you have steel ovaries - but you do. You do need taking care of. Because of that aneurysm, you have no short term memory effectively. If you walked out of the house and went three steps down the street you might not be able to find your way back, or be able to tell a neighbour, a cop, a bus driver what your address was.

I reviewed a book a few months ago - that's what I do now by the way, I review books - called Please Look After Mom. It's a novel and a very huge bestseller by a South Korean writer named Kyung sook-Shin. She was very nice by the way. I interviewed her with the help of a translator. (I do that too - I interview interesting people for magazines and papers. I'll tell you why in a bit.) Her book is about a Korean family's Mom coming to Seoul to visit her children and becoming lost. They never find her. Her family goes through a lot of guilt and pain over that. I don't want that feeling. I don't want you becoming lost. I love you. Or as you'd say to me or the children, 'I love you dammit.'

LOL - I think that might actually be a better title for this than A Letter to Kimberly. I should call this I Love You Dammit. Do you think people would be more likely to buy this if that was it's name?

Buy this. Ah yes, I'd better tell you about that end of things. This letter is going to be a book. That means two things: One, this is going to be a very VERY long letter; and Two, the most personal and private parts of our lives are going to be part of public discourse. I worry, I worry a lot, that may be a wrong thing to do. Am I exploiting a personal tragedy for personal gain?

That's a tough nut to crack and I'm not sure that the answer I've come up with - to write and publish this - is the correct one. People have advised me both ways. Even within our own family I've received different pieces of advice. One told me that it would be embarrassing for me to tell the world our feelings about each other, comments on our sex life, our shared observations on the world. On the other hand, your daughter and my beloved step-daughter Amanda thinks I should just go for it.

Eventually I based my decision by weighing Love on a scale. What is the most loving thing to do? Is it to keep our story private, or is it to share it with the world? I'm going with sharing. Why?

There are a few reasons. I've mentioned that if you were three steps outside our house you might well not be able to find your way home. I repeat that because you've probably forgotten what was written a page or two ago. That's okay. I have patience for my patient (heh heh). Low-rent puns aside, the only way I can bring you home and keep you at home and make us whole again is by being able to make a living while staying at home myself. We needs us the money sweetheart. And, as I'm quite lousy at threading little beads into necklaces, or painting watercolour paintings of the Sleeping Giant, the only skill I have that can be done out of our house is writing. This.

We need the big Deal, the big Score, the bestseller that goes to the Toppest of the Poppest as John Lennon used to say. I think a lot about John Lennon these days. I'll explain that one too. Shortly.

So there's that. To bring you home I need to write and yours/ours is a pretty compelling story. I think it will sell. I bloody hope it will sell! Yet that isn't enough.

Here's the other side of it. You were a healthy person, all strong and in shape from yoga and swimming and working out to the WiiFit until February 8, 2010 when at 11:50AM you were as sick as a person can be. Our lives changed as much as lives can change short of one of us dying. Dying, I dare say, is easier. I'm glad you DIDN'T die! Dear God, don't be getting that one wrong! Death though is the curtain closing on a theatre act. Scene's done, re-set, on with the next. We didn't, we don't, have that. Instead our story goes on without any big crescendo announcing the end of the opera.

And that, as I said way back at the beginning of all this, is hard. As unique as our story is - all stories are unique - lots of people go through similar every hour, every minute, every day. Someone a person loves gets diagnosed with cancer, or has a stroke, or a car accident, or develops depression … it's a nearly endless list. And while there's a medical system in place for the cancer, or stroke, or accident victim, there's that Other Person who needs help too.

I was the one left standing. I was the one who wished he'd fallen.

Do you see? You've always kept your love and compassion right at the surface and shared it without blinking an eye. I remember when one of my best friends for years had a relationship go - Splat! - and he arrived at our door in tears. You hadn't even known him for that long; we hadn't been together that long. Yet, an outside observer would never have known which of us had known him the longest or who loved him the most.

So we, or I, need to do this, to write this book. The message is simple: You're not alone. After all, you know how much I love my Liverpool Reds footy team. I KNOW you remember how I'd sing Amanda's baby Logan to sleep at night with the Liverpool anthem. You'll Never Walk Alone. I'm going to reprint the lyrics so you can sing along and...as Spock said to McCoy - remember:

When you walk through a storm
Hold your head up high
And don't be afraid of the dark

At the end of the storm
Is a golden sky
And the sweet silver song of the lark

Walk on through the wind
Walk on through the rain
Though your dreams be tossed and blown

Walk on walk on with hope in your heart
And you'll never walk alone
You'll never walk alone

When you walk through a storm
Hold your head up high
And don't be afraid of the dark

At the end of the storm
Is a golden sky
And the sweet silver song of the lark

Walk on through the wind
Walk on through the rain
Though your dreams be tossed and blown

Walk on walk on with hope in your heart
And you'll never walk alone
You'll never walk

You'll never walk
You'll never walk alone.

Yes, I'm sure you remember that. And that's why our story has to be shared, so people know that they never walk alone. If I'm wrong, I'm so so sorry. Even if I'm wrong, I hope someone someday thinks I was right, because what we're doing helped.

I'm going to have to take a writing break soon, as our little border collie Stella needs some attention, plus my typing finger is getting worn out. there are a few things I need to tidy up in this first chapter.

By the way - do you remember Stella? That little black-and-white bundle of love sure remembers you. She was just six months old when you fell to the kitchen floor with the aneurysm. I remember her standing over you, watching the ambulance attendants. Oh, and Stella sure is happy when you're home for a visit. When you leave, to go back to Atikokan with your parents, it is always the same thing: she will search through every room of the house looking for you, then she plunks down in front of the front door and I can't get her to move for hours. Stella waits for her 'Mommy' to come home so she can be the first to greet her.

I know how Stella feels.

I mentioned John Lennon earlier. (Look back a couple of pages - you'll find it my Love) I think about John a lot - I usually refer to him on Facebook as 'Johnny Beatle' even though that drives some people right up the wall. I identify with John. Here's why:

- He was angry a lot; I'm angry a lot
- He was funny a lot; I'm funny a lot
- He was a man of peace; I'm a man of peace
- He adored Yoko; I adore you

Sometimes when I'm alone, usually late at night when I have a night off from the job I keep so you can maintain your Health Benefits for all the pills you have to take, I start playing YouTube video after YouTube video of The Beatles or John in his solo career and I start to sing along, just the way I used to sing Logan to sleep when You'll Never Walk Alone didn't do the trick. What song do I sing?, you ask or if you didn't I'm going to pretend that you did because after all *I'm* writing this. I sing the last single Johnny Beatle released before he was shot down; shot down the night before me Dad's funeral. Starting Over:

Our life together is so precious together
We have grown, we have grown
Although our love is still special
Let's take a chance and fly away somewhere alone

It's been too long since we took the time
No-one's to blame, I know time flies so quickly
But when I see you darling
It's like we both are falling in love again
It'll be just like starting over, starting over

Everyday we used to make it love
Why can't we be making love nice and easy
It's time to spread our wings and fly
Don't let another day go by my love
It'll be just like starting over, starting over

Why don't we take off alone
Take a trip somewhere far, far away
We'll be together all alone again
Like we used to in the early days
Well, well, well darling

It's been too long since we took the time
No-one's to blame, I know time flies so quickly
But when I see you darling
It's like we both are falling in love again
It'll be just like starting over, starting over

Our life together is so precious together
We have grown, we have grown
Although our love is still special
Let's take a chance and fly away somewhere

Starting over...

That's the thing. We'll never Get Back. We can Start Over. That's what keeps me alive.

[more]

What is a Soul?

These chapters in this on-going book/blog manuscript generally start with a major event in Kimberly's life, or an observation I want to share. Then I start to write and let the process take me (and you) wherever it leads.

Not this one.

In some ways, I'm not even sure if this chapter even belongs here in this book. This is not part of Kimberly's recovery, although it is prompted by it. I am going to tell you a story that even some of my closest friends have never heard. This is a story about, well, dying.

I am one of those people you hear about who have had what is called a 'near-death' experience. 'Near-death' makes it sound like a scary (but ultimately safe) amusement park ride. Wheeeee! We'll whoop and swoop and sail upside down but we'll end up back at the start minus just a bit of breath and the pocket change that rattled onto the ground.

Well no. No, it's not quite like that. It was June 28, 1989. I'd been hospitalized for five days with severe abdominal pain. Tests had not uncovered the reason, but my white cell count was soaring and something had to be done. That something was exploratory surgery. I was rolled in to the operating room about 1PM. My last words as the anesthetic took hold were to the nurse looking down at me behind her robin's egg blue surgical mask. "You have lovely eyes." I thought if I was going to check out, I might as well go out in style. I've equally been known to whistle in the dark.

The surgeon opened up my abdomen and ...

"Holy s**t," he said. (I don't want spam blockers slamming walls up all over this blog.)

I had, more or less, exploded. Blood, lots of blood, a geyser of blood. It turned out I had diverticulitis and one of the diverticuli had burst. My blood pressure dropped like a crashing stock market, my heart announced it was quitting and I was quite dead for about 90 seconds. Stepped out of life for a breath of fresh air. Most refreshing.

I won't bother with aching descriptions of how it feels to wake up with the sense of a grenade having gone off in your guts, for the significance of the story is in that 90 seconds and how that minute and a half has affected me to this day.

I have been told that it was the morphine. I have been told that this is not unusual. I have been told that it was an instinctive or natural reaction to the high stress of near-death. If you choose to believe any of that, go right ahead. I know what I saw. Onwards.

I remembered it all and was prompted to by a vision of Mary, in a guise of Our Lady of Hope. *A very nice Protestant Minister who I confided in told me that Catholics tend to see Mary and Protestants see Martin Luther. I know what I saw.* She took me back through the memory of those 90 seconds, as I traveled through a long and frescoed hallway, too long and too quickly to actually see the paintings on the wall, although on instinct I believed that they were scenes from my life this far.

Then at the end of the hallway I exited into ... space ... time ... everywhere and nowhere ... neither here nor there but rather here and there. And I knew that this was one passage into post-mortal life. One could, if one wished be one with the universe. This was the first point of puzzlement for me. Bear it in the back of your mind as we continue.

Next, I was shown a more traditional Heaven. There were my grandparents, long gone but now young and in love and heading off for a picnic. Later, I told my mother and my aunt some things I had heard them say and the living confirmed those phrases as typical of what their parents would say.

Finally, I was told or shown (again, both and either) that one could become whatever one wanted: be reincarnated as a person again, an animal, a rock.

There was more, much more. For the first few years afterwards I had frequent premonitions of events great (war in the former Yugoslavia, the tragedies of the Catholic Church, the end of the Berlin wall) and trivial (for some unbeknownst reason I knew one year exactly how the University of Tennessee Volunteers football team would do). I always knew however that I would not be able to profit from these premonitions.

This sort of thing does concentrate the mind. As you might have guessed. It definitely changed me. As you might have guessed. I no longer had the slightest fear of death - why should I? Death seemed like a beautiful, amazing journey. And I do believe I became a much nicer persona as a result, or at least i tried to be so. Your opinion may vary.

But the business about 'choices' still bothered me. How? When? To whom? Or, to Whom? How does God enter into all this and what was God anyway?

I truly started to concentrate on this after Kimberly's aneurysm. Not because I was fearing what would happen if *she* died. I still say with beatific certitude that she is going to survive and recover more or less completely from this ordeal. Changed, obviously (who wouldn't?) but recovered. Now I'm willing to tell you that certitude is based on a premonition. I know how they feel when they come, and this feeling is that of the premonitions past. I'm not delusional. I worked in politics for a time. Believe me, that shakes all smiley-faced delusions out of your system.

But, I was afraid of what would happen if *I* died. I have absolutely no interest in an Eternity that does not involve being with Kimberly. My Hell is every moment away from her. And I am not exaggerating for empathetic "awwwww" reactions. So what does happen in that moment when the body finally and forever announces Tools Down for the last time?

My inability to work this out had, I again admit, reduced my faith in God and the whole religious universe. Despite everything I had been through and had been shown, there was still this Vulcan voice within me that said, 'Not logical, Captain.'

And I had grown to abhor churches and shall we say established religious faiths. They are abhorrent and corrupt organizations that at best tolerate violence, racism and abuse within their ranks. They are feudal in their ability to either ignore or shape laws to their convenience; and have a preening and smug self-confidence in their pronouncements befitting that of a heel wrestler.

You knew wrestling would enter back into the picture.

I ask you, would you not say that The Rock would have made a fine televangelist?

I loved the *message* of religion, I just didn't like how the word LOVE on the great Scrabble Board had its tiles removed and was relaced by WAR. And I had studied Comparative Theology at Queen's University - that and Linguistics should be required courses, by the way. Learn how people think and communicate: that helps in life.

And then, in the absolute reverse of the usual confrontational worlds of Science and Religion, I started to find the answers. Principally, what got me thinking along what I believe is a correct path was a book called *You are Here*. Essentially, a pocket history of the scientific theories of everything as small as sub-atomic particles through to everything as great as the expanse of the universe, it got me noticing parallels existing like Russian nesting dolls.

Pretty much every bright Grade Six science student has noticed how the basic model of an atom looks an awful lot like the solar system. But then beyond that, the galaxy rotates around a centre as do galaxies rotate around a centre; and those centres in turn rotate. Gyroscopes inside of gyroscopes inside of gyroscopes. There too, galaxies collide as sub-atomic particles or atoms collide. That which is small telescopes into that which is large.

Which is, pardon the phrase, logical. Assuming the correctness of the Big Bang Theory, at the end of the first unit of time after time itself began to exist, the exploding particles began organizing themselves into quanta and those happily capturing and circling atoms. Why would this pattern not continue as the size grew greater?

So, if everything that exists is or was contained in this smaller than any definition of small pre-Big Bang ... thing, could there be formed something we would term a Soul? Particles made water, air, rocks, light, gravity and the cute little cat in the windowsill next door. Could they make a Soul?

It has been argued in a slightly bizarre experiment that the Soul actually has mass. I don't quite buy that, as were a Soul to exist it would have to be as practically pure thought, composed of something we have not seen. Like forms of quanta which can appear and disappear and re-appear in two places at one. Hmmm?

That could explain the 'one with the universe' possibility of a hereafter. Everything in the universe was at one point as one with everything else in the universe, therefore the particles which form our 'selves' would return to this endless state.

And what of God? I suspect that the old phrase 'God made man in His image' bore a lot of truth to it. For if God is the logic (that word again) and thought that ordered all those particles, the just as the particles expanded from the Big Bang composing atoms, planets and stars, therefore would it not make sense that the God-Soul would in turn expand, separate and organize into separate Soul units? Us. In other words. The combination of all the Souls in the universe = one God. God actually is within us. Hell of a responsibility. (Every now and then I have to take a 'silly break' from seriousness. Sorry.)

And then I considered metaphysical events - ghosts, apparitions, dogs barking when their masters die many miles away. Something clearly escaped the body and sometimes it stuck around. When this is a book, I'll include many, many examples. For now, I'm sure you can think of several yourself.

Therefore, at the moment of expiration I truly believe that the Soul, quite conscience of itself, chooses its path. It can enter into another, perhaps for re-birth eventually ("He reminds me so much of my Dad. too bad he died without seeing him.") or perhaps as that "voice" one hears when facing a tough decision or an important moment. Or perhaps one might choose to stay in a place or combine with a thing and be its soul for as long as it survives.

What would I do? I would choose to be as one with Kimberly so one day our Souls now twinned might fly away together.

Is this the truth of it all? I don't know, but it is a theory that gives me comfort. And right now, that helps.

Thanks for reading. if you think this will help anyone else, please share.

Be seeing you.

Posted 15th August 2010

A Christmas Story

(You surely didn't think I was going to end there now did you? No, instead let us part with happy thoughts. Every Christmas I would write Kimberly a Christmas Story. This one was from 2008. Peace, good luck and ... Be Seeing You.)

THE WALK-INS

A Christmas Story

By:

Hubert O'Hearn

T'was the night before Christmas and all through the hotel, not a creature was stirring, at least for a while. Outside, snowflakes were falling and the streets looked cold and miserable. Frankly, I was glad to be at work.

No, it was just another December 24th, of no interest whatsoever to anyone outside the mainstream Western religious traditions. I certainly had no one at home wrapping gifts or stuffing stockings. This of course may well be the reason why I was working a midnight audit shift at a small hotel on a night when most of the world was tucking Mama in her kerchief or some such and waiting for the arrival of Santa.

Me? I had no expected arrivals. There were only 10 guests in the whole place and I was looking forward to an uninterrupted eight hours of solving crossword puzzles. But that's life for you. You never get what you're looking forward to...and I apologize for leaving my participles out dangling in the winter cold.

You can imagine my surprise when as I was attempting to deduce the answer to an eight letter word for 'electrically charged (adj.)' a two foot tall stuffed red bear and a one foot tall stuffed grey hippo came waddling into the lobby. It was a shocking experience, comforted only by my instantly solving the crossword clue.

I resorted to my well-honed response, ensconced in me through careful training in the hospitality industry. "Ummm…" (Okay, the 'ummm' was not strictly part of the training) … "How can I be of assistance?" And if that seems a weak response to the situation, I ask you, would it have been better for me to have screamed, shouted, or rolled about weeping on the floor? No, I didn't think so either, although those possible reactions *were* considered.

In any event, the Big Red Bear responded, "Yes, we would like a room please. For one evening, with a big king-sized bed, if you have."

Walk-ins were not unusual at the small hotel, but waddle-ins were. I adopted a professional response. "For yourself and the ummmm….?" I had noticed the hippo grazing away on the complimentary fruit bowl and was momentarily taken aback. But only temporarily, for if I am anything, I am indeed a professional.

"Yes, for two of us," said the Big Red Bear. I thought at first he was winking at me, but then on further observation I noted that he only had one, white, shoe-button eye. There were also little pops along his seams where bits of yellow stuffing showed through. Clearly, this was a much-hugged and much-loved bear.

"Certainly," I said. "Would that be smoking or non-smoking?"

"Oh, non-smoking. We're flammable," the Bear added helpfully. The hippo spoke up, after swallowing down the last golden apple in one sizable gulp. "Do you have anything with warm swampy water? I like warm swampy water."

"Er, I'm sorry. We don't have any hot tub suites."

"Oh," said the hippo. "That's unfortunate," said the Big Red Bear. Little frowns appeared on their brows.

"But!" I rushed to say, "Our bathtubs are large and deep and there is lots of hot water!"

"Oh!," said the hippo. "That's fortunate!," said the Big Red Bear. Little smiles appeared on their faces.

"And!" I said, sensing I was winning the day, "I can give you extra foamy bath suds and a very nice shampoo too!"

The hippo toddled over to the Big Red Bear, the former's little grey ears fluttering in delight. One ear looked slightly chewed, as though a long-ago puppy had once had a longing for stuffed hippo. The Big Red Bear spoke to his companion. "What do you think, Hippie?" (I surmised that must be the hippo's name and I started to fill in the registration form: LAST NAME: *Hippo* FIRST NAME: *Hippie*. MIDDLE INITIAL: *A* seemed appropriate)

"Well Red," said Hippie, eyeing the poinsettias hungrily before remembering that although they are pretty flowers they are equally poisonous. "It has been a long time since we were bathed and shampooed. What's it been? Ten Christmases or twenty for you?"

"Oooo, all of that," said Big Red Bear. "I haven't been bathed in many years. Not since Princess Kimberly was a very little girl and she used to sneak me into the tub. I didn't much like being hung up by my paws on the laundry line to dry out afterwards. But I'm sure her Mum meant well."

"Of course of course," agreed Hippie. "Mums always mean well. It's why they're Mums, after all."

"That my friend is a very sage observation," said Big Red Bear with an approving nod.

"It should be," said Hippie. "I like sage very much. Especially in puddings." He continued, "My young master used to send me for boat rides in cardboard boxes out in the big lake in the summertime…did you know that cardboard makes for a terrible boat?"

"No I didn't." "Oh yes, quite terrible. Falls apart and then you sink."

I interrupted. "I beg your pardon, Mister Bear –"

"Do call me Big Red, or Red for short."

"All right. My name is Max, by the way."

"Pleased to meet you Max Bytheway," said the Bear with both a nod and a bow at his black-belted waist.

"No, umm - I mean - the pleasure is all mine - I think. Did I hear you refer to a Princess? If there's royalty expected, well, we don't have any formal suites, but there are some nice adjoining rooms that we could open up…yes?" (I admit to a certain degree of flustering. Well wouldn't you be?)

The Bear and the Hippo looked at each other and laughed and laughed, hugging each other until they fell to the floor with a tumble. Soggy happy tears of joy rolled down their fluffy faces and as strange as it sounds I was sure that I could smell the sweet mixed smells of baby powder, porridge with maple sugar and lupin petals, all jumbled together. I found myself remembering spring mornings in the garden of our backyard back when I was a boy. I started thinking about the sun on my head, the breeze on my face and the tin footrest on the candy-striped stroller that my mother used to take me for walks to look at the flowers. I couldn't begin to tell you how long it had been since I had remembered such things, assuming I'd ever remembered them at all in all the days since. But it was a very nice memory that the laughing tears' perfume had brought on …

"Er-ERRR!," said Hippie the Hippo, clearing his throat rhetorically. He'd managed to clamber up onto the registration desk and was looking at me with dancing, shiny glass eyes. "That was a most marvelous laugh you gave us. This is clearly a fine hotel –"

"A FINE hotel," agreed Big Red Bear emphatically. Hippie continued, "Quite. But we do owe you an explanation. We don't mean that Princess Kimberly is a Princess in the sense of royal responsibilities, ribbon cuttings, ship christenings and photo features in Hello! Magazine. Rather, *every* little girl is a Princess at least or at best to those of us who love them."

"Oh very good, Hippie," said Big Red Bear, applauding with a thwump thwump thwump of mitteny red paws. "You certainly are speaking well of yourself tonight."

"Thank you Red," said Hippie modestly. "I felt compelled to respond with a rhetorical flourish. You don't think my prose was too purple do you?" Big Red Bear looked carefully at his friend through his one good eye and then shook his head slowly from side to side. "Nooo, you can't possible be purple. You're grey all over from what I can see." "Very good," said the Hippo with a wide, satisfied grin, before frowning, "It's all made me rather hungry though."

"I'll re-fill the fruit bowl in a second," I said, "But if all little girls are Princesses, then what are little boys? Snakes and snails and puppy dog tails?," I suggested. They both looked at me as though I had gone mad. Under the circumstances, that may not have been an irrational conclusion. Big Red Bear asked, "Max, why would you say anything as strange as that?"

"But that's the old phrase: 'Snakes and snails and puppy dog tails, that's what little boys are made of.'" The Hippo and the

Bear looked at me without the slightest hint of recognition. I carried on. "And little girls are made of –" What were little girls made of? I took my best guess. "Silver bells, cockle shells and cups of tea." That was wrong, but it would have to do.

Hippie the Hippo shrugged in disinterested agreement, before dipping his entire face into the bowl of complimentary mints. Between crunches of mint, he informed me that, "Little boys CHOMP CHOMP CHOMP are each and every one CHOMP SWALLOW CHOMP a duke in disguise. Aaaahhh, those were fine candies."

My curiousity was peaked. "Why a duke? Why not a king or a knight?" Hippie was still savouring the minty freshness in his mouth, so Big Red Bear completed the explanation. "Kings have miserable lives, Max. Read your fairy tales. Kings are always having some evil elf or another turn their children into toadstools or foot stools, their kingdoms are fraught with famine and they rarely live happily ever after. Knights are all well and good…provided you like slaughtering dragons, which I do not recommend. A duke is a much wiser thing to be." Well that answered that I guess.

It was at that point that the hotel front door opened and in walked a very busy looking man and an equally busy looking woman, each carrying a dark suitcase and a dark expression. "You have a reservation," the man barked. "Kincaid."

I responded politely. "If you don't mind waiting a few minutes, I'm just checking in these …" Big Red Bear and Hippie the Hippo were now sat just as still as still could be, with neither a breath nor a blink showing from either of them. Could things get any stranger? I rather hoped not.

"Checking in who?", the man barked again. "We're the Kincaids," growled the woman, unnecessarily.

As I have said, I am a professional and I know how to think fast. "I'm just checking in these databases for the finest room we have for you, Mister and Mrs. Kincaid." They made me much more nervous than had the talking Bear and Hippo. "I certainly hope so," said Mrs. Kincaid. She looked with a sniffy expression at the Bear and the Hippo and said, "Your Christmas decorations are old and ragged." I was tempted to put the Kincaids in the room next to the laundry in the hopes of the dryers running constantly from 5AM onwards, but I thought better of it. Instead I just said, "They belong to a little girl who's coming to pick them up."

"They should be kept out of guests' sight!" said Mrs. Kincaid. I like most people, but the Kincaids were proving the use of the word 'most' as opposed to 'all.'

It did not take long to check in the Kincaids (thank heavens) and they left, rolling their dark suitcases with them through the lobby and down the hall. I heard the clunk and slam of their room door and hoped that I wouldn't be seeing any more of them that night.

"They don't seem to be filled with the Christmas spirit," said Big Red Bear dryly. He and Hippie had come back to life and they stretched their little arms and legs as though waking up from a nap.

"You've got that right, Big Red Bear," I said. "Now tell me, if I check you in here, how are you two going to pay for the room?"

"Pay?" said Hippie.

"Pay?" said Big Red Bear.

"I thought you said you'd thought of everything Red," said Hippie with quite a hard stare.

"I guess I hadn't," admitted Big Red Bear.

"Well now what are we going to do!?" said the little Hippo. His hard stare looked as if it was going to turn to tears. I had to do something. Wouldn't you? Wouldn't you do something if you were me?

"I think I might be able to do something for you," I said. "I'd have to charge you for a room if the room itself was available for sale. But I *do* have a room that's temporarily out of order, so I suppose I can just let you stay there for free."

"That's very kind of you Max," said Big Red Bear. "If you don't mind my asking, just what exactly is out of order about the room?" I looked in the maintenance book. "The only problem I see is that the radio isn't working. Will that be okay for you?"

"The bath works fine?" asked Hippie. "Yes, the bath works fine" I answered. "Then we'll take it!" they said together. They each tapped a paw on an ink pad and signed the registration card with their imprint. "You're in room 244," I said. "I don't suppose you'll be needing a luggage cart," I asked as I looked around for any bags or toy boxes behind them.

"Oh no, we travel very lightly," replied Big Red Bear. "I used to carry a lunch box," added Hippie, "But snacks never lasted very long in it, so I don't bother any more. Do you think we could bother you to show us where the room is? We're not very tall and the room numbers are probably well above our heads." How could I refuse such a polite request? It was very nearlymidnight and it wasn't very likely that there would be any more walk-ins. Even if there were, they could wait for a couple of minutes in our lobby's cozy chairs. So I popped the sign on the desk that said:

I AM CURRENTLY ASSISTING ANOTHER GUEST.

I WILL BE BACK IN A FEW MOMENTS.

THANK YOU FOR YOUR PATIENCE.

And with that we set off for the elevator. I could hear their little legs padding along behind me and I realized that what was a very short distance for me was quite a hike for them. I asked, "Would you like to be carried?"

"Ooo yes please," smiled Hippie. "Being carried is just like hugs and cuddles. We love hugs and cuddles."

Big Red Bear seemed sad. "It's been a long time between hugs and cuddles," he explained. I picked them up – the little Hippo in my left arm and the Bear in my right and up the elevator we went. They snuggled in tightly and I felt a happy glow inside. It occurred to me that it had been a long time between hugs and cuddles for me too.

I opened the door to the room, flipped on the lights with my elbow, then laid the two friends down on the fluffy comforter covering the king-sized bed. They looked like they were floating on a big pale blue cloud. "This is a very comfy bed Max," said Big Red Bear. Added Hippie, with great and growing enthusiasm, "Comfy and ... and ... *and* ... **bouncy!!!**" With that he started to spring and sproing about on the bed, turning elegant little front and back flips – THWOMP! "Wheeee!" THWOMP! "Wheee!" THWOMP! "Wheee!" His joyful gymnastics were such that they bounced Big Red Bear right off the bed, and he fell with a soft plunk onto the floor next to the end table. He dragged himself up, brushed off his red fur with his paws then asked quietly yet sternly, "Hippie? Is this what I'm to expect all night?"

Hippie stopped his bouncing and wandered over to the edge of the bed where he could look his friend eye to eye. "I'm sorry Red. I got caught up in the fun. It shan't happen again." And with that he gave Big Red Bear a big slurpy kiss lick. Now dripping wet, Big Red Bear sighed and said, "All right, you're forgiven. Now then we should ... Hippie, what are you up to?"

The little hippo had stuck his head so far under the pillows that only his round grey bum was showing out. It must have been a successful mission, as his small grey tail started to shimmy and shake side to side and up and down. His head then re-emerged with a smile. "I found the Sweet Dream chocolates!" Big Red Bear sighed again and hit himself in the forehead with one exasperated paw. He said to Max, "He's my best friend, but all he thinks of is food."

"And baths!," said Hippie.

"All right, and occasionally baths," Big Red Bear agreed.

"Don't forget cuddles!," added Hippie.

"And...cuddles ... too," said Big Red Bear.

"And your beautiful princess and my master the duke. Oh dear." All Hippie's happiness seemed to drain out of him just then and he sat very still with his head hung low. He even dropped the Sweet Dream chocolates.

Big Red Bear crawled up onto the rumpled bed and gave his friend a hug. "I know," he said simply. "I think of them too. All the time"

It was none of my business and I should have got back down to my front desk. What if the Kincaids had been calling down, asking to have their pillows fluffed? Now I like to think of myself as a dutiful worker – as I said, I am a professional. But although there were hard times in this Christmas of 2008 and good jobs were hard to find and equally hard to keep, I felt so badly for these two odd guests that I simply had to help them any way I could. I sat down next to them on the bed and as I did I felt the chocolate bar in my pants pocket. Taking it out, I divided it into three parts, offering a piece each to the Bear and the Hippo. "Care for a Christmas treat?", I asked. They took the pieces of chocolate, but even Hippie the Hippo just munched on it very slowly.

"Tell me what's the matter," I asked. "Why are you two so sad? And at Christmas time too."

"Hippie?" asked Big Red Bear, "Do you want to tell it?"

"No Red, I'm all out of eloquence. You tell Max the story."
Big Red Bear nodded his head then sat back against two
pillows laid against the headboard. He then started to tell his
story, his one good eye staring up through the ceiling at a
place and time far away.

"Hippie and I have been friends for over three years now," he
began. "I had been with my princess ever since she was a
baby. Her grandmother gave me to her and we stayed
together through thick and through thin ... there was a lot of
thin ... not so much thick. When she was happy she would
toss me up in the air so I felt I was flying and although she
couldn't hear me, I would laugh right along with her. And
when she was sad, I would snuggle in close while she was
asleep and I would whisper the magical words that all well-
loved toys know, so that she would be able to at least have
beautiful sweet dreams, even more beautiful and even
sweeter than the Sweet Dreams chocolates under these
pillows.

"Eventually," he continued, "my princess had a princess of
her very own and then a young duke too. I loved them too, of
course, but always and forever princess Kimberly was my
very best friend. Then there was a very very *very* bad time
and my princess felt lonely and scared. I did my best, but
there were some hard years Max. Hard years indeed.

"One day an Irishman appeared on the scene whose name
was Royston, or Roy for short. Things got much happier then,
as the princess and her new duke fell in love. It turned out, as
of course it would, that the Irish duke had many things in
common with my princess, not least of which (most
importantly in our opinion) being that he too still loved the
stuffed friends from when he was a boy."

"This is where I come in," commented Hippie.

"Yes, this was when I met Hippie. He told me about traveling
with duke Royston to university and to great cities where

they had lived and about how he had always hoped that his master would meet a perfect princess who would love them both. Well he did and she did and Hippie and I took up residence on top of the dresser in their bedroom, where we could watch over them at night. If we were needed, we could always jump down, or 'fall down' if you know what I mean Max, and whisper the magical words to give them sweet dreams."

"It all sounds so perfect," I said. "A real happily ever after story."

Big Red Bear and Hippie the Hippo looked at each other and once again their heads came together in a sad union.

"So we thought," said Big Red Bear. "So we thought too. But then came some bad times. There were job changes and job losses and duke Royston didn't want to admit to princess Kimberly how bad things were which upset princess Kimberly —"

"I don't think we need to tell *all* the details, Red," Hippie interrupted. "No offence to you Max, but it's very hard hearing the story again."

"Oh, I understand," I said. "There were troubles. That's all I need to know."

"Thank you Max," said Big Red Bear gently, "You're a kind man." That was good. I liked being called kind. I asked, "So what brought you to come here?"

"Our hope," said Big Red Bear, "was that they would notice us missing. And if they noticed us missing, we want them to miss us. We want them to miss what they're missing and go find it, in the course of finding us. Does that make any sense to you?" And it did. But I still had another question.

"But…how ever are they going to find you? There must be a hundred hotels or more in this city and how would they know to look in a hotel in the first place? I know that I wouldn't know where to start."

Hippie walked slowly across the bed and put his head on my lap, looking up at me with big, wet eyes. He whispered in a low, slow voice, "We might need a bit of help. From you Max." From me?

"From me?"

"Yes Max," said Hippie. "We spotted that you have the right qualities as soon as we saw you through the glass lobby doors. We have ways of spotting the right sort of person you know."

"That's why we spoke to you," piped in Big Red Bear. "Believe you me it's a rare thing for we stuffed sorts to start talking to you people sorts. Quite the privilege Max, *quite* the privilege." No doubt about it, I had been honoured.

"Look," I said, "I need to get back down to my front desk, but don't you two worry about a thing. I'll figure this all out for you, I promise. You just relax and have a Merry Christmas." Before I left, I asked them Kimberly and Royston's last names, which they told me, and their home address, which they didn't know. That figured. It was not as though they would have received a lot of mail or taken taxi cabs over the years. I turned the television on to Babes in Toyland, which seemed the correct thing to watch on all kinds of levels.

Now was the hard part. How on Earth was I going to locate these two people with just names and no address to go by? Looking in the telephone book, I noticed that there were dozens of people – forty-three to be precise - with Kimberly's last name, but only three with Royston's name. Unfortunately, none of the ones with Royston's name had an initial 'R', so that cast doubt on all of them.

What to do? I couldn't phone forty-three people at random in the hopes that one of them was the sought-for princess Kimberly. What with call display, there would be forty-two rather angry complaints to the hotel manager the next day wondering why a desk clerk was calling them at 11:43PM on Christmas Eve. I stared at the long list of names. There were five with a 'K' before their name, so that helped narrow things down. But which one...?

There was one clue in the story that Big Red Bear had told me. He'd mentioned that Kimberly had two children: a boy and a girl. I didn't know their ages and I rather doubted that Red or Hippie would dare to answer the phone if I called up to their room. I looked again at the telephone book and there it was.

The listing had Kimberly's last name followed by the word 'Family' and the street address corresponded to one of the other 'K' names. There was a chance that might be the right number.

There was a good chance that might be the right number.

I took a chance that might be the right number.

I dialed and as a man's voice answered with a slightly puzzled "Hello?" I suddenly realized that I didn't have a clue what to say. It was at that moment that I became a deeply committed believer in divine inspiration. It was, after all, Christmas. What better time could there be for divine inspiration?

Divine inspiration, even at its best, can take a while to work so I was still a bit shaken when the man's voice again said "Hello?" The tone was still puzzled, but now with an edge of annoyance. It was now or never. I decided I would be both friendly and efficient.

"Yes, I'd like to speak to ... let me see what the name is ... ah yes, is there a Royston there?"

"I'm Royston, or Roy. Who's this?"

"Ah, very good. Roy, my name is Max and I'm calling from the McGregor Inn on the Park."

"Ye-ess?," said Roy doubtfully.

"Well Roy, I've got a bit of a situation here that I was hoping you could help me out with."

"Is this about Amanda? Is she in some kind of trouble?"

"Your step-daughter?"

"Yes. Um, how did you know that?" Yikes! How *did* I know that?

"Well sir, when men express worry about ... about ... girl's names, that's almost always about their daughters and ... oh yes ... as you and Kimberly don't have the same last name I assumed ... I surmised! ... that Amanda was – I mean is – your, er, step-daughter. Yes." I was aware of a certain sweaty moistness growing in the folds of my shirt. "But she's in no kind of trouble. Not that I know of. No."

"That's good to hear. She was staying at her boyfriend's tonight and – say, what's this all about anyway?" It was time for a deep breath.

"You see, there's been an unusual sort of a, well, a package of sorts delivered to us and the instructions are quite specific that you and your wife come down here to claim it. Together," I added with a prim insistence.

"Together?", he asked.

"Yes sir," I replied.

"Me and my wife?", he asked.

"Yes sir," I replied.

"Kimberly?"

"Oh yes, sir. How else would I know her name sir?"

"You don't mean *now* surely? Not on Christmas Eve?"

"I know it's putting you out sir and I do so apologize, but you must see it from the hotel's position. We really can't store these – this! – package. Not when we're short-staffed for the holidays." I wondered if visions of armed security guards mournfully checking their watches were floating throughRoy's head. I thought of one other possible complication. "Are you worried about leaving the children alone sir? I mean, if you have more of them..."

"Oh no. No that would be okay. Bradley's with his Dad tonight and ... can you wait a moment?"

"Of course I can sir." I heard a hand being put over a phone receiver and a muffled calling out. It must have been an animated conversation as every now and then the hand loosened and a few words would sneak through: "Yes tonight", "I don't know", "Your crazy friend Geoff", "Nawww", "Let me see."

A woman's voice took over from Roy's. "Hello? You need us to claim this package tonight?"

"Yes I do and ..." Here's the greatest example of the divine inspiration I spoke of. "...we'd be pleased to offer you a free night's stay if you can make it here in the next half hour. We'll even include a complimentary breakfast." I started smiling as I imagined Hippie chomping down English muffins.

"Well..." she said. "That's very nice. You're sure this isn't a practical joke?"

"Oh no ma'am. The McGregor Inn on the Park *never* jokes." And then to finalize the deal, I said, "Although I'm not at liberty to discuss the contents of the package, I assure you that this does not seem to be anything unpleasant."

Thank heavens they agreed to come down to the hotel. I didn't bother with the elevator, it was too slow. I ran up a flight of stairs and down the hall then let myself into Room 244. Hippie and Big Red Bear looked up from the bed, startled. "They're coming!," I said. "Any minute now!" Big Red Bear smiled and said, "Thank you Max, we knew we could count on you." Hippie added, "Merry Christmas Max!" I wished them both a Merry Christmas, and then ran back downstairs to the desk.

I was just in time to catch my breath and to see the headlights of a car pull in the lot in front of the hotel. Roy and Kimberly – for it was them – were both quite tall. He was tall and grey, she was tall and blonde and did look every inch both of them like a princess and her duke.

In answer to the questions they asked I told them that their package – or packages rather – were in Room 244 and I gave them a key. No, I wasn't sure who had dropped them off. No, there wasn't a note attached. No, I didn't see who had dropped them off. They'd arrived on the previous shift. Could I escort them to the room? (I had to see their reaction.)

Up the elevator we went and I opened the door when we got to the room. The lights were on and there on the bed were the bear and the hippo. Big Red Bear had one paw raised in a Hi! gesture. Roy and Kimberly stood there staring at their childhood friends.

"What are they doing here?", asked Roy.

"Did Amanda do this?", asked Kimberly.

"She must have," replied Roy.

"That's so sweet, to arrange a room for the night for us."

I slipped out the door behind them and made my way back to the front desk. It was now after midnight, officially Christmas Day. My shift had ended before they checked out in the morning so I can't really say how everything went.

But.

Around two in the morning, I had a call from the Kincaids complaining about some kind of party going on above them. They said they heard a lot of laughing and what sounded like a lot of dancing feet. I said, "Maybe its Santa Claus and the reindeer delivering a gift." They hung up, with a harrumph. I hung up, with a smile. Outside, snowflakes fluttered down and in the streetlights they looked like hundreds of bright, shiny eyes …

THE END

ABOUT THE AUTHOR

Hubert O'Hearn is an internationally known essayist, editor and playwright. Born and educated in Canada, he moved to Ireland in 2012 along with his faithful Border Collie named Stella. They currently live in a quiet village in County Mayo. He can be found on Twitter @BTBReviews.